DEVELOPING THE NEXT GENERATION OF MILITARY LEADERS

CANADIAN DEFENCE ACADEMY PRESS

DEVELOPING THE NEXT GENERATION OF MILITARY LEADERS

CHALLENGES, IMPERATIVES AND STRATEGIES

EDITED BY
MAJOR JULIE BÉLANGER AND
LIEUTENANT-COLONEL PSALM LEW

CANADIAN DEFENCE ACADEMY PRESS

Canadian Defence Academy Press
PO Box 17000 Stn Forces
Kingston, Ontario   K7K 7B4

Produced for the Canadian Defence Academy Press
by 17 Wing Winnipeg Publishing Office.
WPO30725

Cover Photo: Combat Camera AR2007-Z041-12

Library and Archives Canada Cataloguing in Publication

Developing the next generation of military leaders : challenges,
imperatives and strategies / edited by Julie Bélanger and Psalm Lew.

Produced for the Canadian Defence Academy Press by 17 Wing Winnipeg
Publishing Office.
Includes bibliographical references and index.
Available also on the Internet.
Issued by: Canadian Defence Academy.
ISBN 978-1-100-19212-3
Cat. no.: D2-281/2011E

1. Command of troops. 2. Military art and science. 3. Military
education. I. Bélanger, Julie, 1972- II. Lew, Psalm, 1976- III. Canadian
Defence Academy IV. Canada. Canadian Armed Forces. Wing, 17

UB210 D48 2011   355.3'3041   C2011-980150-7

ACKNOWLEDGEMENTS

Developing the Next Generation of Military Leaders: Challenges, Imperatives and Strategies is the sixth and latest volume of a series of publications designed to focus on core contemporary military issues. The success of this series has and is founded on the continued interest and effort of the members of the International Military Leadership Association (IMLA), a group that shares the common goal of communicating knowledge to enhance leadership development and in turn, organizational effectiveness. For this, we would like to offer our sincerest appreciation and gratitude to the many dedicated and outstanding professional contributors to this book. Clearly, the effort of these authors will continue to significantly contribute to enhancing our international awareness and understanding of the critical role that leadership plays in modern militaries. It also enables us to better understand how our various militaries, situated around the world, all with different histories and challenges, approach leadership. Again, the collaborative spirit of the IMLA members is paramount, without them this book could not have been written.

It is also important to acknowledge the continued support of the Canadian Defence Academy and in particular, the Canadian Forces Leadership Institute for their continued support to this effort. As such, a special thank you and our gratitude is extended to Mélanie Denis for her outstanding support and guidance throughout this annual project. Because of time-constraints, Mélanie worked relentlessly during the closing days of this project to ensure that the release of this publication would coincide with the annual IMLA conference. Her previous experience combined with her management skills and insights, helped to ensure the success of this project. As with previous volumes in this series, the staff of the 17 Wing Publishing Office in Winnipeg are to again be congratulated for their efforts, under considerable time constraints, to transform this rough manuscript into a high quality and professional document that we are proud to present.

TABLE OF CONTENTS

Table of Contents

FOREWORD

As the host of the 2011 International Military Leadership Association (IMLA) Annual Meeting, I am honoured to present the sixth and latest volume of leadership books produced by IMLA, *Developing the Next Generation of Military Leaders: Challenges, Imperatives and Strategies*. In my opinion, the IMLA has been able to publish leadership books in quite an impressive manner, which reflects not only the high standards of the writers, but also the commendable and successful collaboration effort by IMLA member countries. I believe that only through these kinds of efforts can we solve many of the military problems realized in the contemporary world. In addition, I also would like to convey my continued appreciation to the Canadian Defence Academy, specifically the Canadian Forces Leadership Institute, for its continuing support in making the publication of IMLA books possible.

We can see today that the operational landscape faced by military leaders has changed dramatically since the end of the Cold War. Instead of conventional warfare, military conflicts today are more often characterized by the role of non-state actors, and the lines between politics and war are increasingly blurred. At the same time, this phenomenon can be seen 24/7 on the internet. Therefore, I believe that *Developing the Next Generation Military Leaders: Challenges, Imperatives and Strategies* comes at a most appropriate time. Today's military problems require today's solution, and this also applies to military leadership development. Through the presentation of theoretical frameworks, case studies and applied research, we can see how the militaries of various IMLA member nations prepare their current and future generations of military leaders to lead their soldiers in unchartered terrain, coping with complexity in an interlinked world.

As with the other volumes on military leadership published by the IMLA, I trust that this book will contribute to a more thorough understanding of how military organizations in various parts of the world cope with the challenges of preparing their future leaders for challenges that are very different from the previous generations. The concept of warfare has evolved and requires a realignment of leadership concepts that will help win the war. Seen in this context, *Developing the Next Generation of Military Leaders: Challenges, Imperatives and Strategies* is an important contribution to the debate on what kind of leadership is needed in the so-called Fourth Generation Warfare.

As a final remark, I hope this book not only can provide its reader with insights on how IMLA member nations prepare their leaders for a changing world, but furthermore, how it could lead to the implementation of a joint

Foreword

leadership training and development program. Readers are welcomed and encouraged to contact the IMLA for further discussions on the contents of this volume.

MG Ali Yusuf Susanto, S.IP, M.M.
Assistant for Personnel
Indonesian Army Chief of Staff

PREFACE

The world is changing. This sentiment is expressed so often it has almost become cliché. Yet, the frequent expression about change, or the rate of change, occurs for good reason. Change is inevitable and often difficult. The larger and more complex the organization, the more difficult it can become. However, it is through the process of change that organizations remain viable and position themselves for the future. Failure to adapt or change can be catastrophic for the organization, and for some organizations, like the military, it can literally be a matter of life or death.

At the last meeting of the IMLA, there was consensus that our nations' militaries are facing an unprecedented time of uncertainty and change. In fact, it would be difficult to find anyone connected with any military organization who would dispute this notion. To the point, media sources around the world reveal that our military forces are being called on to do perhaps the widest range of operations (full spectrum warfare to humanitarian operations), at more points around the globe, often operating in unexpected coalitions, than we have seen in our nations' histories. Interestingly, there are certain contextual factors that influence all militaries, even while these varied militaries seek to accomplish different goals. While some of these are obvious to even the casual observer (i.e., technological advances, amount of information available to the soldier), some are much more complex and have implications at all levels of the military infrastructure (i.e., generational differences).

This latest book by IMLA (through the generous support of the Canadian Defence Academy) is designed to examine the implications of some of these changes. Specifically, this book examines the preparation of our future military leaders to operate in an uncertain future. This is done through an appropriate balance of academic investigation and operational experience that is unique to IMLA. This group consists of military members, civilians, psychologists, members of academic institutions, and government agencies from countries around the world. Through this diversity of background and experience, the authors are able to elucidate the challenges that many nations are facing in an attempt to adequately prepare military members to be successful in the Profession of Arms. At the heart of this development is a focus on the leaders of tomorrow. These future leaders will have the overwhelming responsibility to help shape where and how our military forces are fielded. Therefore, the audience for this book includes not only current military members who are being shaped by these changes, but also those that study these populations. These are challenges that will require a multi-faceted

Preface

solution, so it is imperative that all those involved in the developmental and training processes are also involved in the solution.

To illustrate, consider a young soldier leading his/her squad through a small village in southern Afghanistan for the first time (something that happens with great frequency in Afghanistan). The unit has been in country for approximately one week and recently taken over patrols from the unit they are replacing. They will operate "outside the wire" every day and have the responsibility to conduct security patrols in this area as it is a common thoroughfare that is frequently used by the Taliban to move into and out of the mountains. Historically, except for a few skirmishes with the Taliban outside of town, this is a friendly town and is supportive of international troops. In fact, the unit's commander just sat down with the Imam the day before to talk about the positive relationship between the two groups. Nevertheless, on this day, an unexpected explosion in a local mosque splits the squad in two as they pass by.

The squad leader is now placed in a situation where he/she must quickly determine the gravity of the situation and the immediate actions he/she needs to take. A misstep of action in a situation like this can very quickly spiral out of control and ignite a situation with operational or strategic level implications. If he/she reacts too negatively, it could result in civilian casualties that would be denounced by the host country. If he/she reacts too lightly, it could endanger those under his/her leadership. Military leaders must ensure soldiers who face these types of situations are armed with all the information and training they need to react appropriately. Failure to prepare these individuals adequately could have devastating consequences.

While it would be easy to dismiss a book like this as applicable only to those that execute our nation's wars, the implications are far more significant. Naturally, leading in harm's way certainly has implications for many similarly dangerous occupations (i.e., police, firefighters, first responders) that have to prepare for potentially life-threatening situations. However, even more traditional organizations face times of stress and crisis that must be managed. While this typically does not involve the life or death of the individual members of the organization, it could include the long-term viability of the organization. Finally, understanding how individuals and teams react to organizational and environmental change is instructive for all organizations.

There is perhaps no more important task than making sure that when we send our nations' sons and daughters off to conduct military operations, they have the right preparation, development, awareness, and skills to be successful.

Preface

We would like to thank the authors that contributed to this book for shedding light on the challenges of the future so that our respective nations can more effectively prepare for them today. For those that are reading this book, we would like to challenge you to see where you can contribute to the preparation of our future leaders, whatever your field of study.

Lieutenant-Colonel Douglas R. Lindsay, PhD, US Air Force
Deputy Department Head & Senior Military Faculty

Dr. Craig Foster
Full Professor

Department of Behavioral Sciences & Leadership
United States Air Force Academy

CHAPTER 1

GENERATIONAL DIFFERENCES AND THE FUTURE OF THE UNITED STATES MILITARY

*Dr. Craig Foster & Lieutenant-Colonel Douglas R. Lindsay**

When the theme for this book was proposed at the annual meeting for the International Military Leadership Association, it became clear that there were two different ways to consider the next generation of military leaders. The lead author on this chapter interpreted this theme as involving the personal attributes maintained by younger people today. Others viewed this theme as involving the changing nature of military operations. The current volume could have been devoted to either of these viewpoints, but the consensus among the member nations was that neither issue exists independently of the other. To effectively train the next generation of military leaders, one must consider the characteristics of the younger generations in correspondence with the qualities that will likely be required of them in the future. This chapter reflects this approach. We discuss (a) the nature of generational differences in the United States, (b) related changes in United States military operations, and (c) the intersection between the two. In so doing, we hope to provide more than just a description of these issues in the context of the United States. We also aim to elucidate several challenges that can influence the accuracy of generation-based evaluations cross-culturally.

THE PSYCHOLOGY OF ASSESSING GENERATIONAL DIFFERENCES

Assessments of generational differences are often conducted informally. To illustrate, a common analysis of generational differences in the United States would involve an older person lamenting the character of a younger generation, particularly when the younger generation is in its later teenage years. In fact, it is easy to imagine an older man at a shopping mall looking disdainfully at a pack of "Emo" teenagers with their strange hairstyles, lip rings, and excessive eye shadow.[1] This man looks at this group, possibly remembers going to Vietnam when he was almost the same age, and thinks "our country is in fact going to hell." This scenario can illustrate the fundamental challenges

---

* The views expressed in this chapter are those of the authors and do not necessarily reflect those of the United States Air Force Academy or the United States Department of Defense.

Chapter 1

of making fair conclusions about generational differences. There is, of course, the possibility that the older man's assessment is accurate and that his generation is notably "better" than the younger generation. However, these snap judgements of generational differences can be distorted by several psychological processes.

One such process involves the tendency to confound *age differences* with true *generational differences*. Two generations might appear different because the younger generation is in fact substantially different from the older one. In this case, the younger generation is truly different than their elders and this difference would remain evident if the two generations could be compared when they were of the same age. Another possibility is that the younger generation appears different only because they are younger. In this case, the attributes of the younger generation are similar to those of the older generation when the older generation was similarly aged, and the two generations only appear different because the older generation has progressed through additional developmental stages. It is relatively easy for individuals to mistake age differences for generational differences, particularly when older individuals fail to recognize that their attributes and behaviours were conceptually similar to the younger generation when they too were younger. To illustrate, the authors of this chapter are now middle aged. It would be easy for us to view the younger generation critically because of their overzealous enthusiasm for seemingly foolish fads such as letting baggy pants "ride" several inches below their waists, listening to rap that contains way-too-explicit sexuality, and getting too many tattoos. Yet, we might fail to recall our generation's behaviour when we were of a similar age in the 1980s. Many members of our generation wore ridiculous acid-wash jeans, listened to Tone Lōc singing about doing the "Wild Thing," and maintained horrible haircuts that were later dubbed "mullets."[2]

Inter-generational assessments can also be distorted by the psychological process of stereotyping. Stereotypes involve attributing personal characteristics to an individual based on his/her group membership.[3] The concept of stereotyping is often associated with race, gender, or religion, but stereotyping can occur across generations as well. Many hippies from the 1960s proclaimed "don't trust anyone over 30," suggesting, of course, that nobody from older generations was trustworthy (despite hippies' simultaneous focus on peace, love, and understanding). Stereotypes can create perceived differences between groups when true differences do not exist. For example, one research study found essentially no evidence supporting an existing stereotype of only children.[4] Even when stereotypes are based on real mean-level differences, individuals can exaggerate the true differences between groups.[5] This occurs in part due to the outgroup homogeneity effect – the tendency to see outgroup members as more similar (or less diverse) than ingroup members (i.e., "they" are all the same).[6] Stereotypes are also resistant to change because individuals tend to interpret social information in a manner that is consistent with existing stereotypes (a.k.a., a confirmation bias)[7] and can label those who behave inconsistently with a stereotype as an exception to the rule (a.k.a., subtyping).[8] In short, the process of stereotyping suggests that haphazard analyses of generational differences can be overblown or simply incorrect.

It is also possible that members of a particular generation are motivated to see their generation as superior to other generations. This in-generation favouritism might be rooted in social identity theory. This theory begins with the premise that personal identity is comprised of individual-level factors (e.g., seeing oneself as intelligent) and group memberships (e.g., being Muslim).[9] Accordingly, people can maintain self-esteem not just by viewing their own qualities positively, but also by seeing the groups to which they belong in a favourable light as well. Social identity theory is often applied to the major areas of prejudice, like race, sex, and religion, but is easily applied to generations. As the social categorization of generations becomes salient, individuals might be motivated to view their generations more favourably than they view other generations.

There is some anecdotal evidence in the context of the United States Air Force Academy (USAFA) that appears consistent with in-generation favouritism. USAFA faculty and staff will occasionally claim that character issues beset incoming cadets. These concerns might refer to the number of cadets that come from divorced families, the amount of cheating that occurs in high schools today, or other forms of "crisis" that plague younger generations. These characterizations are supported infrequently by any type of legitimate comparative data and these characterizations rarely, if ever, portray the upcoming generation as better prepared than their own. These concerns about incoming cadets once came up in a conversation between the lead author and the USAFA Dean of Faculty. The Dean said, with a laudable amount of sensitivity for the generation younger than her own, that USAFA leaders had expressed similar concerns about incoming cadets in the 1970s. It is possible that cadets in the 1970s were in fact worse prepared for military service than were previous cadets, and contemporary cadets are even worse prepared than were cadets in the 1970s. This would entail a consistent downward trend in preparedness at least beginning with cadets in the 1970s and continuing today. Of course, it is also possible that varying generations of cadets (while differing in many ways) have been similarly prepared for military service and each generation simply sees the next generation as less prepared than their own. This process of disparaging the next generation might also be seen in assessments of USAFA cadets based on graduating class year. Class year is salient to USAFA cadets and graduates. They sometimes reveal this by repeating numbers corresponding to their class years; a member of the class of 1992 might repeat "92" as if it were on a street address. USAFA graduates know well their tendency to claim that they went to the academy when it was tough, and that the subsequent class years are "softer" because they had it easier.[10] Granted, disparaging a subsequent class year involves a much smaller scale than the broad characterizations made between different generations, but this habitual process of seeing the next class of cadets as less competent might be a microcosm of a tendency to inflate one's generational (or class year) ingroup.

To summarize, cross-generational characterizations can be distorted by several psychological processes and this distortion is likely to be negative. Individuals should therefore be cautious about unfairly criticizing younger generations and should also remain skeptical of older individuals who provide offhand conclusions about the shortcomings of younger generations. Uninformed assumptions about generational differences can cause friction between different age groups and possibly undermine the precision of formal and informal organizational processes designed to enhance professional development. However, even while individuals should be careful to avoid the pitfalls of cross-generational characterizations, there are true mean-level differences between generations, indicating that the older gentleman at the shopping mall could be correct, on average, about his characterizations of younger people. We are not arguing that generational differences do not exist. They most certainly do. Our point is that hasty generalizations can easily be misguided.

Fortunately, there is a method for systematically examining generational differences that circumvents the biases that can occur during informal generation-based assessments. Psychology and related fields have created a wealth of data often involving the same measures being used decade after decade. Jean Twenge, author of *Generation Me*,[11] developed a method for using this data to provide more scientifically based conclusions about generational differences. Twenge demonstrated that one could use the information provided in research publications, such as the year the article was published and the age of the participants, to estimate how people born at different times responded to various measures when these groups were similarly aged. The statistics involved with this procedure can be at times more complicated than is necessary for the present paper.[12] Instead, let us illustrate with a simplified example. The majority of psychological research is conducted using college undergraduates. By noting when the research was published, one can estimate the birth year of these participants. After including many such studies that repeatedly use the same survey, the average response of college-aged students can be charted across several years.

This method is critical because it avoids two major issues typically inherent in generational differences research. First, it removes the age confound that exists when a survey is distributed simultaneously to a younger sample and older sample; any mean-level differences obtained using this method could be due to true generational differences or due to age differences. Second, generational differences can also be examined by administering questions to a younger sample and an older sample and asking the older participants to answer the questions as they would have when they roughly the same age as the young sample.[13] Twenge's method removes the errors and biases that accompany such retrospective accounts by comparing responses when those generations were actually of similar ages. With this approach and a broader understanding of generation based assessments, we can now address our leading question: In the United States, are "kids today" different than they were before?

GENERATIONAL DIFFERENCES IN THE UNITED STATES

Generally speaking, the answer to this question is "yes." To begin, college students reported substantially increasing levels of self-esteem between 1968 and 2008, indicating that younger people today experience much greater self-esteem on average than they did in the 1960s and 1970s.[14] This rise in self-esteem brings forth a concern about interpretation. To many, the rise in self-esteem would be clearly positive. In fact, the belief in self-esteem as a cure for many societal and personal failings was the primary basis for attempting to elevate children's self-esteem in the first place.[15] Unfortunately, the evidence supporting the purported benefits of high self-esteem is at best unclear. Baumeister and others concluded in a thorough review that the benefits of elevated self-esteem are minimal and that the "indiscriminate praise" often associated with self-esteem building programs could lead to elevated levels of narcissism.[16] Narcissism overlaps with self-esteem in that it involves a positive self-image, but narcissism includes greater amounts of self-inflation along with additional components like a focus on appearing good to others (e.g., seeming physically attractive, important, or powerful) and a tendency to have less warmth and empathy in interpersonal relationships. Unlike self-esteem, narcissism is more clearly associated with negative characteristics generally involving a reduced concern for others, a willingness to be exploitive, and a propensity for responding aggressively when narcissists' inflated egos are threatened.[17]

Chapter 1

Consistent with the concerns raised by Baumeister and his colleagues, narcissism has also increased substantially among college students during the period from 1979 to 2006.[18] There is also corresponding evidence that members of younger generations tend to care less about the opinions of others and experience reduced levels of empathy relative to older generations.[19]

These findings provide a backdrop for several other generational changes. Younger United States citizens appear to have reduced levels of mental health and well-being.[20] They exhibit greater levels of anxiety[21] and greater levels of depression.[22] These findings might seem at odds with the corresponding increases in self-esteem, but a few psychological processes can explain why the rise in self-esteem and self-focus could ultimately be detrimental. Younger generations also report having reduced locus of control,[23] a variable that measures the degree to which individuals believe that their outcomes are shaped by their personal behaviour (an internal locus of control) or forces beyond their control (an external locus of control).[24] Maintaining an internal locus of control contributes to increased levels of mental health and well-being.[25] As individuals develop inflated perceptions of themselves, they likely find negative feedback to be more threatening, which enhances a tendency to blame failure on external sources (e.g., I failed because the instructor did not like me). This strategy can protect self-esteem in the short term, but this process of externalizing the locus of control could lead to feelings of helplessness and alienation in the long-term.[26] High levels of self-focus might also weaken a sense of community and create feelings of loneliness, ultimately undermining personal well-being.[27] Finally, Baumeister has likened high levels of self-focus to being given a large elaborate house.[28] Owning an impressive house might create positive affect in the short-term, but homeowners typically spend a lot of time and energy maintaining their beautiful homes. These homeowners might fail to notice that they would be happier if they simply had a smaller home which required less attention and allowed more time for other activities like traveling or socializing with others. Likewise, by viewing the self as great and important, individuals devote considerable mental and emotional energy toward continuously confirming these beliefs.

These broad changes that reside at a personality level translate into interesting patterns at the attitudinal or behavioural level. Younger individuals engage in sexual activity earlier and more often,[29] possibly reflecting the reduced concern with others' opinions and increased focus on doing what feels good immediately. Younger individuals also exhibit greater support for racial, gender, and sexual orientation equality.[30] Interestingly, a review of "Millennials at Work"[31] reveals a mixture of positive and negative characteristics. Not surprisingly, this younger generation appears to be more individualistic,[32] less focused on work,[33] and more obese.[34] However, this younger generation might not be different on traits such as wanting to help others[35] and might even offer advantages in terms of willingness to speak openly and work in teams.[36] Others have noted that Millennials report relatively high levels of company and job satisfaction and question whether special considerations for the professional training of Millennials are worthwhile.[37]

One area where younger individuals might excel involves their familiarity with technology.[38] We have focused on personality characteristics and attitudes because these are broad internal attributes that can translate across many situations. These are also the areas that stir the most debate about generational differences. Naturally, there are societal changes, often at the technological level, that are more tangible and less disputable. Younger generations are growing up in a world that is becoming increasingly driven by technology and has exponentially greater levels of immediate media and information availability (e.g., the internet, mobile phones, global positioning devices, hundreds of television channels). These kinds of societal changes surely interact with personality changes in interesting and sometimes concerning ways. Technological experience will increase corresponding proficiency, but the availability of massive amounts of information and entertainment could also undermine levels of self-control.[39] There is also a concern that social networking sites like Facebook promote narcissism.[40]

INTERPRETING GENERATIONAL DIFFERENCES: A FEW CAVEATS

Even though this review reveals noteworthy differences between generations, it is still important to not exaggerate real mean-level differences in the same way that stereotypes can exaggerate differences between groups. Even though individuals born in the 1990s have higher self-esteem on average than individuals born in the 1960s, this does not mean, of course, that every person born in the 1990s has greater self-esteem than every member of an older generation. The younger generation has members with low self-esteem and previous generations have members with very high self-esteem. This should also serve as a reminder not to assume that all members of a generation are similar, even if mean-level generational differences are worthy of consideration.

We also believe it is important to avoid a negativity bias that can accompany legitimate generational differences. There are reasons to be concerned about younger generations. They have learned to be more self-focused, more self-absorbed, and less concerned about other people. This same group also feels lower levels of personal control and exhibits evidence of reduced mental health. At the same time, the self-focus and individualism found in younger generations might have redeeming qualities. Younger generations appear to respect others' individualism by exhibiting greater tolerance for groups different than their own. It is easy for United States citizens to wax nostalgic about previous generations, particularly the generation that fought during the Second World War and then returned home to help create economic and social stability. It is easy to overlook that the civil rights movement and other political movements associated with creating equality in the United States took place after the 1940s and 1950s. While younger United States citizens today have not accomplished the truly heroic deeds associated with a socially popular war, they also did not put Japanese-Americans in internment camps or segregate Black Americans.[41] This suggests that perhaps no generation has done everything correctly and individuals would be wise to maintain some level of generational humility.

It is also important to remember that the generational differences portrayed in the present paper are descriptive of broad changes in the United States. The obvious implication is that these changes are not necessarily descriptive of changes occurring in other nations. Another concern about generalizing these findings occurs not with our peer populations in other nations, but with the sub-population of the United States military. Because the United States maintains an all-volunteer (or self-selected) force, we encounter the possibility that the broad generational differences occurring in the United States do not apply to the United States military. It is possible that the United States military has continued to draw members that have attributes and values similar to previous generations. This would mean that younger or incoming military members could be generationally similar to older military members while becoming increasingly different from their generational peers who remain civilians. It is also possible that the selection process drawing individuals into military service has little interaction with generational changes and younger military members therefore differ from older military members in a manner that parallels generational changes in the United States more broadly. Furthermore, different portions of the United States military (e.g., branch of service, career field, rank) might be less or more representative of the broad changes that are occurring generationally. Unfortunately, we do not have any empirical data to answer this question, although we believe that the generational changes described broadly reflect changes in the average person entering the United States military to a sizable degree. It is difficult to imagine that younger military members have been overwhelmingly exempt from the broad processes that shaped their generations. Nonetheless, future research should consider examining this issue. Nations with higher percentages of military members serving due to compulsory military service (e.g., Singapore, South Korea, and Switzerland) would have reduced concerns about this issue because their military populations would be more reflective of their civilian populations, at least in the age range where military service is required.

THE CHALLENGES FACING FUTURE MILITARY PROFESSIONALS

Just as the type of individual entering military service seems to be shifting, the requirements of military service are shifting as well, possibly in conjunction or in competition with generational changes. The context of United States military operations is in the process of dramatic change. We believe that these changes include four dimensions that have specific relevance to the next generation of military leaders.

The first dimension involves the expanded range of military operations to include roles that would previously have been viewed by military members as non-traditional. This emphasis is reflected in a new lexicon pertaining to United States military operations. Terms such as "counter-insurgency," "peace-keeping operations," "information operations," "remotely piloted aircraft" (RPA; aircraft that are flown from a remote location with no pilot on board the platform), and "improvised explosive devices" have become the "new normal" when discussing ongoing military operations. One of the authors (Lindsay) was recently deployed to Afghanistan and was surprised at how an acronym-heavy organization like the military has developed even more acronyms to describe these new missions and functions. This is not to suggest that the militaries of the past have not participated in such non-traditional activities. Rather, we are simply noting that younger generations should be trained under the assumption that they will experience the entire gamut of military operations. Much of this transition can be encompassed by the notion of asymmetric warfare. Whereas traditional (or symmetric) warfare involves large standing armies competing directly to occupy a piece of land, asymmetric warfare is better described by "the absence of a common basis of comparison in respect to quality, or in operational terms, a capability."[42] In other words, a smaller or inferiorly armed force knows that it is likely to lose a conventional battle, and therefore uses other tactics, techniques, and procedures in order to level the playing field. Smaller forces might use their knowledge of terrain to perform "irregular" attacks that exploit the larger force's vulnerabilities. Ongoing United States military operations (e.g., Operation ENDURING FREEDOM, Operation NEW DAWN) are representative of asymmetric types of conflict. This fundamental difference in the nature of warfare requires an additional set of skills and competencies in military professionals.[43]

One palpable example of the new requirements associated with asymmetric warfare involves the notion of "winning the hearts and minds" of the local population. Military professionals must win over local populations politically, rather than simply dominate them through military strength.[44] While this might seem straightforward in theory, its application is exceedingly difficult. This mission requires that military members understand the local population – their culture, needs, and goals. Without this understanding, military professionals will fail to provide appropriate assistance and create increased animosity, likely increasing the number of enemy combatants. This hybrid of peacekeeping and warfare can also render it difficult to separate combatants and non-combatants.[45] This creates clear challenges for military professionals who must take valuable time to learn and respect the nuances of local culture, many of which are difficult to capture. Also, effective behaviour in asymmetric military operations can be incongruous with effective behaviour in symmetric operations. For example, in the Middle East, one of the factors that help build trust is to put down weapons, remove body armour, and have tea with villagers. The need for this behaviour might appear obvious to an outsider, but this requirement is incredibly stressful (and understandably so) to combatants, because these behaviours put them at great risk. This leaves military professionals in a perpetual dilemma. Failing to do these type of things can undermine the relationship development that is necessary for successful completion of the mission, but these same behaviours, combined with a misjudgement of the current security situation, can cause oneself and others to be killed.

The continued growth of asymmetric warfare contributes to a second dimension of change, which is the delegation of important decision-making processes. Sanders, Lindsay, Foster, and Cook,[46] described this change when they wrote:

> Decisions that were once made at senior levels are now dispersed throughout the military hierarchy. Accordingly, all military members on the 'battlefield' of today must be prepared to make decisions that not only influence the success of the immediate mission, but the completion of the overall theatre mission. For example, a young sergeant that is leading a squad through a village in Afghanistan

can no longer assume that the impact of his/her actions is limited to that geographical location. Poor decisions, such as those that lead to civilian casualties, could destabilize military-civilian relations locally and diplomatic relations internationally. Thus, even when operating at a tactical level, improperly executed decision-making can destabilize the broad military mission. (79-80)

Traditional forms of military operations faced similar situations, where tactical decisions with strategic implications had to be made immediately. Still, the need for strategic-level thinking at all levels of decision-making might be increasing in new forms of military operations.[47] This style of decision-making is incongruous with the traditional rank-driven military process where decisions are made by the commander and then pushed down through the lower levels of the organization. The traditional top-down decision-making system will undoubtedly remain a necessity due to the military's need to react in a swift and organized manner, but an increased emphasis on important and immediate decisions being made at lower levels could cause growing pains. This emphasis might be difficult for higher-ranking military leaders, who are used to having wider decision-making power and to being held accountable for it. This emphasis also has implications for the lower-ranking military leaders, who now face greater responsibility to delineate which decisions are theirs to make and how to make those decisions most effectively. Developing military leaders must become strategic thinkers as well as tactical decision-makers even as they go into harm's way to complete their mission.

The third dimension involves the increased use of technology.[48] Technological expertise is essential to military communications generally and to specific operations such as global positioning systems and RPA. Military professionals must possess a minimum set of competencies just to use and maintain these systems. An interesting example of the intersection between military technology and military psychology involves the growing emphasis on RPA. Remotely piloted aircraft create new challenges associated with this type of weapon system. It is now possible to send an aircraft into harm's way without having to worry about the life of the pilot. What are the long-term abilities required of those who "fly" RPA? Operating RPA does not place physical stress on the body, nor does it elicit the fear and anxiety that can come with directly taking enemy fire. As the use of RPA increases, it might be difficult to maintain an emphasis on a "warrior" type of mindset. It is also important to note that those who fly RPA might need elevated capabilities in other areas. This new form of pilot might need greater levels of "video game skills" especially as the military considers having individuals pilot multiple RPA at one time.[49] Another issue involves a different kind of mental stress that military members might experience when they harm or kill people from such remote locations. It is possible that individuals who operate these kinds of weapons systems will experience fatigue, anxiety, and depression at unexpected times.

A fourth dimension involves the diminishing ability to predict the future of military operations (despite the aforementioned predictions).[50] The rate of change in society appears to be increasing, particularly in the technological arena. As a result, there is less assurance that the capabilities needed in younger military professionals today will remain consistent as they progress through their military careers. This diminished ability to predict the nature of future military operations has been reflected in United States involvement in Iraq and Afghanistan, both of which required substantial adjustment after these operations began.[51] An added challenge is that the United States military is ultimately not responsible for the larger strategic decisions that surround military action, such as when, where, and how the military will operate. This increases the likelihood that military members will engage in operations for which they have had inadequate time to prepare.

The notion of preparing military members for the unknown might seem nonsensical, but two attributes seem chiefly related to this type of preparedness. The first involves the concept of *adaptability*, which is an individual's ability to predict or adjust to changing conditions in the environment while still maintaining an acceptable level of performance.[52] In the military, where change occurs frequently and rapidly, the ability to adjust quickly to a new set of circumstances is critical to mission accomplishment and the prevention of unnecessary harm. A second attribute involves the concept of *openness*. Openness (also called *openness to experience*) refers to an individual's willingness to consider a wide range of values and ideas as well as engage in experiences that are novel, imaginative, artistic or emotional.[53] High scorers on openness tend to be less traditional, less conventional, and more imaginative. If military operations are truly changing at an increasing rate, cultivating openness might be another method of preparing future military leaders for change itself.

YOUNG MILITARY PROFESSIONALS AND FUTURE MILITARY OPERATIONS

Are younger United States citizens better or worse prepared for future military service than were those who preceded them? We believe that the answer is multifaceted, nicely illustrating that the attributes of younger military professionals most likely interact with the changing nature of military operations in complex ways. The clearest negative attribute involves the evidence that younger individuals have on average reduced mental health and well-being. Depression obviously inhibits military effectiveness, and heightened emotional anxiety is likely to interfere with military effectiveness as well. Individuals who maintain elevated levels of anxiety might be sorely tested in asymmetric-type conflicts that require the ability to act as cooperatively and combatively with a local population. Chronically anxious individuals are likely to have less effective decision-making, particularly in stressful situations, and evidence suggests that anxiety is negatively correlated with effective leadership.[54] Another concern is that younger individuals are more likely to be overweight, which is clearly inconsistent with military values. While this is perhaps an easier attribute to remedy, it could have important implications. Younger people who are overweight might be less inclined to see military service as a viable option or to fail to maintain standards while serving in the military.

The increased levels of self-esteem, self-focus, individualism, and narcissism most likely have mixed consequences. The younger generation's enhanced endorsement for celebrating the self and acting independently is clearly at odds with a military organization that typically needs coordinated collective efforts to be effective. Elevated levels of narcissism will cause individuals to be self-promoting, less interested in the well-being of others, and generally difficult to work with. Furthermore, we speculate that elevated levels of narcissism cause individuals to be less likely to endanger themselves to protect others; it is less appealing to risk one's life, when one's self feels salient, unique, and special. Yet, an increase in self-esteem could be beneficial. At this point, it might be helpful to offer a rudimentary distinction between healthy and unhealthy forms of self-esteem. Self-esteem is an effective attribute when it is coupled with a desire to help other people and is separated from the defensiveness, image consciousness, and exploitative behaviours that can accompany narcissism. For example, there is evidence that individuals with high self-esteem are less likely to cheat, but only when they have reduced need for approval from others.[55] Self-esteem, if managed correctly, could contribute to healthy forms of self-confidence that enhance effectiveness. Also, military leaders commonly claim to want honest feedback from subordinates. Younger generations' confidence and informality likely causes them to speak more candidly to superiors. Military leaders might benefit from this candour if they are willing to listen to it and if younger military professionals take care to offer it constructively and professionally.

Chapter 1

Oddly, an offshoot of the self-focus and individualism seen in the younger generations might be useful in asymmetric warfare. Because younger generations generally appear to be more tolerant of intergroup differences, they might also have a better foundation for interacting positively with cultures that are different than their own. For example, older generations appear to have more rooted and negative perceptions of Muslims.[56]   Many of them grew up in a United States where Christianity was the norm and diversity was emphasized less than it is today. Younger generations are more likely to see negative feelings toward Islam generally as prejudicial. In this vein, younger United States citizens might have a better foundation for relationship building that is necessary for not just occupying another nation, but working with other nations as partners. At the same time, it is important to be cautious about this speculation. The reduced levels of empathy[57] and elevated levels of narcissism[58] found in younger generations could cause them to be less genuinely motivated to help others and more susceptible to angry outbursts when working in these contexts.

The younger generation's familiarity with technology should be a clear asset. It seems abundantly clear that technology is and will remain a central part of military warfare.

Concerns about the younger population's preparedness for military service certainly are not new. It would be easy to argue that military operations are unnatural (e.g., risking one's life) and that the military has always had to prepare people for this type of career. We do not wish to discuss this issue generally because it is an expansive issue in its own right and one to which the United States military devotes considerable attention. Instead, we remain focused on the theme of this chapter and how generational changes specifically relate to military preparedness. In this vein, we offer the following suggestions. First, the most significant challenge is creating military professionals with superior mental health, focusing in particular on inhibiting depression and anxiety. Second, the positive self-esteem often exhibited by younger generations should be managed by encouraging empathy, perspective-taking, and service. Each of these could work against the detrimental components of narcissism. Third, younger military professionals, especially military leaders, must be open to new ideas and be adaptable. Fourth, the United States military should leverage younger individuals' technological proficiency. Fifth, the United States military must also continue emphasizing a fitness culture to address ongoing concerns with obesity and physical health generally.

In addition, we also offer two additional variables that appear critical to supporting the expanding roles for military leaders. The next generation of military leaders will have increased need to engage in a variety of roles, some of which are juxtaposing, such as being a warrior versus a peacekeeper. Two of the key variables in managing these varied roles are self-control and ego resilience. Self-control has been described as "the exertion of control over the self, by the self."[59] Ego resilience is an individual's ability to vary perceptual, cognitive, and behavioural strategies in conjunction with the demands of the situation.[60] Individuals high in ego resiliency can increase their levels of self-control depending on situational requirements. Again, the need for military members to exhibit high levels of these variables is not new, but self-control and ego resilience might be increasingly important as military members, especially military leaders, fluctuate between several conflicting roles.

This concept of *ego resilience* should not be confused with the more general concept of *resilience*, which is often used to mean something more like the ability to effectively overcome threatening or difficult situations. A recent issue of *American Psychologist* devoted to comprehensive soldier fitness relied heavily on the concept of resilience.[61] The general concept of resilience does not seem as clearly tied to preparing the next generation of military leaders because resilience has long been critical to effective military operations and there does not appear to be any direct empirical data demonstrating whether resilience has increased or decreased over time. Nonetheless, the concept of resilience might provide a useful overarching theme. Apparent decreases in mental health indicate that younger generations are probably less resilient than previous generations,[62] despite their reported increases in self-esteem. Likewise, the current trends in military operations suggest that the need for psychological resilience could be growing. Thus, while we did not review the general concept of resilience in the context of generational changes, we can only agree that it is a critical part of maintaining ongoing military effectiveness and one that is consistent with the generation-related issues reviewed in this chapter.

The United States military can address these force development concerns in two main ways. One method involves selecting individuals who are fit for this type of service. This process occurs somewhat naturally when individuals who seek military service do so because they possess the correct personal foundation for this type of work. However, the needs for recruiting and the requirements of military service can conflict. Twenge used a chapter title in her book to refer to the "An Army of One" slogan that was adopted by the United States Army in 2001.[63] The notion of being an "Army of One" might appeal to a younger generation that is more self-focused and grew up knowing Rambo and The Terminator. At the same time, this recruiting strategy appears wholly inconsistent with the emphasis on teamwork and collectivism that embodies military units. This reflects a tension that can exist between the need to obtain sufficient numbers of recruits versus obtaining the right kind of recruits. We also caution that an increased emphasis on selecting individuals with certain characteristics could increase the gap that exists between the military and civilians in the United States today. Some differences between the military and civilian populations make sense, such as the ability to take another person's life when necessary, but making these populations too different could be politically problematic.[64]

Preparing the next generation for future military service can also be addressed through training and development. Kowske, Rasch, and Wiley questioned the benefits of tailoring interventions to generational differences in business settings.[65] We appreciate this point of view, because the size of mean-level generational differences can be exaggerated and instituting new training programs comes at a cost. That being said, we do believe that the United States military would benefit from carefully adjusting training programs to address known generational changes. The relative cost of doing so is probably less than typically exists in business organizations considering that the United States military already has numerous training programs. These programs include entire schools, often completed in residence (e.g., Airman Leadership School, War Colleges, etc.), devoted to preparing military professionals for the next phase of their careers. Adapting these programs to address ongoing generational issues does not seem overly costly, especially considering that these programs are constantly being updated anyhow. The United States military must also consider its own version of return on investment associated with these programs. It is exceptionally difficult to quantify how much a slight increase in healthy self-esteem or a slight decrease in anxiety would benefit the United States military. The advantage of considering generational differences, however, is that force development concerns can be anticipated. Thus, using generational changes to tailor development programs should perhaps be viewed not as a cost, but as a method for more effectively *recalibrating* existing training programs to prepare military professionals for upcoming military operations.

CONCLUSION

This depiction of generational differences and the future of military leadership is a United States story. Those outside of the United States will have to determine the degree to which these trends reflect trends in their nations, just as United States citizens can consider whether trends reported from other nations provide insight into our own. However, while generational trends vary in different contexts, we believe that several of the concepts used to analyze generational differences do translate cross-culturally. The psychological processes that distort informal generation-based assessments almost certainly exist across cultures. Mistaking age differences for generational differences and stereotyping are almost certainly universal. The errors and biases that can occur with retrospective judgements surely exist in any culture as well. (If there is a culture where people have substantially accurate and unbiased memories please inform us so we can move there). We hope that our process of examining this issue provides useful insights about accurately assessing generational differences cross-culturally.

Is our military going to experience a precipitous decline as younger generations inherit it? We doubt it. The next generation of military officers has their own pattern of attributes, some of which might weaken military effectiveness while others enhance it. It is also important to realize that these changes have been in progress for decades, meaning that these changes are a growing part of military personnel today, not a dramatic wave that is going to exhibit a sudden stress on the system. Older generations should therefore take some care to not judge younger generations too harshly as the older generation starts handing over the future of the United States military. Besides, lamenting the next generation, rather than partnering with it, could stifle the very development that the older generations wish to create. At the same time, the military should also recognize that there are substantial issues to consider in terms of generational changes, and perhaps it is better for the military to exhibit too much anxiety about the next generation of military leaders rather than too little. We would also encourage military professionals to consider how their generations' upbringing might have given them, as a group, certain strengths and weaknesses in terms of military service. By understanding these attributes, military professionals can consider which attributes are strengths and which attributes are weaknesses that need to be addressed. After all, younger and older members of the United States military have one shared commonality that all should embrace, and that is the acceptance of a profession designed to serve their fellow citizens. The best outcome associated with understanding generational differences is not to focus on which generation is better, but to use this understanding to enhance the effectiveness of all military personnel.

ENDNOTES

1. "Emo" is a term used in the United States to describe a kind of young person who often acts depressed, wears black all the time, and pontificates about deep issues seemingly related to the challenges of life.

Chapter 1

2. A "mullet" is a hairstyle where the bangs in the front are kept short, but the hair in the back is grown long. This hairstyle is sometimes called "business in the front, party in the back."

3. There is some debate about the precise definition of stereotypes. For the purposes of this paper, we believe that this definition is sufficient. For more information, see Shunsuke Kanahara, "A Review of the Definitions of Stereotype and a Proposal for a Progressional Model", *Individual Differences Research*, Vol. 4, No. 5 (2006), 306-321.

4. René Mõttus, Kristjan Indus and Jüri Allik, "Accuracy of Only Children Stereotype", *Journal of Research in Personality*, Vol. 42, No. 4 (2008), 1047-1052.

5. Joachim Krueger, Julie Hasman, Melissa Acevedo and Paola Villano, "Perceptions of Trait Typicality in Gender Stereotypes: Examining the Role of Attribution in the Categorization Process", *Personality and Social Psychology Bulletin*, Vol. 29, No. 1 (2003), 108-116.

6. Patricia Linville and Edward Jones, "Polarized Appraisals of Out-Group Members", *Journal of Personality and Social Psychology*, Vol. 38, No. 5 (1980), 689-703.

7. John Darley and Paget Gross, "A Hypothesis-Confirming Bias in Labeling Effects", *Journal of Personality and Social Psychology*, Vol. 44, No. 1 (1983), 20-33.

8. Zoë Richards and Miles Hewstone, "Subtyping and Subgrouping: Processes for the Prevention and Promotion of Stereotype Change", *Personality and Social Psychology Review*, Vol. 5, No. 1 (2001), 52-73.

9. Henri Tajfel and John Turner, "The Social Identity Theory of Intergroup Behavior" in Stephen Worchel and William G. Austin, eds., *Psychology of Intergroup Relations, 2nd ed.* (Chicago, IL: Nelson-Hall, 1986).

10. A department member co-authored an article that also documents this phenomenon. Steven Samuels and Dena Samuels, "Reconstructing Culture: Privilege and Change at the United States Air Force Academy", *Race, Gender, & Class*, Vol. 10, No. 4 (2003), 120-144.

11. Jean Twenge, *Generation Me: Why Today's Young Americans are More Confident, Assertive, Entitled – and More Miserable than Ever Before* (New York, NY: Free Press, 2006).

12. For a more information about this method see Twenge's book *Generation Me*.

13. See for example Gordon. B. Forbes, Leah Adams-Curtis, Rebecca L. Jobe, Kay B. White, Jessica Revak, Ivanka Zivcic-Becirevic and Alessandra Pokrajac-Bulian, "Body Dissatisfaction in College Women and Their Mothers: Cohort Effects, Developmental Effects, and the Influences of Body Size, Sexism, and the Thin Body Ideal", *Sex Roles*, Vol. 53, No. 3-4 (2005), 281-298.

14. Brittany Gentile, Jean Twenge and Keith Campbell, "Birth Cohort Differences in Self-Esteem, 1988-2008: A Cross-Temporal Meta-Analysis", *Review of General Psychology*, Vol. 14, No. 3 (2010), 261-268.; Jean Twenge and Keith Campbell, "Age and Birth Cohort Differences in Self-Esteem: A Cross-Temporal Meta-Analysis", *Personality and Social Psychology Review*, Vol. 5, No. 4 (2001), 321-344.

15. Roy Baumeister, Jennifer Campbell, Joachim Krueger and Kathlee Vohs, "Does High Self-Esteem Cause Better Performance, Interpersonal Success, Happiness, or Healthier Lifestyles?", *Psychological Science in the Public Interest*, Vol. 4, No. 1 (2003), 1-44.

16. Ibid.

17. See Jean Twenge and Keith Campbell's, *The Narcissism Epidemic: Living in the Age of Entitlement* (New York, NY: Free Press, 2009).

18. Jean M. Twenge, Sara Konrath, Joshua D. Foster, W. Keith Campbell and Brad J. Bushman, "Egos Inflating Over time: A Cross-Temporal Meta-Analysis of the Narcissistic Personality Inventory", *Journal of Personality*, Vol. 76. No. 4 (2008), 875-901.

19. Jean Twenge, *Generation Me: Why Today's Young Americans are More Confident, Assertive, Entitled – and More Miserable than Ever Before* (New York, NY: Free Press, 2006); Sara Konrath, Edward O'Brien and Courtney Hsing, "Changes in Dispositional Empathy in American College Students Over Time: A Meta-Analysis", *Personality and Social Psychology Review*, Vol. 15, No. 2 (2011), 180-198.; Jean M. Twenge, Brittany Gentile, Nathan DeWall, Debbie Ma, Katharine Lacefield and David R. Schurtz , "Birth Cohort Increases in Psychopathology among Young Americans, 1938-2007: A Cross-Temporal Meta-Analysis of the MMPI", *Clinical Psychology Review*, Vol. 30, No. 2 (2010), 145-154.

20. Jean Twenge *et al.*, "Birth Cohort Increases in Psychopathology among Young Americans, 1938-2007: A Cross-Temporal Meta-Analysis of the MMPI", *Clinical Psychology Review*, Vol. 30, No. 2 (2010), 145-154.

21. Jean Twenge, "The Age of Anxiety? Birth Cohort Change in Anxiety of Neuroticism, 1952-1993", *Journal of Personality and Social Psychology*, Vol. 79, No. 6 (2000), 1007-1021.

22. Jean Twenge *et al.*, "Birth Cohort Increases in Psychopathology among Young Americans, 1938-2007: A Cross-Temporal Meta-Analysis of the MMPI", *Clinical Psychology Review*, Vol. 30, No. 2 (2010), 145-154.

23. Jean Twenge, Liqing Zhang and Charles Im, "It's Beyond My Control: A Cross-Temporal Meta-Analysis of Increasing Externality in Locus of Control, 1960-2002", *Personality and Social Psychology Review*, Vol. 8, No. 3 (2004), 308-319.

24. Julian Rotter, "Generalized Expectancies for Internal Versus External Control of Reinforcement", *Psychological Monographs: General and Applied*, Vol. 80, No. 1 (1966), 1-28.

25. Herbert Lefcourt, "Locus of Control" in Alan Kazdin, ed., *Encyclopedia of Psychology*, Vol. 5 (Washington, DC: Oxford University Press, 2000).

26. Jean Twenge, "The Age of Anxiety? Birth Cohort Change in Anxiety of Neuroticism, 1952-1993", *Journal of Personality and Social Psychology*, Vol. 79, No. 6 (2000), 1007-1021.

27. See for example Nazmiye Civitci and Asim Civitci, "Self-esteem as mediator and moderator of the relationship between loneliness and life satisfaction in adolescents", *Personality & Individual Differences*, Vol. 47, No. 8 (2009), 954-958.

28. Roy Baumeister, *Escaping the Self: Alcoholism, Spirituality, Masochism, and Other Flights from the Burden of Selfhood* (New York, NY: Basic Books, 1991).

29. Brooke Wells and Jean Twenge, "Changes in Young People's Sexual Behavior and Attitudes, 1943-1999: A Cross-Temporal Meta-Analysis", *Review of General Psychology*, Vol. 9, No. 3 (2005), 249-261.

30. Jean Twenge, *Generation Me: Why Today's Young Americans are More Confident, Assertive, Entitled – and More Miserable than Ever Before* (New York, NY: Free Press, 2006).

31. David Altman and Jennifer Deal, "Special Issue on Millennials and the World of Work: What You Didn't Know You Didn't Know", *Journal of Business and Psychology*, Vol. 25, No. 2 (2010).

32. Jean Twenge, "A Review of the Empirical Evidence on Generational Differences in Work Attitudes", *Journal of Business and Psychology*, Vol. 25, No. 2 (2010), 201-210.

33. Ibid.

Chapter 1

34. Shari Barkin, William Heerman, Michael Warren and Christine Rennhoff, "Millennials and the World of Work: The Impact of Obesity on Health and Productivity", *Journal of Business and Psychology*, Vol. 25, No. 2 (2010), 239-245.

35. Jean Twenge, "A Review of the Empirical Evidence on Generational Differences in Work Attitudes", *Journal of Business and Psychology*, Vol. 25, No. 2 (2010), 201-210.

36. Karen Myers and Kamyab Sadaghiani, "Millennials in the Workplace: A Communication Perspective on Millennials' Organizational Relationships and Performance", *Journal of Business and Psychology*, Vol. 25, No. 2 (2010), 225-238.

37. Brenda Kowske, Rena Rasch and Jack Wiley, "Millennials' (Lack of) Attitude Problem: An Empirical Examination of Generational Effects on Work Attitudes", *Journal of Business and Psychology*, Vol. 25, No. 2 (2010), 265-279.

38. Andrea Hershatter and Molly Epstein, "Millennials and the World of Work: An Organization and Management Perspective", *Journal of Business and Psychology*, Vol. 25, No. 2 (2010), 211-223.

39. See for example Martha Shaw and Donald Black, "Internet Addiction: Definition, Assessment, Epidemiology, and Clinical Management", *CNS Drugs*, Vol. 22, No. 5 (2008), 353-365.

40. This question has also been raised in Lisa Buffardi's and Keith Campbell's, "Narcissism and Social Networking Web Sites", *Personality and Social Psychology Bulletin*, Vol. 34, No. 10 (2008), 1303-1314.

41. To be fair, not every U. S. citizen from previous generations supported these practices, but younger generations also have members that do not merit blame for the negative characteristics broadly associated with their generations.

42. Montgomery Meigs, "Unorthodox Thoughts about Asymmetric Warfare", *Parameters*, Vol. 33 (2003), 4-18.

43. "Asymmetric" and "symmetric" forms of warfare are sometimes subsumed under the more general term "full-spectrum warfare". For an example of the broad requirements associated with full-spectrum warfare see Wilbur Scott, David McCone and George Mastroianni, "The Deployment Experiences of Ft. Carson's Solders in Iraq", *Armed Forces & Society*, Vol. 35, No. 3 (2009), 460-476.

44. Ibid.

45. This tension is evident in General Infantry graffiti "Better to be judged by 12, than carried by 6" (i.e., Better to face a jury than be killed).

46. Joseph Sanders, Douglas Lindsay, Craig Foster and James Cook, "Ethics in the 21st Century Profession of Arms: A Context for Developing Leaders of Character" in Jeff Stouffer and Stefan Seiler, eds., *Military Ethics: International Perspectives* (Kingston, ON: Canadian Defence Academy Press, 2010).

47. Charles Krulak, "The Strategic Corporal: Leadership in the Three Block War", *Marines Magazine*, Vol. 28 (1999).

48. Tim Robinson, "It's the Network, Stupid", *Military Technology*, Vol. 34, No. 2 (2010), 40-48.

49. Stephen Dixon, Christopher Wickens and Dervon Chang, "Mission Control of Multiple Unmanned Aerial Vehicles: A Workload Analysis", *Human Factors*, Vol. 47, No. 3 (2005), 479-487.

50. Ajay Singh, "Time: The New Dimension in War", *Joint Forces Quarterly* (Winter 1995-1996), 56-61.

51. For a more detailed account of such adjustments, see Sebastian Junger, *War*, (New York, NY: Twelve, 2010).

52. Johnathan Nelson, Stephen Zaccaro and Jeffrey Herman, "Strategic Information Provision and Experiential Variety as Tools for Developing Adaptive Leadership Skills", *Consulting Psychology Journal: Practice and Research*, Vol. 62, No. 2 (2010), 131-142.

53. See for example, Robert McCrae and Paul Costa, Jr., "Validation of the Five-Factor Model of Personality Across Instruments and Observers", *Journal of Personality and Social Psychology*, Vol. 52, No. 1 (1987), 81-90.

54. Timothy Judge, Joyce Bono, Remus Ilies and Megan Gerhardt, "Personality and Leadership: A Qualitative and Quantitative Review", *Journal of Applied Psychology*, Vol. 87, No. 4 (2002), 765-780.

55. Thalma Lobel and Ilana Levanon, "Self-Esteem, Need for Approval, and Cheating Behavior in Children", *Journal of Educational Psychology*, Vol. 80, No. 1 (1988), 122-123.

56. Mohamed Abdel-Moneim and Rita Simon, "Does Age Matter?", *Social Science and Public Policy*, Vol. 48, No. 1 (2011), 41-49.

57. Sara Konrath, Edward O'Brien and Courtney Hsing, "Changes in Dispositional Empathy in American College Students Over Time: A Meta-Analysis", *Personality and Social Psychology Review*, Vol. 15, No. 2 (2011), 180-198.

58. Jean M. Twenge, Sara Konrath, Joshua D. Foster, Keith Campbell and Brad J. Bushman, "Egos Inflating Over time: A Cross-Temporal Meta-Analysis of the Narcissistic Personality Inventory", *Journal of Personality*, Vol. 76, No. 4 (2008), 875-902.

59. Mark Muraven and Roy Baumeister, "Self-Regulation and Depletion of Limited Resources: Does Self-Control Resemble a Muscle?", *Psychological Bulletin*, Vol. 126, No. 2 (2000), 247-259.

60. David Funder and Jack Block, "The Role of Ego-Control, Ego-Resiliency, and IQ in Delay of Gratification in Adolescence", *Journal of Personality and Social Psychology*, Vol. 57, No. 6 (1989), 1041-50.

61. See *American Psychologist*, Vol. 66, No. 1 (2011).

62. Jean Twenge et al., "Birth Cohort Increases in Psychopathology among Young Americans, 1938-2007: A Cross-Temporal Meta-Analysis of the MMPI", *Clinical Psychology Review*, Vol. 30, No. 2 (2010), 145-154.

63. Jean Twenge, *Generation Me: Why Today's Young Americans are More Confident, Assertive, Entitled – and More Miserable than Ever Before*, (New York, NY: Free Press, 2006).

64. Peter Feaver and Richard Kohn, *Soldiers and Civilians: The Civil-Military Gap and American National Security* (Cambridge, MA: MIT Press, 2001).

65. Brenda Kowske, Rena Rasch and Jack Wiley, "Millennials' (Lack of) Attitude Problem: An Empirical Examination of Generational Effects on Work Attitudes" *Journal of Business and Psychology*, Vol. 25, No. 2 (2010), 265-279.

CHAPTER 2

EDUCATION – THE KEY COMPONENT TO THE DEVELOPMENT OF THE NEXT GENERATION OF MILITARY LEADERS

Colonel Bernd Horn *

No organization takes failure more seriously than the military. After all, the consequences of failure are significant. Failure entails serious national and political ramifications, as well as the loss of life. Therefore, the military invests huge effort and resources into preparing its leaders and soldiers for operations throughout the full spectrum of conflict. Intuitively, everyone knows training and experience are key factors in developing leaders. What is less understood is the vital importance of education. Simply put, education is a key component to the development of the next generation of military leaders.

At first glance, one could argue the statement that education is misunderstood or undervalued as a factor for developing future leaders. Virtually no-one would argue that more education is a bad thing. In fact, most would agree that, as a philosophical concept, the more education one has, the richer one is as a person. However, the moment resources or cost enter the equation, the value of education to individuals and organizations often changes. Nowhere is this more evident than in the military, where fiscal pressures inevitably prompt "innovative ideas" that often revolve around cutting professional development, specifically, education. Moreover, these same pressures consistently elicit queries with regard to the value of education, specifically undergraduate and graduate degrees, to the military. Questions such as "Do all officers need degrees?" and "What is the military requirement for graduate degrees?" are frequently floated as a precursor to potential program cuts.

Although the military has historically been an anti-intellectual institution, such discourse seems incredulous considering the contemporary operating environment (COE), which, if anything, will become even more complex in the future. Globalization and persistent conflict, as well as the proliferation of cheap, accessible technology challenge conventional understanding of conflict. Moreover, hybrid threats that include diverse combinations of irregular,

---

* The views expressed in this chapter are those of the author and do not necessarily reflect those of the Canadian Forces or the Department of National Defence.

terrorist, criminal, and conventional forces employed asymmetrically, all operating within populated centres in a variety of culturally diverse environments, are just some of the challenges that have added complexity to conflict. In order to be effective in this environment, military professionals must be adaptive and agile in both thought and action, as well as adept at critical thinking and sound reasoning – all benefits of education. In short, militaries require warrior/scholars who are capable of operating in the complex battlespace of today and tomorrow. As such, education becomes a key factor in developing our future leaders.

A CULTURE OF ANTI-INTELLECTUALISM?

However, this is often easier said than done. The reluctance of militaries to embrace the concept of soldier/scholar, or the importance of education for that matter, is not surprising. The conventional military mind is conservative, functional and skeptical. Above all else, it utilizes experience as the key filter to determine what is possible, what is useful and often what is considered true and real. This is not to denigrate experience, since actual observation of facts or events, as well as the knowledge and/or skill resulting from this, are powerful teachers. Moreover, experience builds confidence, as well as individual and group competence. Quite simply, experience is empirical and tangible; decisions were made, actions were taken and the results were seen if not felt. Rightfully, the military culture reveres and recognizes the experience of individuals. Campaign ribbons, qualification and specialty badges and long service medals provide an instant recognition of an individual's experience and, more often than not, bestow a degree of credibility upon the bearer.

While there is nothing inherently wrong with this approach, it can be dangerous when coupled with overt "anti-intellectualism." Experience is recognized as a critical developmental tool for officers and soldiers. In a crisis, any rational person would prefer to be led by, or teamed with, someone who has previously been tested or has faced a similar menace successfully. However, the military's traditional myopic reliance on experience as the preferred, if not exclusive, professional development tool has arguably created and perpetuated an attitude that has historically shunned intellectualism and scholarship as a useful skill set for officers and soldiers.[1] It is far from unique to state that the military is largely anti-intellectual. Former Canadian Forces (CF) officer, Dr. Sandy Cotton, noted, "Having studied and written and talked to the military culture in Canada for 30-plus years, I would have to say that there is an intellectual stagnation, in some cases an anti-intellectualism."[2] In fact, there appears to be a default mechanism that rejects the concept that warriors can also be scholars.

Recent experience bears this out. The tumultuous decade of the 1990s in many respects ripped the CF asunder. The institution as a whole lost the trust of both the public and the government as a result of a series of scandals that demonstrated an apparent lack of ethical behaviour and leadership, as well as an inability to adapt to, or cope with, significant changes in society and military affairs. This appalling situation led to an in-depth examination of the CF. Tellingly, the review was not entrusted to the institution itself but rather to an external board of inquiry, as well as an array of academics and scholars. One factor that was repeatedly criticized was the absence of intellectual rigor and the lack of higher education in the officer corps.

This should not have been a big surprise. Higher education has never been an important component of officership in the CF, particularly not during the Cold War. Theoretical musings and historical studies, much less a grounding in the liberal arts, were perceived as suspect and downright unsoldierlike. Marshal of France, Herman Maurice, Count de Saxe, mused, "War is a science so obscure and imperfect that custom and prejudice confirmed by ignorance are its sole foundation and support." Simply put, scholarly pursuit was anathema to the true warrior. This attitude was rooted in CF culture. To be fair, it is a criticism that universally fits most militaries.

Respected British historian Sir Michael Howard reinforced the observation. "It is not surprising that there have often been a high proportion of failures among senior commanders at the beginning of any war," he asserted. Howard noted, "These unfortunate men may either take too long to adjust themselves to reality, through a lack of hard preliminary thinking about what war would really be like, or they may have had their minds so far shaped by a lifetime of pure administration that they have ceased for all practical purposes to be soldiers."[3] He argued, "Like the statesman, the soldier has to steer between the danger of repeating the errors of the past because he is ignorant that they have been made, and the danger of remaining bound by theories deduced from past history although changes in conditions have rendered these theories obsolete."[4]

Howard's observations boil down to the lack of importance the military places on education and intellectualism. Norman Dixon, in his seminal work, *On the Psychology of Military Incompetence*, wrote:

> Whether or not intellectual shortcomings lie at the heart of much military incompetence, the fact is that a deliberate cult of anti-intellectualism has characterized the armed services. While its origins relate, as we shall see, to much deeper reasons for military

mishaps than mere ignorance or slowness of mind, the fact remains that its effects have not been helpful. That generals and admirals between the wars who denigrated progressive thinkers and poured scorn on men who wrote books which challenged existing practices must surely have tended to stifle any exercise of intellect by those who wanted to get on, and deterred the gifted from ever seeking a military career.

As Robert McNamara once remarked, "Brains are like hearts, they go where they're appreciated."[5]

Nonetheless, as already stated, anti-intellectualism was endemic to the CF. Although catastrophic events in the 1990s forced a change, arguably anti-intellectualism remains an undercurrent percolating below the surface. Dr. Cotton observed, "officers are generally quite conservative beings, and so are NCOs [non-commissioned officers]….on the social dimension they're profoundly conservative, [and] resistant to change." He insisted, "They tend to get a mindset that locks into certain ways of doing things."[6] It is widely recognized that culture is influenced by what is paid attention to, controlled and rewarded. Cultural values in turn define who we are and what is acceptable thought and behaviour. As a result, the rampant anti-intellectualism that was clearly present ensured that the divide between warrior and scholar remained a deep chasm. The former Chief of Defence Staff (CDS), General Maurice Baril, conceded, "Our approach over the last twenty-five years has focused almost exclusively on the practical side." He stated, "In the arena of officer education for example, there was little opportunity or encouragement for officers to undertake academic study." Baril acknowledged, "It was generally accepted that to take time out for post graduate work was detrimental to your career."[7]

But once again, this admission is not a startling revelation. The attitude was prevalent and overt and could be seen and heard throughout the CF. Streamers, that is those identified with great career potential and destined to attain the highest rungs of the corporate ladder, were normally not posted to schools or required to take time out to attain bachelor, much less graduate degrees, if they were lacking. Those who showed an inclination to pursue higher education had to do so on their own and were still often seen as suspect and their loyalty questioned. Graduate training was seen as self-serving and a step towards preparing an individual for employment on the "dark side," namely, the civilian sector. Predictably, actively seeking higher education became debilitating to one's career.

Paradoxically, the few sponsored graduate education billets that were available were normally given to those on the bottom of the merit list who were nearing the end of their career.[8] Rather than use the opportunity to prepare the future corporate leadership to better command the institution, it was used as a consolation prize, a reward to some of the long serving members who failed to attain high rank. Graduate studies were viewed as an effort to allow those individuals to pad their CVs and prepare them for their second career. The only other accepted rationale for graduate education was to fill a particular requirement, normally a very technical domain such as aerospace engineering. In 1988, Lieutenant-General R. J. Evraire wrote that higher education was not conceived as a way to develop the minds of officers; rather it was a task-oriented function to acquire a skill for which there was an obvious and immediate need, mostly in technical areas.[9]

Annual Personnel Evaluation Reports (PERs) were yearly reminders of the culture's lack of respect for higher learning.[10] Education was of little consequence. It was just not seen as an important component of the military. The successful completion of a Ranger course, not to denigrate its value for tactical training or as a test of personal stamina, was of greater value to a member's future progression, than was the attainment of partial or complete fulfillment of a degree. In addition, when rating personal attributes, whenever scoring limitations precluded a high grading for all attributes, intellect would often be sacrificed for categories such as loyalty and deportment, which were perceived as much more important.

Should there be any doubt of the CF's historic culture of anti-intellectualism then one need only look at the composition of its officer corps. In March of 1997, the renowned Canadian military historian, Dr. Jack Granatstein, reported to the Minister of National Defence (MND) that "the CF has a remarkably ill-educated officer corps, surely one of the worst in the Western World." He pointed out that only 53.29 percent of officers had a university degree and only an abject 6.79 percent had graduate degrees, and these primarily in technical areas.[11] Similarly, professor Albert Legault was equally scathing. "The level of education in the Armed Forces," he argued, "is particularly lacking within the framework of a democracy that thinks of itself as a model or example within the Western world."[12] Former serving officer and current military historian, Desmond Morton, another of the former MND's handpicked consultants in 1997, asserted, "when one Canadian in five completes such a degree [bachelor degree] or its equivalent, this is no longer an elitist pre-requisite for a commission in Canada's armed forces. No self-professed profession would accept less."[13]

It was the gut wrenching analysis of the 1990s that highlighted the importance of education to the philosophical and real health of the CF. As such,

Chapter 2

a virtual phoenix arose from the ashes of the "decade of darkness" and it's myriad of financial, social, operational and leadership challenges. In fact, a large a number of reforms that included: ministerial direction that all officers must hold a recognized undergraduate degree; the CDS appointment of a Special Advisor to the Office of the CDS for Professional Development; the creation of the *Canadian Military Journal* to allow a forum for professional discourse; the creation of a Canadian "war college" course; and the establishment of a Canadian Defence Academy to provide a centre of excellence for CF professional development, to name a few, were all indications that the CF apparently recognized its anti-intellectualism and failure to ensure its personnel received the required education to complement their training.

However, the long bitter war in Afghanistan has once again placed a premium on experience. Moreover, financial pressures have begun to stall, and arguably, even reverse the progress made in the realm of professional development, specifically higher learning. The CF once again seems to be slipping back to its preferred experiential paradigm, which marginalizes the importance of education.[14]

THE FUTURE OPERATING ENVIRONMENT

This apparent retrograde action is disconcerting. After all, in the complex security environment of today and tomorrow, increasingly, education is exactly what is required; education that can put training into the proper context of the particular situation that military personnel may find themselves facing. And, few would argue that we will not continue to face a complex, uncertain, at times ambiguous, but ever volatile, security environment in the future.

The need for education as a mechanism to prepare the next generation of military leaders is virtually self-explanatory. After all, the future will remain largely unpredictable. Conflicts will invariably involve adaptive, dispersed operations against adversaries that are themselves adaptive, agile, networked and innovative. The West will face hybrid threats that will require new solutions and approaches. Geopolitical uncertainties, rapid technological developments and the proliferation of technology and weapons of mass destruction (including chemical, biological, radiological and nuclear (CBRN)) will exacerbate the complexity and threat. In addition, continued social and political instability fuelled by rampant urbanization, competition over scarce resources (e.g. water, food, fuel and other market commodities), climate change and pandemics will feed further disintegration of social order and global stability.

The consequence of that instability will lead to: illicit economic exploitation, the proliferation of weapons, the creation of terrorist training and/or staging bases, criminal activity including trade in drugs and humans, as well as the consequence of population migration and social and political instability, to name a few. The state of global affairs will also continue to invigorate international terrorism, which will continue to grow leaving no nation, including Canada, immune. The threat may become more potent as it becomes more and more difficult to determine who in fact we are fighting. In the future the enemy will often have no clear identity as groups such as Al-Qaeda become more of an ideology rather than a physical organization and morph into a network of networks. In addition, increasing numbers of trained and experienced veteran jihadist fighters returning to their native lands will increase the lethality and sophistication of attacks over progressively larger areas. This trend will also see the threat becoming increasingly more insidious as "home-grown" terrorists who become radicalized on the internet, or extremist institutions within Western industrialized states, lash out at their own societies.

Terrorism itself will continue to evolve as a tactic and a strategy, as well as a way of life – all at the same time. Our enemies will have both virtual (i.e. the internet) and physical (e.g. failed and failing states, rogue state sponsor) sanctuaries. These terrorist networks will behave like a virus, constantly changing and adapting. Terrorist cells will divide, proliferate and separate. Terrorist threats will emanate from individuals or cells, often with no linkage to a greater command node. In the future, our adversaries will be fluid, independent and physically disconnected (i.e. meet on the internet where they will draw motivation and inspiration). They will employ asymmetric strategies in attacks that combine mass bloodshed and economic impact. They will continue to use the tactics of criminality, terrorism and guerrilla warfare in the pursuit of their objectives and will further refine innovative disruptive techniques as well as more traditional methodologies that include suicide bombings, improvised explosive devices and mass casualty events.

The success of the international terrorist networks will be a function of their effective exploitation of globalization (e.g. telecommunications, financing, internet interconnectivity for information operations and sharing lessons learned, techniques, tactics and procedures), as well as the proliferation of cheap technology to enhance their capacity and reach. These organizations will increasingly be networked, multi-layered and complex entities capable of detailed operational planning, synchronization and execution. They will continually learn from their collective experience and will constantly adapt and change, thus, becoming more complex, sophisticated and dangerous.

Importantly, the future threat will be increasingly irregular, if not ethereal, and adversaries will utilize asymmetric methods to conduct persistent conflict and war. We are currently, and will continue to be into the future, in a war of conflicting ideas, ideology and social values against an enemy that is capable of hiding in, and utilizing the rights, freedoms and protections of the very societies that they seek to destroy. The adversaries we face are ideologically, religiously and criminally driven as well as globally networked. Against this new and evolving threat, conventional military responses alone are challenged to bring resolution and rapid effects. In this battlespace kinetic solutions are exponentially less effective and important than non-kinetic methodologies focused on influence, deterrence, information management and exploitation, as well as intelligence.

In addition, the continuing ubiquitous presence of the global media will further challenge military personnel. Instantaneous feeds from operational areas around the globe direct into the living rooms of civilians worldwide in real time (i.e. the CNN effect) will continue to catapult seemingly innocuous tactical situations on the ground to strategic significance. The reporting of ostensibly minor events will have the potential to generate hostility around the world and create international incidents for domestic governments if the actions or words are construed as disrespectful or unnecessary (particularly if taken out of context).

In this ambiguous, complex, volatile and politically, as well as culturally, sensitive environment, traditional approaches, mindsets and responses are increasingly less effective or even acceptable. The U.S. Army has recognized that its competitive advantage is directly related to its capacity to learn faster and adapt more quickly than its adversaries. As such, it hopes to "sustain a capacity for accelerated learning that extends from organizational levels of learning to the individual soldier whose knowledge, skills, and abilities are tested in the most unforgiving environments."[15] In short, there is a recognition that everyone working in the security environment will require new competencies, but especially increased education, to remain effective.

WARRIOR / SCHOLAR

So the question emerges, can, or should, a soldier also be scholar? The apparent predilection for anti-intellectualism in the military, as well as time and resource constraints aside, there is an intuitive understanding why the military mind would focus on training and experience rather than education. After all, education is not tangible. Unlike training, where quantifiable improvements in behaviour and technical prowess can be physically seen, for instance marksmanship scores or proficiency in drills, education is less evident in tangible form. It deals with creativity, critical thinking and reasoning.[16] These qualities are not always outwardly observable. Furthermore, when many in the senior leadership achieved their rank and position without graduate level university education, why should they emphasis such a requirement, a requirement that could be construed as a shortcoming in their personal circumstances and one that did not apparently prevent them from attaining success.

This attitude continues to exist as a result of a complete ignorance with regard to the importance of education to the development of the next generation of military leaders, as well as the military profession at large. Firstly, there still appears to be a lack of understanding of the difference between training and education. The traditional stress on training, that is "a predictable response to a predictable situation," is often confused with, or considered synonymous with, education, defined by Professor Ron Haycock as "the reasoned response to an unpredictable situation – critical thinking in the face of the unknown."[17] Because of the CF's excellent training regime and its current success on operations in Afghanistan, it is easy to be lulled into a perception that believes that the institution's educational needs are quite adequately looked after. What is overlooked, at great peril, is that the prescribed application of ideas and methods, as well as drills and checklists, have a purpose and functional utility, but this methodology is no longer, if in fact it ever was, enough to equip leaders to cope with and function in the complex post modern world.

Simply put, "education," according to Royal Military College of Canada (RMCC) Professor David Last, a former artillery senior officer, "is the shaping of the mind."[18] Education assists in our reasoning ability, which in turn is critical in responding to unanticipated circumstances. After all, as the adage goes, you train for certainty and educate for uncertainty. As the former Commander of the Canadian Defence Academy noted, "The method to get better at what you do is to educate yourself beyond the training you do."[19] In the end, it's about learning, that is, "the acquisition of new knowledge and ideas that change the way an individual perceives, understands, or acts."[20]

Equally important, is the need to understand, and ability to place, the CF's ultimate purpose and its operations within the context of the larger whole

Chapter 2

and the society it serves. The French emperor Napoleon Bonaparte already recognized in the 19th century that "Tactics, evolutions, artillery and engineer sciences can be learned from a manual like geometry; but the knowledge of the higher conduct of war can only be acquired by studying the history of wars and battles of great generals and by one's own experience." He understood, "There are no terse and precise rules at all."[21] In the end, neither the CF, nor any of the components which make it up, exists in and of themselves.[22]

The requirement to comprehend the "the larger picture" cannot be understated.[23] "Professional officers," asserts Professor Last, "are managers of violence." He further explains:

> Their professional education must allow them to understand it. Violence has always been a part of the interconnected human conditions that we label war, conflict, and peace. In the complex world of today and tomorrow, our understanding of these conditions needs to be more comprehensive than in the past. This is more important than technology, doctrine, and strategy, because all are subservient to purpose. There is no purpose without understanding. The officer's understanding must match that of society – otherwise he or she cannot serve it.[24]

This societal connection has another, equally important, dimension. The Canadian Military Ethos demands that the CF remain rooted in Canadian society and reflect its most important values and attitudes. In this regard it is critical to understand that, as Ambassador Paul Heinbecker points out: "we are an extensively educated people".[25] Of the 33 most industrialized economies surveyed by the Organization for Economic Co-operation and Development (OECD), Canada ranked second behind Russia (Japan was third and the US fourth) in the percentage of the population that has attained at least a university or college-level education. The CF must remain very reflective of this leading edge sector of Canadian society if we are to retain the trust, confidence and respect necessary to maintain the essential support of all Canadian citizens.

In addition, the importance of education to the development of the next generation of military leaders, particularly in the post modern world should be self-evident, especially in light of the series of crises that the CF endured during the cataclysmic decade of the 1990s.[26] Paradoxically, it was recognized as early as 1969, by then CDS Jean Victor Allard. "It matters little," he wrote, "whether the Forces have their present manpower strength and financial budget, or half of them, or double them; without a properly educated, effectively trained professional officer corps the Forces would, in the future, be doomed at best to mediocrity, and at the worst, to disaster."[27]

Intuitively, a professional soldier is better prepared to face the unknown challenges of the ambiguous, complex and uncertain battlespace by having a broad knowledge of theories that act as a guide to discretionary judgement rather than a narrow ability in only some of the practical applications of the profession of arms. As one expert concluded, "strategic effectiveness will increasingly be based on the capacity to think like a networked enemy. Therefore, the military strategist needs to understand a complex environment and a diverse range of interests, actors and issues while retaining the capacity to "simplify, focus, decide and execute."[28] Retired American Major-General Robert H. Scales underlined the need for education instead of training when he commented, "This new era of war requires soldiers equipped with exceptional cultural awareness and an intuitive sense for the nature and character of war."[29]

The need for education in today's complex security environment is repeatedly stressed by practitioners who, through the experience in the chaos of conflict, clearly understand that education, rooted in critical thinking, problem solving and analytical research, better prepares individuals to think, as well as cope with problems and situations that are unexpected. It assists individuals to not only embrace change, but adapt to and anticipate it. More importantly, it instills in people the attitude and ability to constantly learn from one's environment and to prepare, as well as react, accordingly. Colonel John Boyd stripped it down to its simplest form. He asserted, "Machines don't fight wars. Terrain doesn't fight wars. Humans fight wars." As such he concluded, "You must get in the minds of the humans. That's where the battles are won."[30]

And, education is the domain of the human mind. Sir Michael Howard wrote:

> ...academic studies can provide the knowledge, insight, and the analytic skills which provide the necessary basis, first for reasoned discussion, and then for action. They provide a forum, and breed the qualities, which enable the student, the teacher, the politician, the civil servant, the moral philosopher, and not least the soldier to reach a common understanding of the problems which confront them, even if inevitably there is disagreement about the solutions. This dialogue is what civilization is all about. Without it societies dissolve.[31]

Chapter 2

Similarly, closer to home, Dr. John Cowan, a former Principal of RMCC, reinforced the necessity of education in relation to the military. "Today, when a young officer may be called upon to be a skilled leader, a technical expert, a diplomat, a warrior, and even an interpreter and an aid expert all at once," he insisted, "there is no question that good training is not enough. Skills are not enough." He added, "The job calls for judgement, that odd distillate of education, the thing which is left when the memorized facts have either fled or been smoothed into a point of view, the thing that cannot be taught directly, but which must be learned. Without the mature judgement which flows from education, we fall back on reflexes, which are damned fine things for handling known challenges, but which are manifestly unreliable when faced with new ones."[32]

Needless to say, as Cowan affirms, there will always be new challenges. This was reinforced by Lieutenant-General Andrew Leslie, a former deputy commander of the International Security Assistance Force in Afghanistan. "Individuals were sent home [from Afghanistan]," revealed Leslie, "Immaturity and the inability to actually think outside the box made them ineffective … What they tried to do was bring their usually very limited experience from somewhere else and apply it the same way that it had been done somewhere else and that didn't work … each mission has got its own unique drivers, cultural conditions, local nuances, relationships with your other allies or other combatants."[33]

Leslie's observation is undisputable. Up until recently the common complaint of any deploying body was that they were prepared for the last deployment not the situation that they faced. But, you don't know what you don't know. Therefore, a culture absorbed solely by experience, whether in the former decades with a reliance on the 4 Canadian Mechanized Brigade Group (4 CMBG) experience of preparing to beat back the Soviet hordes at the Fulda Gap in Germany; or more currently on the Afghanistan experience of fighting the elusive Taliban in Kandahar Province, is oblivious to the value, if not necessity of higher education.

However, General David Petraeus, accomplished soldier and veteran of years of combat in Iraq and a former commander of North Atlantic Treaty Organization (NATO) forces in Afghanistan, supports the need for greater education, particularly graduate studies for senior officers. He affirms "that a stint at graduate school takes military officers out of their intellectual comfort zones." Petraeus believes, "Such experiences are critical to the development of the flexible, adaptable, creative thinkers who are so important to operations in places like Iraq and Afghanistan."[34] He explains that "through such schooling our officers are often surprised to discover just how diverse and divergent views can be. We only thought we knew the contours of debate on a given subject."[35] Petraeus concluded that graduate studies "provide a fair amount of general intellectual capital and often provide specific skills and knowledge on which an officer may draw during his or her career."[36] Moreover, he argued, "graduate school inevitably helps U.S. military officers improve their critical thinking skills."[37]

And so, if experience once again becomes the primary discriminator for advancement, and higher education is again deemed inconsequential, the CF will return to a system where emphasis is placed on progression in a series of key appointments and geographic postings, most notably Afghanistan. As such, successful completion of these tours then once again becomes perceived as sufficient to prepare an individual for the next higher rank and responsibilities. If this comes to pass, then, once again, the CF will fail in preparing the next generation of military leaders.

Unfortunately, this type of myopic outlook and inward focused mindset fails to see the inherent flaw of this model. Experience in itself is valuable and irreplaceable. But it is also constrained by time, geography and memory. One person's experience, particularly at a specific time and place, does not necessarily represent the knowledge or abilities that are needed for an institution to advance into the future. Moreover, the perspective from a shell-hole, turret or command post is so very limited. Service needs become defined in and of themselves without being rooted in their proper societal context. But most of all, a system that values experience as the only true arbitrator of reality suffers from human arrogance and frailty. "We see," wrote Major Seiberg in the mid-1930s, "that the Spanish Civil War has up to now demonstrated nothing really new, and also that men only regard experience as valid when it is their own experience. Otherwise it would not be possible for the same errors that led to failure in the Great War to be repeated."[38] Simply put, those who refuse to open their minds are doomed to suffer the limitations of their narrow, restricted and outdated beliefs.

The truth in this condemnation of professional development based almost exclusively on the experiential paradigm settled home in the 1990s. "Undeniably," wrote General Baril, "the 1990s represented the first strong test of the contemporary CF Officer Corps and we found that part of it was broken." He concluded, "Experience in and of itself was not enough."[39] He later acknowledged that "over the past 10 years ... we constantly found ourselves thrown into the unknown. Complex, ambiguous and politically charged operations tested our leadership and confronted us with ethical dilemmas." Baril further conceded, "here at home we were slow to understand and adapt to the large-scale societal changes associated with the end of the Cold War and therefore were not prepared for these demands."[40]

Quite simply, the warning previously given by General Allard well over two decades earlier went unheeded. As a result, his prophecy came to pass. The predicament was aptly summarized by a former Army Commander, Lieutenant-General M.K. Jeffery. He believed, "the lack of intellectual discipline in the past has got us where we are today [1990s]. If we don't change we will die." He added, "the longer we resist it, the harder we make it on someone else."[41] One former CDS insisted, "Officers need to have the right mindset to change and evolve the profession." He added, "knowledge must be valued as a key ingredient to our growth as individuals and as a profession."[42] After all, as American General David Petraeus correctly identified, "The most powerful tool any soldier carries is not his weapon but his mind."[43]

In the end, every member of the profession of arms must guard against slipping back to old mindsets and ensure that they are ready to meet the challenges that face them not only today but also into the future. So can a warrior also be a scholar? The answer is definitely yes. The many tenets of scholarship, namely precision, detailed research, communications, breadth of knowledge, placing events in a proper economic, political and social context, drawing conclusions and trying to discern themes therefrom, committing those to paper and then articulating them so that others can understand the argument put forward and learn from it, are all skills that are necessary for a soldier.

Equally important, this type of study provides vicarious experience. As already explained, experience is seen as sacrosanct and great emphasis is rightfully placed on it. But, due to real life limitations, experience is often constrained by time and place. Scholarship, on the other hand, allows its virtual experience to be timeless and cover a wider breadth of activity and circumstance. It provides soldiers with a greater repertoire of scenarios, possible solutions and context from which to draw from.

The warrior scholar also contributes to the academic study by providing an intangible element to the understanding of past events. The plight of the soldier, the confusion, desperation, fatigue, fear and loneliness, in short Carl von Clausewitz's friction that is experienced at every level adds to the comprehension of past events. Those who have experienced it firsthand can understand and possibly offer a more accurate interpretation of historical events by being able to draw on their own experience. Conversely, the study of the past and a scholarly analysis of why things went wrong may assist the warrior in trying to mitigate a repetition by using intellectual skill to control, correct or manage as many of those faults as possible.

Furthermore, education arms the warrior with the ability to deal with the ambiguity and complexity that our soldiers face in the battlespace of today and tomorrow. Beyond the practical there is also the intangible. That is to say, a greater breadth of knowledge, tolerance to alternate interpretations and ideas, a comfort with critical debate and discussion, the honing of analytical skills, as well as the exposure to complete new bodies of literature and thought that expand the mind just make the warrior that much more capable. General David H. Petraeus pronounced, "The future of the U.S. military requires that we be competent warfighters, but we cannot be competent warfighters unless we are as intelligent and mentally tough as we are aggressive and physically rugged."[44] It is no different for the Canadian Forces.

So, is the warrior scholar an irreconcilable divide? Absolutely not! Unfortunately, these two entities have for too long remained divided, when in fact they should be fused to strengthen both disciplines. In the end, indisputably, education is a key component of the development of the next generation of military leaders.

ENDNOTES

1. Professional development is normally recognized as a combination of education, training, experience and self-development.

2. Charles "Sandy" Cotton in John Wood (ed.), *Talking Heads Talking Arms: No Life Jackets* (Toronto: Breakout Educational Network, 2003), 176. Cotton observed, "It is very, very rare for an officer with an advanced graduate degree, particularly at the doctoral level in Canada, to rise above the rank of lieutenant-colonel. Contrary to the United States for example."

3. Michael Howard, "The Use and Abuse of Military History", *The Army Doctrine and Training Bulletin* (Summer 2003), 21.

4. Ibid., 21.

5. Norman Dixon, *On the Psychology of Military Incompetence* (London: Pimlico, 1994), 161.

6. Cotton, 172.

7. General Maurice Baril, "Officership: A Personal Reflection" in Bernd Horn and Stephen Harris, eds., *Generalship and the Art of the Admiral* (St. Catharines: Vanwell Press, 2001), 139.

8. For those who served during the 1980s and 1990s this statement is not a revelation. John Fraser, the Chairman of the Minister's Monitoring Committee expressed of the period, "a lot of [senior] officers felt it wasn't important to have a degree." John Fraser, interview with Dr. Bill Bentley and Colonel Bernd Horn, 21 February 2011. Former CDS, General Ray Henault admitted, "I remember the days when a person with a Masters or PhD were not considered warriors – they were seen as having gone over to the other side." General (retired) Ray Henault, interview with Dr. Bill Bentley and Colonel Bernd Horn, 9 November 2010.

Chapter 2

9. Lieutenant-General Richard J. Evraire, *General and Senior Officers Professional Development in the Canadian Forces,* (October, 1988), 75. The anti-intellectual attitude was not restricted to merely higher education. Equally telling was the lack of tolerance for new ideas, criticism or self-examination. Conformity and loyalty were valued over intellect and critical thinking. Challenging the prevailing beliefs and pushing the envelope on future developments were not career enhancing. Innovation may have been applauded, but conformity was consistently rewarded.

10. The whole issue of the subjective nature of PERs can be summed up by Lord Palmerston's comment, "Merit? The opinion one man holds of another." See John A. English, *Lament for an Army* (Toronto: Irwin Publishing, 1998), 55. See also Brigadier-General Ken Hague, "Strategic Thinking General / Flag Officers: The Role of Education" in Bernd Horn and Stephen Harris, eds., *Generalship and the Art of the Admiral* (St. Catherines: Vanwell Press, 2001), 516-517.

11. Jack Granatstein, *A Paper Prepared for the Minister of National Defence by Dr. J.L. Granatstein Canadian Institute of International Affairs,* 25 March 1997, 19.

12. Albert Legault, *A Paper Prepared for the Minister of National Defence by Professor Albert Legault Laval University,* 25 March 1997, 40.

13. Desmond Morton, *A Paper Prepared for the Minister of National Defence by Desmond Morton McGill Institute for the Study of Canada,* 25 March 1997, 23-24.

14. This statement is admittedly somewhat subjective as there is no "smoking gun" directive that underscores this statement. However, one need only look at the high number of requests for equivalency for Development Period 4 (senior officer) courses; the efforts to develop easily achievable accreditation options for those senior officers lacking requisite education; the reinstitution of programs to enroll officers without degrees; the efforts of the environmental commands to repeal the need for officers to hold degrees, and the pressures to achieve savings through the elimination or curtailment of educational programs. A former CDS who served during the 1990s, upon hearing these indicators, conceded it represented a disturbing backwards trend.

15. United States of America, Department of the Army, *The Army Learning Concepts for 2015.* DRAFT. 20 April, 2010, 1.

16. "Creativity is critical requirement for adaptation. We need creativity because: When things change and new information comes into existence, it's no longer possible to solve current problems with yesterday's solutions. Over and over again, people are finding out that what worked two years ago won't work today. This gives them a choice. They can either bemoan the fact that things aren't as easy as they used to be, or they can use their creative abilities to find new answers, new solutions, and new ideas." Richard King, "How Stupid are We?", *Australian Army Journal* (Summer, 2009), 186.

17. Dr. Ronald Haycock, former Dean of Arts, Royal Military College (RMC), "Clio and Mars in Canada: The Need for Military Education", presentation to the Canadian Club, Kingston, Ontario, 11 November 1999.

18. Major David Last, "Educating Officers: Post Modern Professionals to Control and Prevent Violence", in Lieutenant-Colonel Bernd Horn, ed., *Contemporary Issues in Officership: A Canadian Perspective* (Toronto: Canadian Institute of Strategic Studies, 2000), 26.

19. Rear-Admiral (retired) David Morse, interview with Dr. Bill Bentley and Colonel Bernd Horn, 6 October 2010.

20. This is the Canadian Treasury Board definition. See Canada, *Policy on Learning, Training and Development.* Treasury Board Secretariat, 2006, retrieved 2 November 2010 from <http://www.tbs-sct.gc.ca/pol/doc-eng.aspx?id=12405&section=text#cha4>.

21. Quoted in Murray Simons, *Professional Military Learning. Next Generation PME in the New Zealand Defence Force* (Canberra: Air Power Development Centre, 2004), 43.

22. This is why the US military believes that "successful operational adaptability depends upon educating and developing leaders, training soldiers, and building cohesive teams who are prepared to execute decentralized operations in and among populations in coordination with Joint, Interagency, Intergovernmental, Multinational (JIIMP) partners." United States of America, Department of the Army, *The Army Learning Concepts for 2015*. DRAFT. 20 April 2010, 2.

23. Major-General Don McNamara asserted that advanced-military professional education is required "to get people to think in two ways. One, to think strategically so that they're not commanding a ship anymore, they're commanding a force, and that is a mindset that is not easy for a lot of people to change. The second thing is that they are now thinking in terms of dealing at the highest national levels and not at the level of an individual military formation. These are two major changes that are not easy for people to assume without getting some experience before they actually have to assume it." Don Macnamara in John Wood (ed.), *Talking Heads Talking Arms: No Life Jackets* (Toronto: Breakout Educational Network, 2003), 155.

24. Ibid., 9.

25. Paul Heinbecker, *Getting Back in the Game: A Foreign Policy Playbook for Canada* (Toronto: Key Porter Books, 2010), 23.

26. For details on the "decade of darkness" see Bernd Horn and Bill Bentley, "The Road to Trans-formation: Ascending from the Decade of Darkness," in Robert W. Walker, ed., *Institutional Leadership in the Canadian Forces: Contemporary Issues* (Kingston: CDA Press, 2007), 1-25; or Bernd Horn and Bill Bentley, "The Road to Transformation. Ascending from the Decade of Darkness" *Canadian Military Journal*, Vol. 16, No. 4 (Autumn, 2007), 33-44.

27. Department of National Defence, *The Report On The Officer Development Board* (Rowley Report), Ottawa, March 1969, v.

28. Colonel Roger Noble, "'Beyond Cultural Awareness': Anthropology as an Aid to the For-mulation and Execution of Military Strategy in the Twenty-First Century," *Australian Army Journal,* (Winter 2009), 67.

29. Emily Spencer, *Solving the People Puzzle: Cultural Intelligence and Special Operations Forces* (Toronto: Dundurn Press, 2010), 115.

30. Colonel John R. Boyd, (USAF Ret) cited in Major Jason Hayes, "Preparing Our Soldiers for Operations within Complex Human Terrain Environments," *Australian Army Journal,* (Winter, 2009), 104.

31. Michael Howard, *The Causes of War* (New York: Harvard University Press, 1984), 83. Major-General, the Honourable W.A. Griesbach stated, "Since wars cannot be arranged to order merely to train officers, it follows that, after a long period of peace , the officers of an army must get their military education from reading and study." "Military Study: Notes of a Lecture," *Canadian Defence Quarterly*, (October 1931), 19.

32. Dr. John Scott Cowan, RMC Convocation Address, 4 October 1999, Kingston, Ontario. See also Eliot Cohen and John Gooch, *Military Misfortunes. The Anatomy of Failure in War* (New York: Vintage Books, 1991), 233-237.

33. Spencer, 72.

34. David H. Petraeus, "To Ph.D. or Not to Ph.D...." *The American Interest* (July/August 2007), 16.

Chapter 2

35. Ibid., 18. He further insists, "This is a very valuable experience in and of itself for those of us in uniform who will work and live in other cultures overseas. If the range of views within our own country is greater than we supposed, that can only help prepare officers for an even wider range beyond our shores."

36. Ibid., 18.

37. Ibid., 19.

38. Major Sieberg, "Tank or Anti-Tank? Does the Spanish War Show Which is Superior?" Translation of an article appearing in the "Militar-Wochenblatt" of 11 February 193, National Archives, MG 31, G6, Vol 9, File: Articles, Papers, Speeches – U.

39. Baril, 140.

40. Canada, *Canadian Officership in the 21st Century (Officership 2020). Strategic Guidance for the Canadian Forces Officer Corps and the Officer Professional Development System* (Ottawa: DND, 2001), foreword, iii.

41. General Maurice Baril, covering letter, "Canadian Officership in the 21st Century," (Officership 2020) Launch Implementation, 2 May 2001, 3.

42. Lieutenant-General M.K. Jeffery, address to the Commanding Officers Course 2001, 21 June 2001, Fort Frontenac, Kingston, Ontario.

43. Petraeus, 16.

44. Ibid., 20.

CHAPTER 3

FOURTH GENERATION WARFARE: WAR IN PARADOX, STRENGTHENING THE CUBICAL FORCES AND LEADERSHIP COMPETENCIES PREPAREDNESS

*Major Ardisutopo Endro Tjahjono**

> *Destroying and winning in every battle is not the perfect victory. The ultimate victory is whenever you can destroy your enemy's defence without any battle.*

Sun Tzu

INTRODUCTION

War is an armed conflict resolution, decided by the state after all peaceful efforts have been exhausted.[1] In war, the state is responsible to win, by empowering the necessary national resources to defend national interests, and to guarantee the readiness and preparedness of its military forces. With the advent of globalization however, the characteristics of conflict has changed. Many pundits have stated that the future battleground will no longer be characterized by direct confrontation between armed forces. They believe that, in term of the spectrum of conflicts, future warfare will tend to be non-linear. For instance, in order to achieve certain strategic goals and targets, such as the downfall of a political regime, or the meltdown of an economy, a state can use non-regular components of power, in which non-physical dimensions, such as changing public opinion or eroding international support, can become the weapons of choice.

This so-called *4th Generation Warfare* (4GW), was first introduced by William Lind and his colleagues of the United States Marine Corps in 1989 to classify and characterize the dynamic trend of warfare of the future after the collapse of the Cold War era.[2] 4GW as a new concept of warfare, basically has its foundation in the emerging concept of globalization, in which people from different countries across the globe are connected and no longer

---

* The views expressed in this chapter are those of the author and do not necessarily reflect those of the Indonesian National Defense Forces or the Indonesian Army.

constrained by a physical territorial barrier. This global connectedness is facilitated through information technology, the main driver of globalization. In the context of warfare, a country can empower all of its political, economical, social and military resources available to create an offensive strike against the enemy. The objective of 4GW is to change the minds of the enemy's policy makers, so that their "will" to fight is diminished.

Originally conceptualized as a response to 3GW, in which big gaps in terms of capability and weapons, driven by technology, have resulted in a considerable weaponry imbalance among nations. This imbalance has forced weaker nations to create new strategies and tactics of warfare, so that they can continue fighting against stronger adversaries (i.e., conventional warfare is not possible). This model of warfare often is also referred to as *asymmetric warfare* or *unconventional warfare*. In other words, compared to previous warfare, the utilization of technology and great armed power in this era no longer guarantees advantage (i.e., of the David versus Goliath scenario).[3] Consequently, according to the basic concept of 4GW, states with stronger political will are capable of defeating countries with greater economic and military power. Lieutenant-General Johanes Suryo Prabowo, the current Chief of the Indonesian Armed Forces' General Staff, considers 4GW as a form of warfare that effectively utilizes the long-term political and social network. Armed forces will only be "selectively" used and will attack "selective targets" which have significant impact in the international political front.[4]

In practical terms, 4GW is the implementation of non-traditional ways to destroy the enemy (i.e., economic, diplomacy, media, etc). For some, 4GW has also been simplified as "*a war on terror*", a global war on cellular organizations and action groups with certain ideological threats. Basically, these groups and organizations are trans-national in nature and have the ability to implement very sophisticated psychological warfare, including media manipulations. In fact, some strategists claim that 4GW in the modern context is the evolution of the conflict in the Iraq and Afghanistan War, when the US military forces and its allies had to face the power of non-state actors.[5]

Probably in reference to John Naisbitt's concept of "*Global Paradox*" (1994), 4GW is more aptly to be called "*war in paradox*". Certainly, 4GW has some contrasting elements. Those very same elements however, are in fact working out together. The contrasting elements are related to the use of high-tech weaponry, the subjects or actors involved in the warfare, the object to conquer, the form of conflict that will ultimately transform into insurgency and terrorism, the means used during the war, and the spectrum of conflicts. Therefore, to avoid becoming the loser in 4GW, each nation must pay added attention to the means of warfare used by the enemy, including the substantially different weapons and techniques, the potential national weaknesses that could be exploited by the enemy, and the national resources that can become potential targets of direct attack by the enemy.

This chapter will discuss an alternative way of deterring 4GW through the systematic use of soft power to win the war. This concept is basically a lesson learned from the Indonesian Army's experiences performing its territorial function. In addition, strategies to develop leadership competencies related to this context will be explored.

4GW: A NEW FORM OF BATTLEFIELD

Current military strategists classify warfare in generational terms. In the first generation (1GW), warfare was conducted in open field, using line and column tactical formation. Military forces faced each other on the battlefield, within striking distance of the weapon systems, with limited flanking movements by both infantry and cavalry units. Examples of this kind of warfare can be found in the Napoleonic war. Second generation warfare (2GW), although still using the linear lines of battle, witnessed increased utilization of flanking movements. With the development of flight technologies, offensive movements could be achieved with the help of air to surface weapon systems. In this generation of warfare, in order to win the battle, infantry and artillery units were required to work seamlessly, and the three to one ratio of attacking forces against defensive forces was introduced. Examples of 2GW includes the two World Wars. Third generation warfare (3GW) further developped 2GW. It is characterized by the use of superior weapons technology with massive destructive powers and high mobility manoeuvring tactics. Because this kind of warfare is expensive and complex, only countries with highly developed economies and superior technologies could implement it.

Basically, 4GW is an asymmetric and non-linear system of warfare, which utilizes all of the available infrastructure and weapon systems in order to destroy the will of the enemy to fight. Consequently, in 4GW, the battlefield need not be a physical battlefield where armies are fighting against armies as in the previous generations of warfare. With globalization, the internet, and 24/7 news channels, the front lines could be political, economical, social and military. The method could be insurgency, separatism and/or terrorism. In short, psychological warfare to weaken the enemy. Therefore, the scope and objective in 4GW is not physical destruction *per se*, but includes action to change in public opinion, transnational

Chapter 3

support, a change in government, and the upheaval or replacement of a political system in a certain country. In 4GW, superiority in warfare technology could, arguably, no longer be considered as a source of strength, but the ability to inflict fear in the enemy's centre of gravity. The September 11, 2001 attacks on New York and the Pentagon by Al-Qaeda are a current example of 4GW. The following graphical representation is based on John Robb's excellent description of modern 4GW.[6]

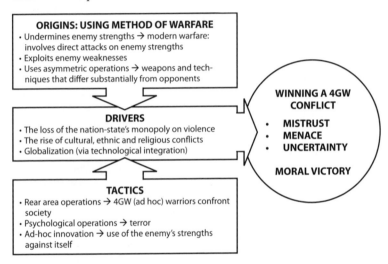

Figure 1 – Modern 4GW[7]

4GW: CUBICAL FORCES AND THE INDONESIAN ARMY'S TERRITORIAL CAPACITY-BUILDING

At the moment, most countries still base their defence system on 1GW, 2GW or 3GW concepts, anchored by strong land, sea, and air forces – in short, hard power. Certainly, in the context of 4GW, these warfare concepts are no longer effective or as effective as they once were. Military powers that depend solely on hard power must be transformed to be able to utilize soft power in order to neutralize the effects of 4GW. Elements of soft power that can be developed are information, media and people power, among others. In addition, we can also add aerospace power, which can be construed as the pinnacle of hard power (in the form of space stations and satellites), and soft power (such as media coverage). If all of the tangible hard powers and the intangible soft powers are combined, then military powers can be seen as cubical forces as follows.

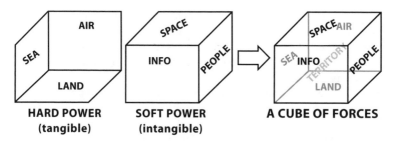

Figure 2 – Cubical Forces of Military Power

The Indonesian Army, which is responsible for the land defence of the country, has the duty to identify the possible threat spectrum, both from the result of external transnational trends, and also from the internal dynamics within Indonesia. Indonesia itself is a very strong candidate for 4GW as it is a developing country with a large population and a highly pluralistic society. The treat of separatism exists and terrorist acts have been committed in the country, with strong international repercussions, especially when the players aimed to maximize their impact through the international media. One method to defend the country against 4GW is the so-called Territorial Capacity-Building (*Pembinaan Teritorial* or *Binter*). This concept was formulated based on the Indonesian Army's experiences during the colonial war, when the guerrilla army became *one with the people* so that it could live on its own without support from the central command.

It was largely due to the Japanese legacy of creating a territorial army to defend Indonesia from an external aggressor that possessed a professional armed force and technologically advanced weaponry and technical skills, coupled with the Indonesian Army's own experience in implementing a successful guerrilla warfare strategy during the war of independence, that the doctrine of "*total people's resistance*" was developed.[8] Within this doctrine, the Indonesian Army established a system of military districts called *Wehrkreise* (adapted from the German system during Second World War), in which the entire Army would abandon linear defence and retreat to non-urban areas in order to wage guerilla warfare.[9] Under this system of circular or regional defence, each regional commander had full authority to operate against the Dutch forces by utilizing the assets available in the district under his command.[10]

Consequently, in each military district, soldiers were required to unite with the people, so that the people would be willing to supply them with the necessary logistical support as well as provide information on the movement of the Dutch soldiers.[11] Realizing the political pitfalls that might arise with this system, General Nasution, one of the greatest thinkers in the Indonesian Army, further developed this doctrine. In essence, his contributions created an Indonesian version of a guerrilla warfare doctrine that excluded the political outlook that existed in the people's army concept of most communist countries (i.e., this refined doctrine did not justify or envision the Army to mirror the politically-oriented armed forces that existed in those countries).[12]

Referring to this historical background, Territorial Capacity-Building can be understood as the effort of the Indonesian Army to prepare all of the resources in the territory to be used to defend the country. Again this was based on the concept of "Oneness With The People" (*Kemanunggalan TNI-Rakyat*).[13] The objective is to create an emotional bond with the people so that they will feel that they are in the same boat with the Army, and consequently, be willing to defend the Unitary State of the Republic of Indonesia.[14] Accordingly, based on the 3rd Bill of Law on National Defence, the Indonesian Defence system is based on a Total Defence System (*Pertahanan Semesta*).[15] To achieve this objective, Territorial Capacity-Building requires certain competencies such as a territorial management system, social communication, and a quick reporting system, both at the individual soldier and unit level.[16] One of the unique functions of the Territorial Capacity-Building is the implementation of social services for the people in the territory.

A good example of the effectiveness of Territorial Capacity-Building was the spontaneous involvement of the people during the rebellion of the Darul Islam movement, which aimed to create an Islamic State in Indonesia in the 1960s. At that time, the Indonesian Army implemented the Territorial Capacity-Building Strategy to win the heart and minds of the people. This strategy focused on convincing the people that the form of Islam practiced by the Darul Islam movement was alien and different from the Indonesian mainstream, which is more tolerant and accomodates local traditions. As a result, the people in the area of the rebellion were willing to voluntarily help the Army by localizing the insurgency, creating "fences of people" (*pagar betis*) to prevent the rebellious group from fleeing their position, and providing the logistical support for the Indonesian soldiers who were conducting operations in the area.

Returning to the concept of Cubical Forces, Territorial Capacity-Building cannot be considered as an independent power, but can be seen as the cumulative result of all the forces in the cube. This is the essence of this concept. All resources, be they soft or hard power, must be empowered, so that the capacity will depend on the ability to expand each side of the cubes. This concept of warfare is considered very relevant for Indonesia since the country does not possess an offensive strategy that can be implemented outside its territorial boundary. The main objective of the Indonesian Defence system is to protect the territorial integrity of the country. In order to achieve this end, the Indonesian Territorial Defence System is divided into several Territorial Areas, which are classified as Strategic Compartments (from the highest structure which parallels the provincial government, to the lowest level, which parallels the village apparatus). These territorial commands are required *to become one with the people*, so that they will be ready to defend the country against internal and external threats. In terms of the Cubical Forces, the figure below demonstrates the Territorial Capacity-Building concept.

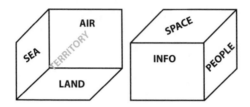

TERRITORIAL CAPACITY-BUILDING

Figure 3 – Cubical Forces of Territorial Capacity-Building

DEVELOPING TERRITORIAL LEADERS

In modern times, research conducted at the University of Indonesia showed a high degree of trust among the Indonesian people toward the Territorial Command (*Komando Territorial*).[17] Some of their reasons for this trust, among others, include practical benefits, such as ensuring safety, providing protection, controlling the behaviour of other law enforcement officers, becoming a source of information for the people, and as a driver for national potential. In addition, the Territorial Command can provide an ideological benefit. According to the research, the people viewed the Territorial Command as a supporter of democracy, as a guardian of the Unitary State of the Republic of Indonesia, as an agency that promotes nationalism, and as a buffer against the negative effect of globalization. Lastly, the Territorial Command was perceived as trying to create a positive image through showing a caring attitude toward the people, demonstrating empathy, and reacting quickly to the problems faced by the people. Apart from these results, the research also showed that most of the people still accepted the military's line that military operations conducted against separatism are for the benefit of the Unitary State of the Republic of Indonesia. Therefore, it is only logical that strategic

Chapter 3

leadership development models in the Indonesian Army, especially in the context of 4GW, should be formulated based on the leadership competencies required for the Territorial Command.

At the moment, the Psychological Service of the Indonesian Army has developed Assessment Centre programs based on job analysis and competency mapping of District and Resort military commanders. District military commanders are senior lieutenant-colonels responsible for the operational aspects of a territorial area the size of a mid-size Indonesian city. Most of them are former battalion commanders of combat units. They must possess competencies such as analytical thinking, decision-making, communication skills, risk taking, tolerance for differences, conflict resolution skills, initiative, negotiation skills, strategic networking skills, leadership and teamwork skills. District military commanders must be able to develop the capacity of the military potential in the territorial area under their command. To do this, they must be able to interact and work with the local government, influence the people and the media, be on good terms with Non-Governmental Organizations (NGO) and educational institutions in the area, etc. Conversely, Resort military commanders hold the rank of senior colonel and lead several District military commanders. Most of them are former brigade-level commanders of combat units and, apart from the competencies of District military commanders, they must also possess additional soft competencies such as sensitivity, cross-functional competencies and strategic thinking as they are responsible for the strategic aspects of the Territorial Commands.

Candidates who are successful during the selection process will then complete the appropriate courses. Development programs for the Resort military commanders are conducted at the Army's Staff and Command School, while the Centre for Territorial Education is responsible for developing District military commanders. Hard competencies are developed through familiar methods such as command post exercises, case studies and short lectures, while behavioural competencies are developed through experiential training. On the other hand, values that reflect institutional competencies are inculcated through social projects in which candidates are given hands on experiences to solve problems in the community.

CONCLUSION

Social and technological changes have brought about new paradigms in how warfare should be conducted. Currently in 4GW, players, especially non-state actors, emphasize the use of the non-military infrastructure to achieve their objectives. Therefore, military power alone will not be suffice and armed forces around the world must, as a result, be prepared to use soft powers as required. Based on the historical nature of the military operations conducted by the Indonesian Army, the territorial concept of war-fighting is a method that should merit attention for military strategists. Indonesia, as a multicultural nation, has complex problems that can potentially be exploited in 4GW. To face these challenges, the Indonesian Army must have competent Territorial Commanders who can implement Territorial Capacity-Building. In order to achieve these goals, assessment and development program for District and Resort military commanders have been conducted, and could become the future model for leadership development programs in the era of 4GW.

ENDNOTES

1. Johanes Suryo Prabowo, *Perang Darat* [Land Warfare] (Jakarta: Agung Printing, 2009), 1.

2. William S. Lind, Keith Nightengale, John F. Schmitt, Joseph W. Sutton and Gary I. Wilson, "The Changing Face of War: Into the Fourth Generation," *US Marine Corps Gazette,* (October, 1989), 22-26.

3. Jeffrey Record, "Why the Strong Lose?", *Parameters* (2005).

4. Johanes Suryo Prabowo. *Pokok-pokok Pemikiran tentang Perang Semesta* [Thoughts on Total Defence] (Jakarta: Pusat Pengkajian dan Strategi Nasional, 2009), 32.

5. Ninok Leksono. *Hidup di Era Perang Asimetrik* [Living in the Era of Asymetric Warfare], paper presented at the "Seminar Perang Asimetrik" [Asymetric Warfare Seminar], Dewan Riset Nasiona, Jakarta, 27 September 2007.

6. John Robb, "4GW – Fourth Generation Warfare", *Global Guerrillas,* posted on 08 May 2004, retrieved on 11 April 2011 from <http://globalguerrillas.typepad.com/globalguerrillas/2004/05/4gw_fourth_gene.html>.

7. Ibid.

8. Kelompok Kerja SAB, *Sedjarah Singkat Perdjuangan Bersenjata Bangsa Indonesia* [Short History of the Armed Struggle of the Indonesian People] (Jakarta: Staf Angkatan Bersendjata, 1964), 74.

9. Petra Groen, *Marsroutes en dwaalsporen. Het Nederlandse militair-strategische beleid in Indonesië 1945-1950* [Lines of march and wrong tracks: Dutch military strategic policy in the Dutch East Indies 1945–1950]. (Den Haag: SDU, 1991).

10. Nugroho Notosusanto, *Pejuang dan Prajurit, Konsepsi dan Implementasi Dwifungsi* ABRI (Jakarta: Sinar Harapan, 1984), 55.

11. Himawan Soetanto, *Yogyakarta 19 Desember 1948: Jenderal Spoor (Operatie Kraai) versus Jenderal Sudirman (Perintah Siasat No. 1)* (Jakarta: Gramedia Pustaka Utama, 2006), 269.

12. Robert Cribb, "Military Strategy in the Indonesian Revolution: Nasution's Concept of Total People's War in Theory and Practice", *War and Society*, Vol. 19, No. 2 (2001), 144-154.

13. Mabesad, *Buku Petunjuk Induk tentang Pembinaan teritorial* [Field Manual on Territorial Capacity-Building], (Indonesian Army HQ, 2007), 40.

Chapter 3

14. Mabesad, *Naskah Sementara Buku Petunjuk Lapangan Kodim tentang Binter* [Temporary Field Manual for District Military Command on Territorial Capacity-Building] (Indonesian Army HQ, 2007), 3.

15. Setneg, *Undang-Undang RI no 3 tahun 2002 tentang Pertahanan Negara*, Indonesian Bill of Law Number 3, 2002 on National Defence.

16. Mabesad, *Buku Petunjuk Teknik tentang Lima Kemampuan Teritorial* [Field Manual on the Five Territorial Capabilities] (Indonesian Army HQ, 2007), 29.

17. Lestrata. "Analisa Tanggapan Masyarakat Terhadap Peran Komando Teritorial" [Analysis of Society's Attitude Towards the Role of Territorial Commands]. "Memahami Peran Koter Dalam Sishankamrata." *Yudhagama Jurnal*, Media Informasi and Komunikasi TNI AD [*Yudhagama*, Journal of the Indonesian Army] (December, 2005), 79-86.

CHAPTER 4

FROM "LEADING FROM THE FRONT" TO "LEADING FROM THE SHADOWS": DEVELOPING A LEADERSHIP CULTURE FOR THE STRATEGIC LEVEL

*Dr. Nick Jans**

> *Leadership is about the organizational power to achieve ends, not about "leading" per se. The exercise of power involves appreciating and utilising a number of different sources of power, such as resources, connections, opportunities, and people who can help you, as well as your own formal authority, with the appropriate mix contingent on the situation.*[1]

INTRODUCTION

This chapter addresses senior leadership development, in terms of the development of a leadership culture.

A *leadership culture* is an environment in which certain "enabling" factors operate in ways that make it possible for leaders to get things done. Most of these factors – whether enabling or "dis-enabling" – are usually so well established that most people don't think about them; they have become simply "the way we do things here". This is the nature of culture. They are all the more powerful for being so. And although we usually talk about *leadership culture* in positive terms, a leadership culture is quite likely to contain "dis-enabling" factors that impede leadership and performance.

Leadership becomes increasingly complex at the senior organizational level. Stepping up to the strategic level involves a professional transition which is markedly different from the relatively seamless transitions at more junior career levels.[2] A major reason for this is the discrepancy between the sound leadership culture that operates at the operational level and that in the defence bureaucracy. The challenge therefore is to create an equivalent, but necessarily different, leadership culture at the strategic level.

---

* The views expressed in this chapter are those of the author and do not necessarily reflect those of the Australian Defence Force.

Chapter 4

This chapter will argue that the key to "leadership development" for senior leadership is to focus less on developing the leaders as individuals and more on developing and strengthening the leadership culture in which they work.

THE BIG TASK

Contemporary defence leaders must both "manage today" and "manage tomorrow." In an environment of political and economic uncertainty, they must provide ongoing strategic leadership while simultaneously pushing through fundamental organizational reforms aimed at improved organizational agility and efficiency. And both tasks must be achieved in the light of impending demographic and social changes that will sharply increase the difficulty of resource acquisition and management, especially in personnel recruitment and retention.

Happily for Australia, it has leaders who are equal to the task. For the last 15 years, there has been a concerted effort to develop leaders with a beyond-the-unit perspective; with the perspectives and skill sets for joint operations.

But having the right *leaders* is not the same as having the right *leadership*. If innovation in defence is often tortuous and inconclusive, this is not because its leaders lack skill or intelligence. Nor is it because they are "conservative" (because, most – in the current generation anyway – are not). Rather, the sluggish pace of innovation is a consequence of organizational practices that inadvertently constrain the pace of change by promoting a short-termist and incremental approach to strategic problem solving. In short, the issue is not with variability in the leadership abilities of leaders, but with deficiencies in the leadership culture in which they find themselves.

The crucial career step up to one-star (i.e., Brigadier rank and equivalent) is dramatic and, for many, daunting. When people join the Senior Leadership Group (SLG), they find themselves engaged in an appreciably different culture to those of earlier career stages. Professional achievement at this level requires both a new set of skills, especially in terms of exerting influence in the absence of formal authority, and a markedly different approach to being a "leader" and to the concept of "leadership".

The expectation that leaders will lead-from-the-front, and a set of leaders who are willing and able to do so, are important strengths for a military organization. But, like most cultural characteristics, such strengths also contain the seeds of weakness. The fundamental argument is that effective leadership at this level depends less on the qualities and efforts of "leaders" than it does on the presence of a strong "leadership culture."

Studies on this topic are rare. The primary subject in writings on military leadership is "command", and the shelves of Defence libraries groan with books about command, leadership and military operations. But, despite the obvious fact that not all senior officers will command on operations, virtually all get involved in Defence Headquarters (HQ) staff activities and all contribute to crucial decisions on strategy, policy, management and resource-allocation, there are very few studies of organizational behaviour in the senior HQ/bureaucracy arena.

THE CONCEPT OF LEADERSHIP CULTURE

Imagine this: you are a career officer, and you are on your way to take up an operational command appointment at the lieutenant-colonel (or equivalent) level. Chances are that you are feeling apprehensive, but you will also probably be excited and confident. What is it about the nature of this impending career opportunity that makes you feel so positively towards it? Now, imagine a similar situation, but this time you are on your way to take up a senior position in the Defence HQ bureaucracy. Again, how do you feel about the impending posting and how well do you think you will perform?

When I've posed these questions in presentations to officer audiences, a predictable pattern of answers emerges. In respect to the first question – relating to an impending operational command – the responses are always upbeat. Everybody is confident that they will perform well; and the reasons they give for such confidence fall into four main categories. Most talk about the solid preparation that their previous career experience has given them, and their strong motivation to succeed; they are extremely keen, and thoroughly schooled in the theory and practice of leadership and command within the relevant operational discipline. Others mention the support that they are likely to get from the other members of the ship or unit – that is, from their subordinates. They expect to find a strong ethos of "followership", with subordinates who will be ready, willing and able to give support and assistance to the Commanding Officer (CO) as the person in charge. A third area that will be mentioned is the sense of cohesion, trust, mutual respect and teamwork that is likely to exist in the unit, and the advantages of members of the unit sharing a common view of the world and common formative career experiences. The final area that is mentioned is the unit's command infrastructure, in the form of technology – well-established operational and communication procedures and the like will help you make things happen quickly, and

Chapter 4

accurately – and people often also mention the great advantage derived from the "parallel command structure", in the form of the Senior Sailor/NCO system, and how that establishes flexibility, resilient, and depth in the leadership process that is critical in communications and operational agility.

In respect to feelings prior to taking up a senior staff appointment, the responses are much less optimistic and upbeat. But again a similar pattern of reasons for feeling like this emerges. Again, these reasons can usually be categorized in terms of leadership, followership, command architecture, and social capital. However, in this particular case, these will perceived as being relatively weak in comparison to the situation that typically exists in operational military units.

The labels I give to these four areas are, respectively: leadership, followership, command architecture, and social capital. These are the four key elements of leadership culture.

The strong features of these factors, as they exist in operational units, evolved as the results of experience across centuries, and are now so much part of our "conventional wisdom" that we wouldn't expect military units to operate effectively without them. However, if this is so self-evident that it scarcely needs stating, we might wonder about why it was only comparatively recently that the Australian Defence Force (ADF) engaged in a concerted program to tackle these dis-enabling factors.

TRYING TO BRING OUT THE "LION" IN THE LIONS

A few years ago the then Chief of the Defence Force (CDF) and the Secretary established a systematic program to improve the situation for the SLG. The program had a strong focus on leadership and social capital in particular. In respect to leadership, senior leaders were given exposure to "advanced leadership ideas" that were purportedly being used in private sector "best practice"; in respect to social capital, there was a concerted attempt to build a cohesive senior leadership group, through compulsory attendance at the senior leadership days, where mixed groups of senior officers and senior public servants worked in syndicates on various issues. The CDF and secretary also communicated their desire to "reduce red tape", "speed up decision-making", and the like, with a series of exhortations around the theme of "reducing bureaucracy."

This reform program had mixed success. Its strongest successes were in the area of social capital, with a demonstrably closer knit senior leadership team progressively evolving. But it had much less success with leadership and very little success with reducing bureaucracy (or, in terms of our model, strengthening command architecture). The main reason for the lack of success in improving leadership was that the program was focusing on improving the abilities of individual leaders who, firstly, were already skilled and savvy in terms of their leadership abilities and, secondly, were unlikely to learn much that would fundamentally improve their performance in the comparatively short snatches of time that were allocated. If anything, these senior leaders needed greater functional expertise in the particular programs that they were ostensibly leading. For example, those in senior positions in personnel functions would have benefited from greater depth of experience in and understanding of the personnel function, and likewise for most of the other functions that were not closely aligned to the conduct of operations.

But the biggest weakness continued to be in respect to followership. We'll get to the reason why this is such a big weakness shortly, but first another personal story – or, rather, an account of a trio of responses that I obtained during an interview survey of members of the SLG in early 2003.

The situation is exemplified in the comments that came from three particular interviews as part of a large-scale interview survey that was being conducted within the defence bureaucracy. "X", "Y" and "Z" had each once worked in the same Director General-level team.[3] We begin with X, the most junior, talking about how well Z, the most senior of the three, had performed in a key senior policy development role:

> Z was doing a vital job that few other people had been able to do well. But after only 18 months in the job he was posted to command [an Australian-based formation]. The reason given was that the CDF needed "well-rounded candidates for Chief of […]".

Next, Y, the one-star who had succeeded Z:

> I think that I am well equipped for this appointment but I was fortunate in that I took over from Z. He had set up an infrastructure to help get things done: a hand-picked staff, including experienced "old stagers", all of whom had been well-briefed about what you needed to do to be successful in the bureaucracy. I'm now into my third year and this long tenure is really paying off. It takes 5 to 6 years to change things in Defence. Without continuity of direction, focus and leadership, it's hard to achieve very much.

Chapter 4

Finally, Z himself:

> I just did what I thought was sensible. I was fortunate in that I had served in Canberra before and I knew a lot of my civilian counterparts. I'd acquired a sense of how the Australian Public Service (APS) works and thinks. I spent a lot of time talking to them, to find out their views and where they were coming from. But it was still hard work! What was frustrating was that many of the barriers to getting things done were actually within the system's control. First, tenure: I was given only 18 months in the job. That is ridiculous. If you want people to be accountable for results, then for heaven's sake leave them there for long enough for their accountability to become evident. Second, very few of my staff had been trained for their huge resource management role, because they were being career-managed as generalists. This meant that their career prospects plunged if they were not picked for command. I had a number of really useful officers working for me but then the "command list" came out and some of them saw that they were not on it. Within 6 months, they had all left. What a waste!

These extracts are revealing as much in what they do not say as in what they do. If Z really was "doing a vital job that few other people had been able to do well", why was he moved on after only 18 months in the job? Does Y's being "now into my third year" make him unusual? Given that careful career development is a distinctive feature of the early and middle professional military career, why was that very few of Z's staff had been trained for their "huge" resource management role? Why did not being on the "command list" have such an influence on the career decisions of so many of his subordinate officers? And above all, why does it take "5 to 6 years to change things in Defence"?

The leadership culture model allows us to analyse the X, Y and Z responses in terms of the leadership culture model, especially in terms of leadership and followership.

LEADERSHIP

Attempts to improve leadership in the defence bureaucracy have invariably been hampered by the consequences of the generalist career development policy. This had been the rationale for moving Z on after only 18 months in a vital job. Virtually all senior military officers are managed with an eye to enhancing their competitiveness for promotion to the next rank. This means that they are managed according to what is essentially a "generalist" model of career development, in what is essentially an up or out program aimed at developing and selecting the best small panel to be considered for Chiefs of Service. This not only directly affects all military members of the senior leadership group that also has indirect effects on those at the lieutenant-colonel/colonel level immediately below them.

The consequences of this policy are profound. First, it shapes the way that both followers and leaders view their roles. Military officers see their *raison d'être* as "command" and their professional identity as a "warrior". Most expect to make their reputations in command roles and support the use of command performance as a major criterion for career advancement. In the early career stage, they are encouraged to practice the so-called "heroic" leadership style: "direct, public, aggressive, exemplary and risk-taking."[4] As a consequence, those who advance are impressive, confident and assertive professionals, highly regarded by members of the government, the public, their peers, and by their subordinates. Even when senior officers move up to joint appointments, the profession still tends to view them on the basis of how they performed as a "warrior chief" and still expects them to exercise traditional forms leadership relevant to that role.

The will and the skill to take charge in uncertain situations are not only admirable virtues but are also essential for organizational performance in the contemporary business environment. *Prima facie*, this should apply to the armed forces more than any other organization; and, to a large extent, it does. The danger of this ethos, however, occurs when both leaders and followers become over-reliant on the top people "taking charge" and "leading from the front."

Why is this a "danger"? The answer lies in the different kind of leadership style that is needed for work at this level. While it is true that the function of "command" continues to be important in many roles at the SLG level, the working environment in the defence bureaucracy tends to favour somewhat less direct and less formal styles of authority and leadership to those which were used in earlier career roles. Leaders who want to exert genuine influence need to rethink their concept of "leadership", in terms of the connection between "command" and "authority". They need to consider the possibility that they will often achieve more if they develop the skills of "indirect leadership" or "leading-from-the-shadows."

To begin with, senior officers who continue to act in accordance with traditional assumptions about the rank-authority nexus (for example, that "the senior person knows best") do themselves and their programs no favours. The functional network at the top of defence is diverse and pluralistic and – despite advances in SLG team-building – lacks a common set of values. The SLG itself contains equal numbers of Service officers and civilians, so its members are now exposed to a wide range of disciplines and sources of professional expertise. Beyond this, the SLG deals with a host of other external contacts and stakeholders, including government and other government agencies, allies, and major contractors. All such stakeholders can be expected to have varying perspectives on goals and priorities and varying preferences on how these should be pursued.

In this sense, it is useful to think of the SLG as a system of political coalitions in which individuals and sub-groups vie for power and influence.[5]

> At this level, you have to exercise "influence" rather than "authority"; you have to build consensus rather than exercise individual direction; you often have to use organizational politics rather than tackling a problem directly.

> One way of looking at defence is in terms of a "Federation": a collection of sub-agencies, each with its own purpose but united under a single overarching purpose and bound by a common set of standards. The key task of leadership is the process of leveraging the strengths of each element of the Federation: change management is the leadership of process. Change happens through networking and politics. People exercise influence not by virtue of their rank but by virtue of their authority. The two are different. Rank, or formal position, is only one element in the possession of organizational power.

Professional achievement in such situations requires not just a new set of skills but a markedly different approach to getting things done. The environment rewards leaders who are confident with the new, and alert to the possibilities presented by alternatives; it rewards those with the ability to "get above" a problem, to appreciate its dimensions and the perspectives of different stakeholders; it requires political sensitivity (both small "p" and big "P") and pragmatism; and, above all, it requires the ability to be influential even in situations where the formal trappings of command appointments, such as superior rank, greater experience and the legal authority to act unilaterally are lacking.

Executives cannot, of course, avoid taking charge in many situations, since they are bound by certain procedures, especially those relating to government policy and accountability for using resources. Beyond this, however, they also have the responsibility of making the bureaucracy responsive and less "bureaucratic." For this task, influence is a matter not just of "*what* you know" but also of "*who* you know." The formal hierarchy matters much less at this level, and personal influence depends more on reputation, knowledge, expertise, access to and control of information, and membership of alliances and groups. Encouragingly, many of defence's senior leaders have adapted their behaviour along these lines.

Even when leaders learn to operate in this way, however, many continue to assume that it is their responsibility to "know the answer" for the majority of problems with which they deal. But effective strategic leadership doesn't depend just on being a good networker. Much more importantly, effectiveness depends on accepting that, at this level, one has entered the zone of "Leadership Without Easy Answers".

Leadership Without Easy Answers is the title of a must-read book by Harvard leadership scholar, Ronald Heifetz.[6] It is a "must-read" for two reasons. First, Heifetz explains, with copious case studies and examples, how leaders can get things done in situations of strategic crisis and stakeholder conflict where doctrinal guidance and precedent are lacking. Second, he demonstrates the futility – and the dangers – of assuming that leaders and leadership teams must continually be able to produce immediate answers to complex issues.

The reason why leadership at the strategic level is such a challenge for both leaders and followers, Heifetz argues, is because leaders *and* followers need to accept a different way of thinking about how "leaders" can help solve "problems". His fundamental tenet is that leadership at this level generally requires leaders to begin, not by providing solutions, but by asking questions, *even in situations where followers demand that leaders show decisive leadership.*

As Heifetz points out,

> ...in a crisis we tend to look for the wrong kind of leadership. We call for someone with answers, decision, strength, and a map of the future, someone who knows where we ought to be going – in short, someone who can make hard problems simple. But many problems are not simple. Instead of looking for saviours, we should be calling for leadership that will challenge us to face problems for which there are no simple, painless solutions – problems that require us to learn new ways.[7]

These remarks are particularly pertinent to the situation faced by senior military professionals. The archetype of a military leader is the "follow-me" combat leader, heading the charge, rallying the troops, directing operations from a field headquarters. Make no mistake, direct and decisive leadership *is* important in situations of crisis. Over the longer term, however, leaders' *indirect* activities – the "leadership you can't see" – have at least as much effect on performance and morale than the charismatic leadership that is characteristic of the heroic model.

Encouragingly, as the interview quotation below shows, many Australian defence leaders recognize this:

> The role of the people at the top is really to facilitate the exercise of leadership by encouraging all of those in the process to play their parts. They need to generate the enthusiasm and engage the motivations of those within the organization to achieve the goals that have been established, communicated and agreed.

> As a senior leader, you are a steward: you are in charge of this organization for a limited period and it is your task to develop it and nurture it, and hand it on to the next leader in good shape. Then you are an enabler: you must be the control of the process, but not core to the process. That is, you are not one of the workers or operators: you've got to set up an environment, and assemble the resources, which make it as easy as possible for others to get on with things. Then you must stand back, directing operations as necessary, but letting others do the detailed work. Understand that you're not the most important person in the organization. The leader gets things done by relying on others.

BUILDING FOLLOWERSHIP: SUPPORTING THE LIONS WITH LION CUBS

The sensible strategy for development of high performance at the senior levels of the bureaucracy is to concentrate much less on "leadership" *per se* and much more on "followership".

Followership is arguably the biggest weakness in the leadership culture at the top of the defence organization. As noted, the generalist career model as a consequence of having virtually all officers in a continual rotation cycle. The military has always known this would have a performance consequence in staff organizations, but these consequences were accepted for their supposed benefits (which, however, it has never bothered to quantify). Moreover, the cost-benefit trade-offs have invariably been perceived in terms of the direct effect of frequent job rotation on senior leaders, whereas, it is just as pertinent to examine the indirect effect of frequent job rotation of the senior leaders' supporting staff on senior leaders' performance.

High rates of officer job rotation negate much of the considerable public investment in their education and other forms of career development.

> At least 10 of my 30-plus years of full-time service, if not more, were spent doing things for which I was demonstrably ill-prepared in terms of both education and experience. I had to become, if you like, an auto-didact. In retrospect it all seems a little amateurish – much time spent training for things I never did and much time spent doing things for which I was never trained.

> We don't want style to become more important than substance but there is a serious risk that this will happen, especially in the situation where officers are being moved from job to job frequently. Because they only have a short time to make an impression their focus is on making an impact in the short term. With the best will in the world it is hard for them not to see an eighteen-month posting in terms of three phases: six months of getting on top of the job, six months of getting things done, six months to prepare for moving into another job. The reality is that, in many if not most senior appointments, you need five years to initiate and see-through important organizational changes and programs.

Even if time-in-job were not related to *individual* performance, it would be remarkable if the overall effect of this were benign or even neutral. Having virtually *all* those responsible for directing and shaping organizational change continually moving from job to job and from function to function adds an additional burden to the change process in an already challenging situation.[8]

Most importantly, such mobility makes it difficult for leaders and their staffs to detect and act on long-term issues that require near-term action, especially for issues of a non war-fighting type. Detecting a strategic issue and assessing its implications usually takes both a well-informed eye and sophisticated judgement. Service leaders have very well-informed antennae for military issues, but their appreciation of social, managerial and economic factors outside their field of expertise is not so well-honed. It would not be surprising if, under all the circumstances of the work pace and variety of problems, a number of important long-term issues escaped their notice.

The problem doesn't end there. Even if a perceptive individual or team detects an issue and decides to act on it, such action then has to be initiated and steered through. As the frequently-cited and widely-advocated Kotter change management model tells us, the first steps in leading change are to *Establish a sense of urgency* and *Create a guiding coalition*.[9] But it is difficult to develop an appropriate "sense of urgency" when leaders expect that they and their staff will have short tenure within any particular job in any particular program, and especially when many don't or won't recognize a long-term issue. And it must be even more difficult to "create a guiding coalition" when the top people and one's counterparts in other programs are in the same situation.

> Given that Secretaries are now on short-term contracts, there is now much less of the "frank and fearless" approach to giving advice. And, bizarrely, the Secretary of Defence is on the shortest contract of all: whereas other heads of departments are on five-year contracts, the Secretary of Defence (the agency where long-term planning is most important) is on a three-year contract. At least subliminally, that sends a message.

> The Services show great timidity in developing leaders' non warfighting skills. We go from this course [Centre for Defence Strategic Studies: the highest-level military career development program run in Australia] into appointments that will often involve managing projects of millions of dollars, but we are not well equipped for such roles. It is little wonder that we find ourselves contracting out to the same small group of contractors, avoiding off-the-shelf solutions, and generally applying an excessively conservative and time-consuming approach.

A few years ago, some colleagues and I set out to analyze the performance effects of continuous job rotation.[10] We surveyed officers in mid-career roles, differentiating between those in operational units and those in staff units, asking each group a series of questions that assessed how well they thought they were performing.

The first thing that we found were that those in operational units and those in staff units had quite different patterns of time-performance related changes across appointment tenure. The performance of those in operational units did not change significantly between those in the first year, those in the second and those in the third, whereas the performance of officers in staff units progressively improved over time (i.e., performance in the second and third years was significantly higher than that in the first.)

Second, even though those in staff units improved their performance over time, their average performance ratings in the second or third year never reached those of their counterparts in operational units; i.e., performance was lower at all tenure stages compared with those in operational units.

The reasons for these two differences are not difficult to explain. Those in operational units were performing a function for which they had had previous training and experience and in which they were supported by experienced and motivated subordinates. In contrast, those in staff units were appreciably less likely to possess these advantages. Further, those in staff units began at a relatively low level of experience that progressively improved as they gained experience in what for most was a novel functional area. In contrast, their counterparts in operational units had "hit the ground running": they had a good sense of what they had to do even before they got to the unit, and the unit was ready for them to perform that function from the very first day.

And it is not just a matter of differences in individual performance. Competent people working with competent colleagues will have the advantages of competent and effective teamwork: competent and experienced colleagues will be aware of what they have to do to contribute to the team and what they can expect from other team members. Take away the competence and you considerably reduce the efficiency and effectiveness of the teamwork.

Moreover, having a critical mass of competent subordinates, who possessed between them a sufficient amount of "corporate memory", makes it feasible for their leaders to apply the "leadership without easy answers" approach. Those leaders can pose the questions with a reasonable expectation that useful responses will be forthcoming.

SOCIAL CAPITAL AND COMMAND ARCHITECTURE

Both social capital and command architecture are comparatively minor factors here. To begin with, programs aimed at the improvement of cohesion and teamwork in the SLG are continuing, and continue to strengthen the sense of unity and common purpose at that level. Second, improvements in leadership competence and confidence will tend to have a natural flow through to both social capital and command architecture. Thus, to a large extent, both these factors can be left to be improved by natural forces.

Chapter 4

SOME CONCLUSIONS, SOME ANSWERS –
AND SOME FURTHER QUESTIONS

Leadership, in all its manifestations, is fundamental for success at the strategic level. However, the kind of leadership needed at the top differs in significant ways to that which is associated with earlier career stages. Few officers who advance to the highest levels find it easy to make the adjustment, especially as most continue to be subjected to a generalist model of career development that requires them to move between appointments and often between functions every two years or so.

The key to making all this work is to improve the competence of the support staff officers immediately below the senior leadership group. Having a proportion of those with tenure stability and functional expertise will be the basis for a critical mass that will have a number of follow-on benefits.

The most effective kind of leadership is the kind that you can't see. Strategic leadership is very much about developing a "leadership culture", in which performance happens as a matter of course. If the culture is strong, people will perform with minimal leader intervention. But if the culture is weak, or sends contradictory signals (such as "use your initiative" but "don't make any mistakes"), performance outcomes are likely to be deficient. Even the most charismatic leaders are comparatively ineffective in these conditions.

Happily for Australia, Defence has the leaders it deserves. For the last 15 years, there has been a concerted effort to develop leaders with a beyond-the-unit perspective and a keen appreciation and skill set for joint warfare. But there is another, less complimentary, sense in which "Defence has the leaders it deserves". Defence might have the *leaders* it deserves, but does it have the *leadership* it deserves? As individuals, the SLG has an impressive array of energy and talent, but this isn't being tapped fully. Quite simply, current senior staffing arrangements make it difficult for senior leaders to develop an appropriate leadership climate and drive organizational change at the rate and level that both Government and the current situation demand. Such conditions, however, are not created overnight.

There has never been a more important time to rethink the reform process and the ways that human capital, especially at the senior level, can be better leveraged. Given the right conditions, Defence's leaders will continue to do Australia proud in the enormously challenging years that lie ahead. Creating the right conditions may well be both their greatest leadership challenge and their greatest potential legacy.

ENDNOTES

1. The italicized quotations in this chapter come from a 2003 survey of members of the Senior Leadership Group in the Department of Defence. A series of in-depth interviews was conducted with senior officers from all three Services and senior executives of the Australian Public Service.

2. Walter F. Ulmer Jr., "Leadership, managers and command climate", in *Military Leadership: In Pursuit of Excellence* (3rd Ed) eds. Robert L. Taylor and William E. Rosenbach (Boulder, CO: Westview Press, 1996): 196-203, 199.

3. None were aware that the others were also being interviewed. In fact, it was a happy coincidence that all three volunteered to be interviewed.

4. From a quotation by British historian John Keegan in the New York Review of Books, Vol. 36, No. 13 (17 August 1989), in which Gordon Craig reviews a number of books on military history. See <http://www.nybooks.com/articles/3925#fn5>.

5. See: Rosabeth Moss Kanter, *The Change Masters: Corporate Entrepreneurs at Work* (London: Unwin Paperbacks, 1983); Herminia Ibarra, "Structural alignments, individual strategies, and managerial action: elements toward a network perspective of getting things done", in Nitin Nohria and Robert G. Eccles, eds., *Networks and Organizations: Structure, Form, and Action* (Harvard, MA: Harvard Business School Press, 1992, 171); Ronald A. Heifetz, *Leadership without easy answers* (Cambridge, MA: Harvard University Press, 1994); Nick Jans with David Schmidtchen, *The Real C-Cubed: Culture, Careers and Climate and How They Affect Capability* (Canberra Papers on Strategy and Defence No 143. Strategic and Defence Studies Centre, Australian National University, Canberra, 2002).

6. Ronald A. Heifetz, *Leadership without easy answers* (Cambridge, MA: Harvard University Press, 1994).

7. Ibid., 2.

8. An officer who commented on an earlier draft of this report noted that, in his recent six years within a particular Defence function, he saw five changes of the two-star Head and four changes of one-star Director General. The turbulence at the top of this function, he believed, took its toll on organizational performance.

9. John P. Kotter, *Leading Change* (Cambridge MA: Harvard Business School Press, 1996).

10. Nick A. Jans and Judy M. Frazer-Jans, "Career Development, Job rotation and Professional Performance", *Armed Forces & Society*, Vol. 30, No. 2 (2004), 255-278.

CHAPTER 5

THE NEW ZEALAND ARMY LEADERSHIP FRAMEWORK – REINVIGORATING LEADERSHIP

Lieutenant-Colonel Rob Hoult & Dr. Peter Greener*

> *Leadership is the achievement of a task or mission through the willing and cooperative efforts of others.*

New Zealand Army Leadership Manual[1]

INTRODUCTION

In the New Zealand (NZ) Army, as with all military forces, leader selection and development have always been seen to be important enablers to military capability, yet one could argue that the execution of leadership development has been somewhat incomplete. Perhaps surprisingly, until 2007, the NZ Army did not have its own leadership doctrine. The Australian Army had long been the prime source of leadership doctrine,[2] and it would seem that this had served the NZ Army adequately.

Nonetheless, and especially since the 1980s, there have been multiple calls for a more systematic and considered approach to leader development in the NZ Army. In an absence of a formalized and coordinated organizational approach, individual leaders at times introduced leadership training initiatives *ad hoc*, out of frustration over organizational inertia.

Beginning in 2007, there has been a deliberate and coordinated revolution in the style and substance of NZ Army leader development. The Army Leadership Framework (ALF), introduced in late 2007, has profoundly changed the nature of leadership development, and arguably the paradigm of leadership itself within the NZ Army.

This chapter will outline the NZ Army experience of introducing the leadership framework into an environment where none previously existed. This chapter will also examine the context into which the ALF has been

* The views expressed in this chapter are those of the authors and do not necessarily reflect those of the New Zealand Defence Force.

applied, explore the leadership development culture and practices that existed pre-2007, and explain the steps that were taken to design what has proved to be a robust, holistic and credible leadership framework. The components of the ALF, the manner in which it was implemented in the NZ Army, and the lessons that were learnt in this process will also be examined. Finally, the chapter will conclude with a look to the future and explore the next steps that the NZ Army will take in order to capitalize on the gains it has made, as well as the challenges of developing pan-NZDF leadership doctrine.

WHY DO WE NEED LEADERSHIP ANYWAY?

Leadership is to the military what the brain is to the human body – we wouldn't function particularly well without a brain, and the military cannot do so without leadership. Similarly, our understanding of leadership is somewhat akin to our understanding of the brain – we have our theories on how each works, but the body of knowledge is in no way complete. Indeed, the father of transformational leadership, James Burns, has written that "*leadership is one of the most observed and least understood phenomena on Earth.*"[3]

For a phenomenon that is not well understood, leadership is nonetheless a remarkably well represented topic – a Google search on leadership will reveal a lifetime's worth of reading, and the shelves of bookshops bulge with contributions to the subject. Thinking on leadership has evolved considerably since Carlyle's theory on the *Great Man* in 1882,[4] progressing through theories associated with traits, behaviours, situations, contingencies, transaction and transformation. A 2003 review[5] of leadership theory and competency frameworks found that whilst militaries typically continue to select officer candidates using the trait approach, there has been a shift to emphasize the importance of the leader's role in relation to followers, and a greater emphasis on relationships as the foundation for leadership. In this respect, leadership can be expressed as the dynamic that exists between leader and follower when certain conditions are met. These conditions could include, but are by no means limited to, mutual respect, two-way open communication and mutual trust.

THE NZ ARMY LEADERSHIP CONTEXT AND OPERATING ENVIRONMENT

Leadership is the NZ Army's centre of gravity – the one thing above all else that underpins organizational success, most tangibly demonstrated by the achievement of meeting agreed outputs, and experienced internally through internal processes and practices. Because leadership also shapes organizational values, culture and behaviour, it is arguably the area that warrants the most attention and investment.

Leaders in the NZ Army are busy. As of 30 May 2011, The NZ Defence Force (NZDF) had 578 personnel deployed in sixteen peace-keeping operations, United Nations missions and defence exercises across ten countries.[6] When it is considered that for every serviceperson deployed there is another serviceperson preparing to deploy and another serviceperson regenerating from a recent deployment; around 17% of the regular strength of the NZDF is committed to operations at any one time.[7]

Whilst the military cannot assert that it has a monopoly on the need for leadership excellence, it can lay claim to a unique combination of characteristics that sets its leadership requirements apart from other professions. From a New Zealand military standpoint, the characteristics that define the context of military leadership include:[8]

- The basic unit of an Armed Force is a small team with built-in redundancy amongst that team and throughout the service.
- Every individual must be able to believe in the ability and trustworthiness of those around them, which will be enhanced by continual training and a common set of values.
- The expected employment environment of, and skills used by, any one person can vary immensely from day to day.
- All personnel are expected to live within a paradox of high individual initiative in a highly disciplined structure.
- To maintain discipline and teamwork within highly stressful situations, a very clear line of command and communication must be established and maintained.
- Those personnel vested with command responsibility must strive to maintain high personal standards and credibility as well as supporting both the organization and the individuals under their command.
- Failure in battle is unacceptable.

LEADERSHIP DEVELOPMENT PRE-2007

In 1985, the NZ Army Chief of General Staff (CGS) directed the Commander Land Forces, Brigadier Ian Burrows, to commission an Army Leadership Study[9] into the standard of leadership in the NZ Army. In the background to his report, Brigadier Burrows noted that:

Chapter 5

For some time now it has been of growing concern that the standard of army leadership at all levels has been eroding. This view has been expressed in various forums and has often been given recently as one of the reasons for soldiers taking premature release.

The major conclusion drawn from the Army Leadership Study by Brigadier Burrows was:

Leadership is being formally taught in the Army without centralized direction. There is a need to establish an overall philosophy, confirm the levels at which it should be taught, ensure course content is appropriate and provide for progressive continuity.

History shows that very few of the recommendations made in the Army Leadership Study were accepted, let alone adopted. The words "disjointed," "uncoordinated" and "haphazard" could best be used to describe the conduct of leadership training in the NZ Army from the mid-1980s through until 2007. This is not to say that both leadership development and progression in how the NZ Army developed its leaders did not occur – both occurred, and with some good effect. What did occur however tended to come about through the initiative of the officers and soldiers working in the schools formally tasked with leadership training, rather than through any strategic input from the Army's senior leaders.

Yet, the recommendations from the Army Leadership Study were not completely ignored. One positive outcome was the establishment of the Army Adventurous Training Centre (AATC) in 1986. This initiative occurred through the drive of the then-Chief of the General Staff, Major-General Tony Birks. Birks, a Sandhurst graduate, drew upon his British Army experience, and recognized that military training needed to incorporate opportunities for officers and soldiers to experience physical and mental challenge aimed at the development of resilience, with emphasis on the ability to manage thinking and behaviour in situations of high perceived and/or real risk, where physical harm and even death were possible.

Initially, the AATC delivered resilience courses using the mediums of rock climbing, white water kayaking and mountaineering, with courses being open to volunteers of any rank, officer or soldier. A decade later, in the mid-1990s, a growing focus on leaders was emerging, through a realization that the most organizational value would be achieved through focusing on developing junior leaders. Scenario-based leadership courses complimented the more traditional skills-based courses, and were embedded in officer training at the Officer

Cadet School of New Zealand (OCS (NZ)) and NCO and Warrant Officer (WO) promotion courses conducted at The Army Depot (TAD).[10] By the mid-2000s, these courses had been refined, and were significantly enhanced through the AATC's mix of military and civilian instructors gaining expertise as facilitators, and a concentration on the development of self-awareness as a key enabler to leadership success. The AATC had also unofficially introduced situational leadership theory into its leadership development scenarios; with the intention of building on from the only official leadership model is use at that time – John Adair's *Functional Leadership Model* – now more commonly known as the *Action Centred Leadership Model.*

The OCS made a major contribution to the concept of values-based leadership in the late 1990s, paving the way for the identification the NZ Army values that were to emerge in 2006. The OCS values of *Courage, Loyalty, Initiative, Integrity, Pursuit of Excellence and X-factor* (i.e. charisma) formed the acronym of CLIIP-X, and served a useful role in guiding and assessing officer cadet behaviour. The NZ Army values of *Courage, Comradeship, Commitment and Integrity* (C[3]I) grew through this period and now form an important component of the ALF.

Despite these essentially local initiatives, there remained a lack of a coordinated approach to leadership development for the officer and soldier streams, and a distinct lack of top-down direction on philosophy. Indeed, whilst the AATC worked on an agency-basis providing leadership development activities, the OCS and TAD tended to avoid the sharing of ideas, the opportunity to work collaboratively, or even share a common picture of how the Army's leaders should be developed.

Indeed, it could be said that leadership was inferred by decree – having been appointed as the commander, leadership was assumed. The prevailing view at the time appears to have been that leadership was something that the leader delivered, rather than leadership being the phenomena that emerges as the product of the two-way relationship between leader and subordinate.

In 2006, momentum was growing for the more effective development of leadership doctrine and delivery of leadership development across the NZ Army. The Military Studies Institute (MSI) initiated a discussion paper[11] to examine the need for the establishment of an Army Leadership Centre, prompted by the effort allied militaries were demonstrating in this area. The MSI paper concluded that the establishment of a leadership centre was warranted, and would contribute to more effective leader development. In late 2006, the Commander of the Army Training Group built on the MSI discussion paper with specific recommendations for the vision, mission and structure for an Army Leadership Centre.

THE IMPERATIVE TO BUILD THE ARMY LEADERSHIP FRAMEWORK

In 2006, The NZ Army was battling an attrition rate approaching 20%. A buoyant economy with plentiful employment opportunities was causing an unsustainable drain of human capital, most noticeably with those in their first five years of service, and more critically, in the areas of junior leadership. The NZ Army's reliance on bottom-up recruiting and development meant that significant gaps were emerging, with limited opportunity to redress the issue.

Analysis of climate survey data in late 2006 revealed some harsh truths – among other factors, a significant number of staff was leaving for reasons that were able to be clearly linked to gaps in leadership competence across all levels of the organization. The realization was that leadership wasn't "broken" – it just wasn't of the collective standard that had been expected, or indeed required by an organization that requires excellence in leadership behaviour. Moreover, the NZ Army had done little to ensure that leadership development matched the increasingly complex requirements of the 21st century – what was done in 2006 was in effect little different to what had been done for previous generations, despite the ever increasing complexity of the military environment.

Figure 1 is the "anomie"[12] model that emerged from this research, and which provided the catalyst for the NZ Army to critically question a number of assumptions concerning leader development and performance.

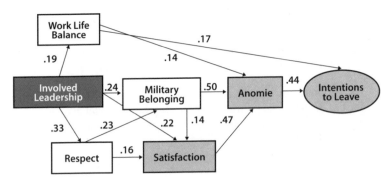

Figure 1 – The Anomie Model

This model provides a cause and effect chain of the conditions that can lead to a service person declaring his/her intention to leave the NZ Army, or for that matter, any organization. It highlights the pivotal role of leadership in this equation, and the consequences of a lack of leadership. Whilst the labels of *work life balance*, *respect*, *satisfaction* and *intentions to leave* are self-explanatory, those of *involved leadership*, *military belonging* and *anomie* warrant explanation in order to allow this model to be better understood.

- *Involved Leadership* is determined by three aspects:

  - clear task assignment, standards to perform and providing feedback;

  - being trustworthy and interested in the career progression of people; and

  - showing leadership and ensuring that the workplace co-operates and delivers.

- *Military Belonging* is internalized, but is often readily observable:

  - pride in the organization;

  - pride in work done;

  - feel part of the Army *whanau* (family); and

  - care about the organization and its mission.

- *Anomie*[13] is the product of a lack of involved leadership, and the loss of military belonging. It is defined as *a condition of instability resulting from a breakdown of standards and values or from a lack of purpose or ideals.*

This research work, with its compelling relationship of regressive coefficients, was completed by a consortium of Winsborough Limited[14] and the Bismarck Foundation[15] and said as much about what leaders weren't doing as what they were doing.

Faced with these facts, the Chief of Army initiated a review of leadership and specified the requirement for the establishment of the ALF. This work took place over late 2006 and through 2007, and involved a significant body of research and analysis. A comprehensive interview program of representational groups at every level of the Army was completed alongside an intensive examination of contemporary leadership doctrine and practice from a wide range of other military, public, private and academic fields in the international arena. Critically, the consortium identified the positives of the then-current NZ Army leadership environment, understanding the value in retaining the tried and tested aspects of organizational practice.

In creating the ALF, the NZ Army sought a framework that provided:

- an overarching theoretical construct against which leadership development would occur;

- a description of the leadership related tasks and associated skill, knowledge and attitude sets required for each rank/level of leadership across Army;

- a coherent leadership development regime for each rank stream presenting the competencies as a progression of development, along with required learning outcomes at each step of development; and

- supporting tools and documentation for training developers, trainers, immediate superiors and commanders.

THE ARMY LEADERSHIP FRAMEWORK PHILOSOPHY AND COMPONENTS

The ALF is concerned with leadership – and the tasks that leaders must do in order to be successful. It is less concerned with command and management, although there is an unavoidable blurring of the three at times. The role of, and necessity for command is reinforced through the ALF, but the ALF is careful to differentiate between the two. The essential argument is that command concerns *role-vested* authority, whereas leadership concerns *personally-earned* authority. Command is bestowed from above, but the right to be called a leader is earned, from below. Similarly, many of the decision-making and change management tools and techniques that are embedded in the ALF could indeed be considered in the domain of management theory, yet they become effective leadership tools when combined with influencing skills and knowledge, and with a moral compass aligned to the NZ Army ethos and values.

The ALF is founded on eight key philosophical tenets:[16]

> **1. Leadership development is founded on the development of strong individual character that has at its heart the NZ Army ethos and values**. The ALF embraces the notion that leaders must be first and foremost "good people." This tenet aligns itself strongly to contemporary leadership thinking evidenced by Robert Hogan and Rodney Warrenfeltz's *Domain*

Model of Managerial Skills,[17] which provides a taxonomy of leadership and managerial skills. The Domain Model has as its foundation intrapersonal skills – self-awareness, self-control, emotional maturity and integrity. This reinforces Stephen Covey's notion of primary and secondary greatness[18] – the concept that primary greatness concerns strength of character, and secondary greatness concerns learned responses of positively influencing others – the interpersonal skills found in the second of Hogan and Warrenfeltz's domains. Similar findings concerning character were reached by Jim Collins in his book *Good to Great.*[19]

2. Leadership development is a continuous process embedded in daily routine, rank relationships and the unit culture, as much as on formal courses. This tenet acknowledges that we can teach theory, models and tools on a formal course, but leadership is learned at the workplace in everyday interactions. As such, leader development is predicated on the provision of continuous coaching and guidance.

3. The same definition of leadership is used throughout all NZ Army material. One framework guides the understanding and development of leadership at all levels, in both the officer and soldier streams. Consistency in theory, language and application are the building blocks of developing an organization-wide understanding and practice of leadership.

4. Officer-soldier leadership teams are the base functional unit for all leadership levels, from leading platoons to leading the Army. The officer-soldier partnership is seen as a critical enabler at every level of the Army. This recognizes that whilst there can only ever be the one commander in each unit, there can be two leaders who complement each other. At the unit level, the Commanding Officer is the commander, but together with the Regimental Sergeant-Major leadership is a shared function.

5. Greatness in leadership is not achieved by an absence of weakness. Fault-checking is not the path to great leadership. Leaders build on their and others' strengths. Leaders must however be self-aware and understand any significant derailers – what Zenger and Folkman[20] would term "fatal flaws." The disciplined use of 360-degree reporting, personality profiling, reflection and peer feedback are essential tools in this process.

6. Leadership is a privilege and not a job. The responsibility of leaders does not end when they leave the military base at the end of each day.

The willingness and ability to be a role-model 24/7 is a key component of military leadership.

7. Continuous and constructive coaching is the best medium to develop leader capability for the level of the role. Leaders have to understand, and demonstrate, that their most important job is developing their subordinate leaders. This is not a job that can be put off for want of being too busy.

8. Leadership is a practical art and development should reflect the realities of the role. Training must be realistic – it must reflect the tasks that a leader has to do in order to be successful at his/her current level, or one-up if being prepared for promotion. This requires an understanding that the nature of leadership changes as one ascends the ladder of hierarchy. Emphasis must focus on what differentiates each successive level of leadership, and in particular the concepts of increasing discretionary time and increasing complexity. This places increased cognitive demand on leaders and leader selection and development must reflect this reality. In this respect, the ALF draws on the learning of Elliott Jaques' *Requisite Leadership*[21] theory and the application of his stratified systems approach to leadership.

THE ARMY LEADERSHIP FRAMEWORK
OPERATIONAL TRIANGLE

All leaders need a sound understanding of context in order to make informed decisions about the deployment of their team. Figure 2 depicts the operational triangle and the three components of context a leader must understand in order to direct and guide the team to complete its mission. These components are as follows:

The context of leadership is **integrated.** Leaders must operate effectively in an integrated world. Integration will typically occur at three levels: within the NZ Army and between the various battle operating systems; across the wider New Zealand Defence Force; and finally with other military forces, agencies of the United Nations, local and Non-Governmental Organizations.

The context of leadership is **current.** Leaders ensure that they, and their teams, understand their current mission and tasks. The real issues and problems in the workplace must be identified and dealt with by the leaders. They act to achieve the mission and do not wait for "the ideal conditions". Facing the reality of a situation means being flexible and adaptive in adversity – and not indulging in wishful thinking or despair. Operational tempo, shortage of resources and under-manning all pose challenges to teams. Effective leaders face these factors squarely, engage the team in finding solutions and stay focused on maintaining their level of optimum capability.

The context of leadership is **future oriented**. Leaders not only master the current environment but are also future focused. Operating only in the current realm will lead to a short-term, crisis-oriented environment. Leaders must act to maintain and build capability for the future, putting in the groundwork for success that may occur beyond the tenure of their posting or career. Leaders must also help their teams to understand what the future holds and what changes will be required and why. Leaders coach their subordinates through adaption, improving skill and capability for the future.

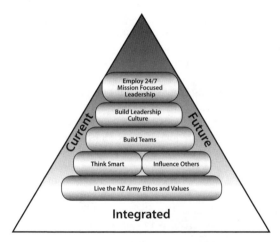

Figure 2 – Army Leadership Framework and the Operational Triangle

ARMY LEADERSHIP FRAMEWORK ELEMENTS

The ALF comprises forty two leadership "tasks," grouped into the six elements shown in Figure 2. Most of these 42 tasks apply at any level of leadership, although seven are concerned primarily with the NZ Army's strategic level of leadership.

Chapter 5

The six elements of the ALF are:[22]

- Live the NZ Army Ethos and Values. The NZ Army values are at the heart of the framework. Strong values are what you prioritize, defend and want least to sacrifice. Values influence goals and form the touchstone for decision-making. Internalizing these values, modelling them and instilling them in the everyday lives of soldiers are at the core of leadership.

- Think Smart. Some leaders work by setting the pace for their teams – showing through personal example what the team needs to do, and how it should be done. This *pace-setting* style of leadership is often self-taught, but the leader hasn't yet learned to add value to the team by doing work different to them. In the NZ Army that is the opposite of what is required. Instead, leaders need to add value through thinking ahead, but being creative and prepared to experiment and to consider the consequences of their and their team's actions.

- Influence Others. The nature of modern conflict and warfare almost always brings NZ soldiers into contact with a wide range of cultural contexts (ethnic, tribal, religious) in operational theatres. Changes in migration to NZ and the changing demographic and generational mix of the NZ Army also throws people from very different backgrounds together. Good leaders are respectful of and make an effort to understand other cultures. In addition, they are able to make and maintain relationships with a wide variety of people and in the most trying of circumstances. They use modern tools of psychology and anthropology to influence and persuade.

- Build Teams. Good leaders create, focus and maintain effective teams. This is the first task of a leader and remains unchanging at every level in the organization. Teams form the core building block of effective military units. Training as coherent, tight knit units is critical to the development of a healthy NZ Army culture.

- Build Leadership Culture. To build a strong leadership culture in the NZ Army the foundation must rest on a shared value base, strong professional identity and a clear sense of leadership mission. Having a strong, shared culture binds members of the organization close, supports morale and encourages the growth and emergence of future leaders.

- Employ 24/7 Mission-Focused Leadership. Leadership is not a job. It is work, but the work doesn't stop when the job finishes. Leaders accept they are responsible for the people under their command, and they discharge those responsibilities in all circumstances and at all times. They accept that the nature of NZ Army life is its mission focus. Results are what matters and leaders accept that the lives of their followers are often at risk because of their command decisions. They learn to control impatience in themselves and others and apply mission command as necessary. Finally, leaders adapt to the changing demands of warfare. Fourth generation warfare requires leaders to accommodate blurred front lines, combatants who are indistinguishable from civilians and refugees, the complexity of multi-agency and multi-force involvement and the pressure of real-time media exposure.

A key principle of the ALF is that it offers competencies, defined as tasks. Leaders are expected to perform certain tasks in order to be successful, however the manner of how the leader performs these tasks is not necessarily prescribed. What the ALF does offer is awareness, theories, models, tools and techniques that may be employed to achieve these tasks, but it leaves it to the leader's discretion to determine the best fit for the task at hand, based on the context of the situation. The grab-bag of awareness, theories, models, tools and techniques are grouped by transition level according to where they are most likely to be relevant and effective. A building-block approach allows previous knowledge to be leveraged and expanded as the nature of leadership becomes more complex the higher one rises in the organization. Much of the leadership knowledge and skill learned as a junior leader remains equally as valid in strategic leadership roles.

The ALF utilizes a *Leadership Transitions Model* as shown in Figure 3. There are three key components to this model that represent a shift in thinking about the nature of leadership in the NZ Army. First, the model highlights that *Self-Leadership* is a requirement for all leaders. Leadership begins with the self – mastering one's self-interested desires and doing what is needed for the team and the mission. This requirement transcends rank, and is as important for the newest recruit as it is for the Chief of Army.

Second, at each and every level of the Army, leadership is provided by a *leadership team*. In all but one case, this involves an officer and a soldier – at the most basic team level, the leadership team is comprised of two NCOs, a Corporal and a Lance Corporal. At every other level, an officer and soldier work together to provide leadership to their immediate team and wider organization. This takes nothing away from command – the officer is still appointed and held accountable as the commander. Leadership, however, is a shared responsibility between the officer and soldier, whether this is

Chapter 5

the Platoon Commander and Platoon Sergeant, or the Chief of Army and the Sergeant-Major of the Army.

Finally, the model orients leaders to the changing nature of leadership. As a leader ascends the hierarchical stairway, leaders are reminded that leadership must be exercized in increasingly complex domains, and that the requirements for successful leadership will involve new knowledge, skills and attitudes. Equally importantly, there is the recognition that some of the leadership behaviours that brought success at lower levels may no longer be appropriate.

Whilst the model must align itself to military rank, it is more concerned with the job size and complexity that each successive level represents. As an example, in the NZ Army, corps schools (such as the Combat School for infantry and cavalry officers and soldiers) are commanded by Chief Instructors in the rank of Major, and assisted by School Sergeant-Majors, normally in the rank of Warrant Officer Class One (WO1). These officers are responsible for delivering training across the army, despite their relatively junior rank when compared to other armies. They are working at the level of *Lead Capability*, one transition higher than the majority of their peers.

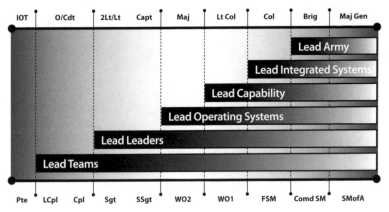

Figure 3 – Leadership Transitions

IMPLEMENTATION OF THE ARMY LEADERSHIP FRAMEWORK – THEORY TO PRACTICE

In late 2007 the NZ Army established a fully dedicated Leadership Project Team (LPT) to implement the plan of embedding the ALF across the Army, with the expectation that this task would take up to three years. As the initiator of frequent pan-organizational projects and programs, the Army understood that project team stability, continuity and focus are key drivers of success. The project head reported directly to the Chief Human Resources Officer (Army), and was thus able to readily access key stakeholders across the Army.

In keeping with the principles of the ALF, the LPT was headed by a leadership team of a Lieutenant-Colonel and a Warrant Officer Class One, and were assisted by two experienced training designers in the ranks of Warrant Officer Class Two and Staff Sergeant respectively.

The LPT remained intact for the first two years of the program, losing one training designer once momentum had been established and a successful outcome was assured. Three additional full-time team members were added in mid-2008, with these staff becoming the nucleus of an Army-wide training team that grew to 150 trainers over the life of the project, and incorporated leaders at every level of the organization.

One of the major success factors of the implementation was the adoption of a "leader-led" approach. Early in the project it was understood that leaders would most readily accept new ideas coming from successful leaders whom they knew and trusted. Over the life of the project, some 150 "trainers" were identified, trained and utilized in a part-time capacity. Typically, these trainers would act as facilitators on workshops one level below their current rank, allowing them to speak with some credibility of the leadership challenges present at that rank.

The implementation of the ALF incorporated five major tasks, with outcomes programmed to occur in a deliberate sequence:

- The conduct of "catch-up" workshops for every leader in the NZ Army. These were of five days duration, and designed to achieve three major outcomes:

  - Socialize to all NZ Army leaders the reasons behind the introduction of the ALF, and its main components;

  - Introduce the key leadership success factors for participants' current rank; and

  - Introduce the key leadership success factors for the participants' direct reports (i.e. one level of leadership down) in order that the participants can focus their leadership coaching to best effect.

- Modification and/or building of "business as usual" leadership development courses, to provide the long-term mechanism for leadership education. These courses have historically existed at most levels of the organization, but required work for alignment with ALF outcomes where this was different from existing content. These courses would prepare leaders for advancement to the next level of responsibility, and relied on participants having attended a "catch-up" workshop at their current rank as a prerequisite.

- Formalize and refine experiential leader development activities. For many years, the NZ Army had developed leader self-awareness through challenging outdoor activities delivered by the NZ Army Adventurous Training Centre. These activities were aligned with the ALF, and target the development of the intrapersonal and interpersonal behaviours that are critical enablers to leadership in stressful environments. Prior to the introduction of the ALF, there was a degree of organizational resistance as to the need for, let alone efficacy of, such development. However, the growing body of research highlighting the role of character and personality in successful leadership has put this argument to rest.[23]

- Stand up an Army Leadership Centre (ALC) to carry on the work of the LPT. The ALC would be responsible for doctrine development, lead the delivery of leadership education as the NZ Army leadership centre of excellence, and validate and moderate the effectiveness of leadership practice across the NZ Army. As this paper is written, the success of the ALC has prompted the Chief of the NZDF (CDF) to accelerate the establishment of a NZDF Leadership Centre, and the standardization of leadership doctrine across the three services (NZ Army, Royal New Zealand Navy [RNZN] and Royal New Zealand Air Force [RNZAF].

- Build a positive organizational culture. Through the development mechanisms outlined above, leaders are now expected to apply their learning and lay the foundation for long-term positive growth in organizational culture in the work place. With much greater visibility on leadership expectation at all levels, leaders are being held accountable from below for effective leadership.

METRICS – MEASURING IMPLEMENTATION EFFECTS

Measurement of the effectiveness of the "catch-up" workshops occurred throughout the project, in order to ensure that the workshops delivered the desired outcomes. One of the most significant Key Performance Indicators concerned whether the workshop participants believed the training was adding value, in terms of being relevant and useful to their current responsibilities as leaders. Across all the workshops (in excess of 2500 participants), validations consistently showed that over 95% of the participants believed that the workshop content was both useful and relevant. These positive results have continued with the business-as-usual courses. Significantly, for 60% of the participants, at least 50% of the content on their workshop represented new knowledge and skills.

Climate surveys completed since the introduction of the ALF also paint a positive picture. Organization-wide ratings for leadership behaviour have trended up. Whilst that is positive, the NZ Army is taking a longer-term view on judging the success of the ALF. On initiating the ALF in 2007, the Chief of Army expressed his expectation that the benefits of the project would take a decade to be realized – it would be the NZ Army's new leaders who would carry the new leadership culture into the future, free from many of the current paradigms.

But metrics only tell part of the story. The first three outcomes are largely mechanical – formal processes have been put in place, and leaders are directed or encouraged to take part in the range of ALF activities. It is the last outcome – the building of a positive organizational culture – that paints the most compelling picture.

Leadership across the NZ Army has been re-invigorated. This has been evidenced through many forms, but six visible examples are:

- The "language" of leadership has been raised into the NZ Army's consciousness – leadership concepts and theories are commonly referred to in everyday conversation. Most evident has been the catch-phrase "24/7," which in the context of the ALF refers to leaders being conscious of their responsibility to act as role models 24 hours a day, seven days a week.

- Leaders have been observed to create the time for deliberate discussions, feedback and planning on how their work areas can continue to grow a more positive culture, in order to become more enjoyable and productive workplaces.

- Leaders are more open to giving and receiving feedback, and building self-awareness. A growing number of leaders are utilizing tools and experiences that assist them in growing their leadership capability – this has become an open and accepted practice, and something that would have challenged previous generations of NZ Army leaders.

- The value of deliberate coaching and mentoring are becoming self-evident, as leaders embrace their role as talent agents. The NZ Army's largest camp is nearing completion of a pilot mentoring program for leaders, with the expectation that this will be exported across the Army through 2011.

- The ALF has reinforced that all members of the team add value. This has been made evident through the recent (January 2011) extension of full voting rights to the Warrant Officer of the Defence Force (WODF – the NZDF's senior non-commissioned leader) on the Defence Leadership Board – the Defence Force's executive decision-making body. The WODF now holds the same voting rights as the Chiefs of the Army, Navy and Air Force. Previously, the WODF enjoyed associate member status with this board, without voting rights.

- As the LPT grew into the ALC, the NZ Army increased its demands on the ALC to directly assist units and act as a conduit for leader education and organizational culture development. This extended from formed units through to *ad hoc* teams formed for overseas operational deployment.

ARMY LEADERSHIP FRAMEWORK SUCCESS FACTORS – THE STICKINESS FACTORS[24]

The ALF has been successfully embedded across the NZ Army primarily through the success of the "catch-up" workshops. The success of the workshops exceeded expectations, and became the catalyst for widespread change in many areas of NZ Army practice and culture. A retrospective examination of the project implementation identifies a significant number of success factors, some not fully appreciated at the outset. These are:

- Letting success speak for itself. At the commencement of the project there was command pressure for a major project launch. This was resisted, however, as the project team was mindful of creating unrealistic expectations in a program that was going to take at least two years to deliver. Instead, the project team choose to focus on delivering a quality program, trusting that participants would become the program's biggest advocates. This "fly-wheel" approach worked, with momentum creating a desire to be involved, and be part of the solution.

- Plan in detail, execute with flexibility. Over 250, five-day residential "catch-up" workshops were conducted during the project. Workshops were synchronized around key NZ Army activities and were often run concurrently in multiple locations, and at multiple levels. Sequencing was constantly adjusted to take account of other demands, and the logistics of the project challenged the project team to remain agile and adaptive.

- Leadership starts at the top. "Catch-up" workshops started top-down, as did the new regime of experiential leadership activities. The Chief of Army led the way and this challenged leaders at every level to step up to the plate, in the knowledge that actions speak louder than words.

- Workshop trainers were hand-picked, irrespective of rank. The sheer quantity of "catch-up" workshops meant that trainers would need to be drawn from throughout the NZ Army, and deliver workshops to their peers or immediate subordinates. The project team believed that the quality of workshop trainers was the make or break of workshop success, irrespective of the quality of workshop content. Trainers needed to be recognized leaders – credible and respected, with excellent interpersonal skills. In a noticeable break from tradition, the project team chose to "look up" when selecting trainers, taking as a priority the subordinate view of a more senior leader, rather than a top-down approach. This gave a more accurate take on leader behaviour and brought transparency to the process.

- Workshops were conducted in a mixed-rank setting. Traditional NZ Army practice has been that officers and non-commissioned officers follow separate pathways of leadership development, and yet were expected to work together in mixed-rank leadership teams as previously explained. Despite some initial scepticism about the efficacy and prudence of such a proposal, a legacy of this decision is the greatly enhanced depth of communication and trust between the officer and soldier streams.

- Learning is enhanced through perceptions of equality. An early decision was taken to conduct the workshops in civilian clothes, as a mechanism for forcing participants to look beyond the uniform and badges, and see the person. This was important for the mixed-rank aspect of the workshops, but also in breaking down stereotypes associated with trade and specialization, although it did expose a degree of insecurity with many leaders. The wearing of civilian clothes also effectively highlighted the 24/7 nature of leadership – leadership behaviours shouldn't be predicated by whether one is in uniform. Validation of the workshops highlighted this decision as being critical in allowing free and frank participation.

- Facilitation, not instruction. Considerable effort was expended in developing the facilitation skills of the trainers. It was critical to workshop success that participants were made to feel that their prior knowledge and experiences about leadership were relevant and valued, and that involvement in discussions would aid the learning of all. Participants were welcomed to challenge new ideas and develop their understanding through exploration and debate. A formal learning environment of lessons or lectures would have stifled learning.

- Good leaders engage. Senior NZ Army leaders were made welcome at every workshop, whether to join in discussions, or offer their opinion on leadership theory and practice. The only caveat on their involvement was their need to respect the opinions and leadership experience of the participants, and to recognize that rank did not necessarily make their opinion more valid. Targeted appearances by the Chief of Army, Deputy Chief of Army and the Sergeant-Major of the Army reinforced the importance of leadership development, and the investment in the ALF, and provided a powerful informal opportunity to share ideas and intent.

- Guest students add diversity and aid learning. All uniformed NZ Army leaders were required to attend a workshop specific to their worn rank. As the workshops progressed, the project team looked to widen the participant audience in order to provide a greater variety of views and experiences. Spaces were increasingly made available for non-uniformed military staff, members of the other two services, the New Zealand Police, and a number of other public service organizations.

- Minimize disruption to the individual and family. For the vast majority of workshop participants, workshops were attended in their home location. Aside from the desire to reduce disruption to participants, this plan also enabled the achievement of two aligned factors. First, participants would see standing in front of them trainers who were generally already known and respected as competent leaders, thus lending instant credibility to the program. Second, participants could experience an environment with peers who were already known, and build on the relationships that already existed.

- <u>Linking learning to application.</u> The final activity in every workshop was an exercise where every participant would express to their fellow participants and trainers their most significant learning moment and their "next-step" on returning to the workplace. In the latter stage of the project implementation, participants were encouraged to document their intentions. The "next-step" activity was for many participants a powerful experience, as it forced reflection on current leadership behaviour, and served as a prompt for change. Significantly, many stories have emerged subsequent to workshops of immediate and positive work-place changes in leader behaviour.

LESSONS LEARNED – APPLYING LESSONS FROM THE PROJECT TO BUSINESS AS USUAL

A range of lessons were learned through the life of the project that either reinforced earlier learning, or were adopted as worthy practices for the future. The more significant lessons were:

- Business-as-usual leadership courses have adopted a three-way partnership approach in terms of "ownership"; the facilitation role is shared by trained facilitators drawn from working units, staff from the ALC, and staff working at the Army school conducting the leadership course. This has created an expectation that leadership exists across the NZ Army and is "owned" by no one element.

- Any substantive change takes time; the bigger the organization, the longer it will take. Attempting to force a culture change is unlikely to be successful; at best, it will be short term and compliance driven. Long-term change occurs when it is internally driven and accepted.

- For many generations, leadership in the NZ Army was an unspoken assumption. Talking about it in a meaningful and positive way had brought it back into full consciousness. Leadership exists when it is a topic of conversation.

- Existing organizational culture can both assist and hinder change. It is prudent to leverage off the positive attributes of culture, and avoid tackling any negative aspect of culture head on.

- The NZ Army's reputation for leadership excellence has been reinforced. A growing number of public and private entities have sought advice and/or assistance with leadership development for their own organizations as a direct result of the exposure of the ALF in the wider community.

COMMON LEADERSHIP DOCTRINE FOR THE NEW ZEALAND DEFENCE FORCE

Building on the success of the ALF is the challenge to realize similar achievements across the wider NZDF. The RNZN and the RNZAF conduct their own leadership development regimes utilizing their own doctrine. Whilst there is a high degree of consistency of leadership doctrine and practice across the three services there is, perhaps not surprisingly, a degree of institutional reluctance to agree to a common framework and common expectations, let alone common training. It would appear that both perceived and real differences in service culture lie at the heart of this resistance, yet there are indications that as the frequency of the three services working together increases, the need for a common language of leadership emerges. The CDF's expressed intent to move towards common leadership doctrine for the NZDF and the establishment of a NZDF Leadership Centre pave the way for the future.

The catalyst for change appears to lie in joint training and joint education through the medium of the NZDF Command and Staff College. The 2011 Joint Junior Staff Course (JJSC) provided the platform for a trial of the ALF in a tri-service forum, and as a precursor to the modification of the ALF as the basis for a Defence Leadership Framework. The JJSC is a mid-level course required for promotion to Lieutenant-Commander (RNZN) and Squadron Leader (RNZAF), but not yet mandated as a requirement for promotion to Major (NZ Army). The Lead Operating Systems level of the ALF (Army Captain to Major transition) was introduced and found general acceptance as a framework of leadership knowledge, skills and attitudes. Student fears of the ALF being too "green" were proved to be largely unfounded.[25]

The key to establishing common leadership doctrine, let alone combined leadership training, is trust. Each service must trust that they won't lose anything of value – be it culture, skills or knowledge. With a history of working well together in the past, and with cultures that are more alike than they are different, there would appear to be little philosophical reason why the initiative would fail.

CONCLUSION

Leadership is the NZ Army's centre of gravity. The quality of leadership at every level of the NZ Army sets the stage for operational effectiveness, and this is achieved through the practice of involved leadership and the establishment of an appropriate leadership culture.

In hindsight, one could be forgiven for asking why the NZ Army had been so reticent in its formal development of leadership. For something so important, there seems to have been an almost remarkable organizational acceptance that junior tactical leaders would grow into the organization's strategic leaders through osmosis. Even though this issue seems to have been well recognized in some quarters, and prompted the well-researched Burrow's Report of 1985, little effort was made to rectify any shortcomings. The only significant advance that occurred in these decades of inertia was the creation of the Army Adventurous Training Centre in 1986. The AATC became a platform for leader development and it is perhaps fitting that it now forms an essential component of the Army Leadership Centre.

The ALF has reawakened the language of leadership in the NZ Army, and heightened awareness and expectations for sound leadership. The ALF has created the platform that enables a shared understanding of what one must do in order to deserve the title "leader." It is better accepted that leaders require development in order to successfully progress though leadership transitions, and that leadership is not developed through osmosis. Equally important is the philosophical shift in who "owns" leadership development. The triad of partners (Army Leadership Centre, Army schools and working units) now combine to teach the theory of leadership, with working units continuing leader development in everyday work.

The six ALF elements of *Live the NZ Army Ethos and Values, Think Smart, Influence Others, Build Teams, Build Leadership Culture* and *24/7 Mission Focused Leadership* provide a simple, unavoidable and powerful image of a leader's tasks. The concept of *leadership teams* has sparked a renaissance in the relationship between officer and soldier – awareness of a shared leadership responsibility for leadership outcomes has clarified role expectations and responsibility.

The success of the ALF has only been achieved through considerable effort across the organization, and through the collective effort of many leaders. Long-term success relies on maintaining momentum – effort and energy must continue to be applied if the ALF is to continue to guide the development of NZ Army leaders. Effort and energy equate to resourcing the ALC with appropriately talented staff and with the top-down mandate to hold the organization's leaders and leadership culture to account.

Chapter 5

Finally, the success of the ALF can provide a springboard for enhanced pan-NZDF leadership doctrine and development. Herein lays a significant challenge, but also significant opportunity. The simple act of intending to move to common doctrine and training paves the way for rich rewards in the form of a more connected NZDF, and the promise of enhanced operational effectiveness maximizing the utility of the fighting elements of which New Zealand is most proud – its personnel.

ENDNOTES

1. New Zealand Army, *NZ Army Leadership Manual* (Wellington: New Zealand Army, 2007).

2. For many years the two key leadership manuals were the *Australian Army Handbook on Leadership* (1973) and the *Australian Army Leadership Theory and Practice* (1973). More recently, the Australian Defence Force has produced a range of useful leadership manuals, including *Junior Leadership on the Battlefield* (Canberra: ADF, 1994), *Land Warfare Doctrine 0-0 Command, Leadership and Management* (2003), *and Australian Defence Force Publication 00.6 Leadership* (2007).

3. James M. Burns, *Leadership* (New York, NY: Harper & Burns, 1978).

4. Thomas Carlyle, *On Heroes, Hero-worship and the Heroic in History* (New York, NY: Fredrick A. Stokes and Brother, 1882).

5. Richard Bolden, Jonathan Gosling, Antonio Marturano and P. Dennison, *A Review of Leadership Theory and Competency Frameworks* (Exeter: Centre for Leadership Studies, University of Exeter, 2003).

6. *NZDF Deployments*, retrieved on 15 June 2011 from <www.nzarmy.mil.nz/army-overseas/deployments/default.htm>.

7. The strength of the regular component of the NZDF as at 1 April 2011 was 9,782. Source – *Personnel Summary*, retrieved on 15 June 2011 from <www.nzdf.mil.nz/at-a-glance/personnel-composition.htm>.

8. Presentation to 2011 New Zealand Defence Force Command and Staff College by Colonel Alan McCone, Director Training and Education Directorate, New Zealand Defence Force, June 2011.

9. Ian Hamilton Burrows, *Army Leadership Study* (Auckland, New Zealand Army, 1985).

10. The Army Depot is the NZ Army unit responsible for all-arms (or common) soldier training. This includes recruit training and command, management and leadership courses for non-commissioned officers and warrant officers.

11. Dan Riley, *Leadership Development Discussion Paper* (Military Studies Institute, New Zealand Army, July 2006).

12. The anomie model is a causal analysis diagram developed through analysis of data from 1450 climate surveys examined during research into the causes of attrition. Working from left to right with regressive coefficients, one can trace the "drivers" of why an individual may leave the service.

13. Anomie definition retrieved on 15 June 2011 from <www.britannica.com/EBchecked/topic/26587/anomie>.

14. Winsborough Limited is based in Wellington, New Zealand and provides organizational and clinical psychology services.

15. Bismarck Foundation Limited is based in Wellington, New Zealand and provides learning analysis and design services.

16. New Zealand Army, *NZ Army Leadership Manual* (Wellington: New Zealand Army, 2007).

17. Robert Hogan and Rodney Warrenfeltz, "Educating the modern manager," *Academy of Management Learning and Education*, Vol. 2, No. 1 (March, 2003), 74-84.

18. Steven R. Covey, *The Seven Habits of Highly Effective People* (Old Tappan, NJ: Simon & Schuster, 1989).

19. John Collins, *Good to Great* (New York, NY: Harper Collins, 2001).

20. John H. Zenger and Joseph Folkman. *The Extraordinary Leader: Turning Good Managers into Great Leaders* (New York, NY: McGraw-Hill, 2002).

21. Elliott Jaques, *Requisite Organization* (Arlington: Cason Hall & Co., 1988).

22. Verbatim descriptions from *NZ Army Leadership Manual*, 22-29.

23. Robert Hogan and Robert B. Kaiser, "What We Know About Leadership," *Review of General Psychology*, Vol. 9, No. 2 (2005), 169-180.

24. Malcolm Gladwell coined the phrase "stickiness factor" in his book *The Tipping Point* (Little Brown, 2000). The "stickiness factor" refers to what makes something compelling to the consumer – enough so to overcome resistance to buying the item, and leading to widespread consumer acceptance and demand.

25. 2011 Joint Junior Staff Course validation.

CHAPTER 6

COPING WITH COMPLEXITY – PREPARING MILITARY LEADERS FOR AN INTERLINKED WORLD

*Dr. Stefan Seiler & Dr. Andres Pfister**

INTRODUCTION

Armed forces in many developed parts of the world are generally well trained and equipped. These forces also display high levels of tactical and operational competency as well as the ability to execute tasks. Two recent developments, however, have resulted in major challenges for modern military organizations. The first development is related to military operations: modern military interventions are not only related to core military capabilities, but increasingly to highly complex operations in postwar environments with overlapping military and civilian tasks and responsibilities. The second development is related to political decision-making: financial restrictions and changing political opinions about the form and relevance of military forces have led to restrictive parameters and shifting conditions for senior military leaders in terms of technological modernization, people development, and organizational structure. As such, this chapter focuses on challenges for military leaders related to complex and unpredictable environmental changes rather than on specific military capabilities.

During the Cold War period, the economic, political, and social developments of a nation were often linked to or driven through partnering with either western allies or the Eastern Bloc. By closely observing the behaviour of important agents and gathering information from the networks of the opposite side, many developments became quite predictable. Predicting future developments made it possible to prepare for and react to unwanted developments at an early stage. Since the end of the Cold War, military leaders have been confronted with a multi-polar world with different nations, organizations, and agents pursuing very different goals.[1] The modern world is becoming increasingly complex, interlinked and global, and leaders and their organizations are confronted with rapidly changing environments,[2] with events in one

---

* The views expressed in this chapter are those of the authors and do not necessarily reflect the official policy of the Swiss Armed Forces.

part of the world producing unforeseen effects around the globe. This poses a new challenge for military leaders and for military organizations as they are required to monitor and interpret the behaviour of several independent but interlinked actors within a certain region or around the world to identify key developments, new threats, and to determine their own strategy. In recent years, military, political, social, religious, and economic leaders were surprised by several important global developments (e.g., the financial crisis in Greece and/or Ireland). Although some early signs were present, policy-makers and experts were not able to predict the magnitude and impact of these developments. In the context of national security, it is of vital interest and paramount for military leaders to effectively detect and correctly interpret changes, at an early stage, in order to react appropriately, and ensure troop, civilian, and national safety.

Two developments exemplify the importance of detecting changes at an early stage. First, the financial crisis which hit economies around the world illustrates the nature and reality of unpredictable major events which have an impact on civil societies and the military. The direct consequence for many armed forces was reduced military budgets, the result of increased national debts, and the need to cut government expenses. This has a direct influence on military capabilities – military leaders are urged to actively interact with political decision-makers as professional advisors on decisions related to technological investments (e.g., new weapon systems), human capital (e.g., officer training and education), or organizational structure (e.g., conscript, professional, volunteer). A second recent example is the outbreak of pro-democratic movements in Northern Africa. This development was even less predictable than the financial crisis. Without notice, a large region became emerged in turmoil, leading to dramatic government changes in Tunisia and Egypt, as well as a massive military intervention by an international coalition in Libya. The developments in Libya are especially difficult to predict as multiple stakeholders within Libya and the allied forces pursue different goals and agendas (e.g., Ghadafi Clan, European Union, the United States of America, North Atlantic Treaty Organization, Arab League, Al-Qaeda).

Several early signs hinted toward the development of these two described events. Few experts, however, predicted or anticipated impending future developments and dangers, and most scientific, political, economic, social, and military leaders failed to accurately predict these events. Since military leaders are responsible for the protection and security of their nation and society, they have a vital interest in being aware of and prepared for such global, complex and sudden changes. They need to be able to accurately recognize and correctly interpret signs of impending change, both region specific, and on a global scale. Without argument, if experts around the world were not able to predict such events, can we realistically expect military leaders be able to do so and equally important, how can they prepare for such events, if they do not know what the future will look like?

COMPLEX ADAPTIVE SYSTEMS AND NETWORKS

We approach this challenge by analyzing how complex adaptive systems (CAS) and the corresponding networks of agents react to environmental changes. Based on complexity theory,[3] organizations can be seen as CAS with the people in the system being defined as agents.[4] These agents are members of a network which constitutes the CAS. Each agent feeds the network with information and changes its own behaviour based on the information that is acquired within the network or due to changes in the external environment.[5] The external environment of a CAS mostly consists of other CASs, or other networks which a member agent can also be part of (i.e., other groups and organizations).[6] Beyond other CASs, several other environmental factors influence the behaviour of agents within a network (i.e., political, social, economic developments, weather conditions, etc.).[7] Developments in the external environment can eventually lead to changes in the behaviour of an agent within a CAS.[8] While more and more agents change their behaviour on the basis of new information or external events, the CAS as a whole also adapts to environmental changes.[9] It is difficult to determine how changes within a system take place as each system has a great deal of complexity due to the mutual relationships between the agents within the networks. Contrary to adapting to new developments, each CAS also strives for stability.[10] Once a CAS is established (e.g., a functioning group or organization), the system tries to maintain its stability as long as possible, sometimes despite internal or external pressure for change. Smaller adaptations, which do not threaten the overall stability, are constantly taking place.

As complex as these systems are, it is important to understand that early and important signs of potential change of individual network agents or parts of the system can be identified by observing the adaptation process within the network. As more and more agents change their behaviour, the behaviour of the network, and the CAS as a whole, adapts to the new environment.

In the military context, the specific challenge for military leaders is threefold. First, military leaders have to gain access to the myriad of networks in political, economic, religious, social, and scientific areas within a region, country and worldwide. Second, they have to actively participate within these networks, become a respected and trusted member, develop competency to identify important information signifying change as well as the ability to detect changes in the behaviour of the network agents. Being a member of different CASs makes it possible to understand the dynamics of the network and to determine whether it is primarily seeking stability or is in the process of change. This helps to determine causes for behavioural changes of network agents. Third, military leaders have to be able to integrate their knowledge of different networks and discover the underlying environmental change process. In doing so, they acquire the ability to influence a system, better prepare for adaptations and reduce or mitigate against the likelihood of being surprised by sudden change.

This leads to a new challenge for military leaders; they need to understand the requirement for and to become a valuable and trusted member of other military and non-military networks (e.g., the military networks of other nations, political networks and parties, scientific and economic networks, and the networks of regional leaders in other countries).

NETWORK ACCESS, PARTICIPATION AND COMMUNICATION

Gaining access to a network can be a difficult endeavour and simply be the first step in the process. More importantly, however, is becoming a valued and trusted member of the network with unfettered access to important information and the ability to influence the system. We consider the following three characteristics necessary conditions to achieving access and influence capability or status: similarity, trustworthiness, and stability.

Group or organizational members who constitute a network generally share similar experiences and goals, a common group or organizational culture, norms and rules, and a certain way of thinking (e.g., a world view).[11] Each network has its own communication style as exhibited through the use of specific terms, abbreviations and non-verbal communication behaviour.[12] Additionally, network members generate a certain amount of pressure to conform to the prevailing culture and world view.[13] Valued members are seen as trustworthy and reliable in terms of congruency, the pursuit of network goals and orientation, and are able to build stable relationships over time.

How then do military leaders gain access to networks outside their military environment and become valuable, influential members? First of all, one has to actively seek out contact with members of a new network. Finding a "common ground," for example, by sharing similar experiences, interests, norms, goals, or world views should represent a critical first step. This requires demonstrating a certain amount of understanding and interest in other people's and organizations' needs and goals. For example, if international coalition forces make decisions with regard to adapting local safety procedures, clan leaders from that area should be integrated in the problem-solving process and treated with respect. This will help to maintain the confidence bestowed on them by these clan members. In such cases, discussions may take longer and be more complicated; however, it is the recommended course of action and possibly the only path to achieve the long-term support and buy-in of the local people. Through the creation of strong relationships with specific network members, network access, over time and as trust becomes established, can be achieved. Although some non-verbal communication behaviour, rules and norms can be learned before entering the network, much is acquired while actively participating in the communication process.[14] The ability to interact with network members and applying their rules and norms is crucial; one will not become a member of a network if one is not able to use the appropriate verbal and non-verbal communication style and terms.

Once membership is acquired, it has to be nurtured. Inactivity or a lack of participation generally leads to a gradual exit from that network and can result in increased effort to reactivate member status. Hence, if a military leader is part of a network, he/she has to remain an active member in order to have continued access to network resources. Remaining a trusted and accepted member of a network also implies feeding useful and valuable information into the network. At times, this requires the need to carefully manage the need for military confidentiality against the desire for sharing information with other network members. The problem of regaining member status in a network frequently occurs when a military leader who has access to several local networks in a specific region is replaced. A network membership cannot easily be transferred to others as it is often tied to a specific person. Hence, a new military leader will be required to earn access to the existing networks, even though he remains the representative of the same coalition. This refers to the problem of stability in personal relationships versus institutional relationships. This transfer can be supported by a formal introduction of the new representative to the network members by the current position holder and by briefing the new person about network specifics.

For example, if a military leader can gain access to a network of Afghani or Iraqi clan leaders, becomes accepted as an external network member and remains active within the network, he/she could acquire early information from the network on environmental changes such as increasing insurgent activities as well as the actions the network is planning to take. Similarly, being part of a political party network at home offers the possibility to gain early access to information on emerging political developments. Besides gaining early access to information, being an accepted member of a network allows one to actively influence the networks decision-making process. According to complexity theory, leadership within a CAS is a self-developing interactive process in which, arguably, any active agent can take over a leadership role, independent of their hierarchical status.[15] Hence, a military leader has the opportunity to influence the adaptation process of a CAS by actively participating and communicating his/her opinion during the change process. As such, military leaders no longer react to environmental changes, but have a chance to influence the direction of future changes within the system.

INFORMATION INTEGRATION AND TREND ANALYSIS

Understanding developments in a single network helps to understand the environmental change a specific CAS is adapting to. But as shown in the examples at the beginning of this chapter, global developments like the financial crisis or the sudden outbreak of the pro-democratic movement in North Africa were not predictable by changes in the behaviour of one network or CAS alone. Several different CASs changed and adapted their behaviour simultaneously. These CASs are interlinked and each CAS is part of the environment of another CAS.[16] As such, they mutually influence each other. Hence, some changes in one network are due to changes in another. To discover and correctly identify such fundamental developments, military leaders have to integrate the information gathered from several different networks and analyze the linkages and interrelations between different CASs.

For example, being a member of a village clan leader network will enable the detection of changes in this network through concurrent membership in the clan leader networks of other villages, the military leader network of coalition forces, and the regional political network. As such, this allows the agent to identify behavioural changes and adaptation processes across several related networks. Understanding how the networks of the village clan leaders, the regional government, and coalition forces are interlinked and interacting with each other helps to identify relevant changes early. This knowledge can then be used to prepare for possible future developments and to influence the networks in a particular direction.

Military leaders also have to gain access to important political and other networks in their home countries. With certainty, developments in the home country affect military leaders' as much as operational challenges. Defence budget cuts due to increasing national debt or changes in political priorities with regard to the form and size of the armed forces can have severe influences on military capabilities. Military leaders must therefore have the ability to interact, consult, and advise political and other network members, who make important decisions for the future development of the armed forces. Preparing military leaders for this additional task is a major challenge for the armed forces.

CHALLENGES FOR THE ARMED FORCES

The challenge for the armed forces is to prepare military leaders for this highly demanding task, which is not in the traditional realm of military leadership professional development nor does it take place in a classical military setting or network. In addition to expert knowledge in military domains, leaders need to be educated and trained to interact with and influence agents in different networks. More specifically, this means military officers must be educated in a variety of disciplines to include but not limited to political, social, economical, technological, strategic, historical, juristic, and cultural science. This also implies an interest and understanding of changes in societal cultures and values (e.g., the impact of popular culture on younger generations). Further, military leaders have to be able to effectively communicate with various agents. This not only requires sufficient language skills, but also the ability to interact successfully in different cultural environments. The armed forces can support the development of such competencies. First and foremost, the teaching of the relevant languages and network nuances is essential. Further, critical basic behaviours can be learned before trying to access a network (e.g., through role-plays). For example, knowing how to appropriately greet an Afghani clan leader, how to approach political leaders, how to show respect, understanding what behaviours are acceptable and expected, or viewed as highly disrespectful, helps to gain or initiate access to networks. Clearly, final adjustments will have to be learned during the interaction with the various network agents. In such an environment, it is important to be able to have a certain degree of cultural empathy, in other words, the ability to understand and see the world through the eyes of other network members without losing one's own standpoint and focus on a mission. This requires interest, openness, polycentrism and cultural knowledge[17] (e.g., understanding why in certain cultures respect for local authorities [e.g., clan leaders] is higher than that for government authorities). Such competencies can be developed through professional training or rotations to other military branches (e.g., army, air force, navy), participating in international military training programs, or spending time with other organizations the military works with (e.g., NGOs, police, firefighters, etc.). This exposes

Chapter 6

military officers to different organizational cultures and potentially leads to a better understanding of the need for partial behaviour adaptation while exposed to different settings. During such internships or job-rotations, officers learn that different communication styles are appropriate in different settings; that organizations may set different priorities while experiencing the same situation; and that people have different motives and interests. Such experiences help to develop behavioural skills that can be applied across various settings and awareness for organizational and individual differences. It is important to note that the success of such a learning process is dependent on a person's ability to reflect on these experiences. Officers need to reflect on the effects of behaviours and interactions in different settings and draw the right conclusions, test their hypothesis, observe other successful people in particular networks, and learn from them. Purposeful reflection of their own behaviour and observation of other peoples' behaviour can increase a person's ability to interact successfully in new networks.

In addition, military leaders also need to better integrate non-military related issues in their military problem-solving process and military intervention plans. Consequences of military interventions have to be analyzed from effects on the CAS, not only from a military effectiveness perspective. An additional important aspect is related to a person's intrinsic motivation to interact with people in various CASs. In order to establish successful relationships in complex, multi-cultural environments, military leaders need to be self-motivated to gain access to such networks and understand the dynamics within and outside these networks. The armed forces can actively foster this motivation by generating an individual interest for non-military areas or by actively supporting the already existing interests of military leaders. Generating an individual interest can be achieved through increased professional development in fields described in the previous paragraphs. Qualified professors and instructors with a focus on operational relevance and a well-structured curriculum are essential. The goal should be to foster interest and self-learning in various military as well as non-military topics. As well, the military selection process, the general interests of potential future military leaders should be assessed – people with multiple interests should be preferred over people with limited interests in complex cause and effect interactions. In addition, having a unified, yet diverse officer corps with various interests and backgrounds helps to broaden the horizon of the organization and each individual within the organization. If military leaders do not understand the importance of being connected to various people in different networks or are not intrinsically motivated to seek the challenges related to accessing different CASs, they will most probably fail to become valued members in these networks.

The final task for military leaders and the armed forces lies in the integration of the acquired information obtained from various networks to develop a combined and complete picture, and discovering and recognizing the important underlying environmental developments. Military leaders have to be able to integrate knowledge gathered from different networks. Based on strong analytical skills, they have to be able to evaluate the underlying reasons for behavioural change in the different networks, reflect on potential consequences, propose the right and necessary actions to be prepared for new developments, and develop strategies to influence different networks in the desired direction. The environmental developments and adaptation processes of any CAS, however, are dynamic processes that can be influenced to a certain degree, but never fully controlled. Every influence on a network provokes further reactions, which are sometimes difficult to predict in advance.

CONCLUSION

In a globalized, interlinked, and complex world, military leaders have to play an important and influencing role in more than just their own network. They have to be able to influence others, identify early signs of system changes and understand the consequences of these changes. In doing so, it will help to mitigate or protect their troops, the nation, or the world community against undesired effects, leading to a more polarized and less secure world. In summary, military leaders;

- need to be experts in core military domains;

- need to have strong analytical skills;

- need to be well and broadly educated to understand the complex interactions and dependencies between military and non-military systems and activities;

- need to master a wide repertoire of behaviours, ranging from listening skills, subtle influence skills, negotiation skills, diplomatic appearance, to firm command and control authority;

- need to have (cultural) empathy;

- need to reflect on their own behaviour and observe successful others in their interactions; and

- need to be motivated to work in such an environment.

Chapter 6

In sum, military leaders need to be able to adapt their behaviour to various situations and groups without losing a clear identity and profile.

ENDNOTES

1. Feng Zhongping, Robert Hutchings, Radha Kumar, Elizabeth Sidiropoulos, Paolo Wrobel and Andrei Zagorksi, "Global Security in a Multipolar World", *Challiot Paper* (2009), 118; Lisbeth Aggestam, "The World in Our Mind: Normative Power in a Multi-Polar World" in André Gerrits, ed., Normative Power Europe in a Changing World: A Discussion (The Hague, Netherlands: Institute of International Relations Clingendael, 2009), 25-36.

2. Daniel Katz and Robert L. Kahn, *The Social Psychology of Organizations* (New York, NY: Wiley, 1978); Marguerite Schneider and Mark Somers, "Organizations as Complex Adaptive Systems: Implications of Complexity Theory for Leadership Research", *The Leadership Quarterly*, Vol. 17 (2006), 351-365.

3. Benyamin Lichtenstein, Mary Uhl-Bien, Marion Russ, Anson Seers, James Douglas Orton and Craig Schreiber, "Complexity Leadership Theory: An Interactive Perspective on Leading in Complex Adaptive Systems", *E:CO*, Vol. 8, No. 4 (2006), 2-12.; Mary Uhl-Bien, Russ Marion and Bill McKelvey, "Complexity Leadership Theory: Shifting Leadership from Industrial Age to the Knowledge Era", *The Leadership Quarterly*, Vol. 18 (2007), 298-318.

4. Uhl-Bien, Marion and McKelvey, "Complexity Leadership Theory: Shifting Leadership from Industrial Age to the Knowledge Era", 299.

5. Lichtenstein *et al.*, "Complexity Leadership Theory: An Interactive Perspective on Leading in Complex Adaptive Systems", 3; Stefan Seiler and Andres Pfister, "Why Did I Do This? Understanding Leadership Behavior Based on the Dynamic Five-Factor Model of Leadership", *Journal of Leadership Studies*, Vol. 3 (2009), 41-52.

6. Lichtenstein *et al.*, "Complexity Leadership Theory: An Interactive Perspective on Leading in Complex Adaptive Systems", 3.

7. Kathleen Carley and Vanessa Hill, "Structural change and learning within organizations", in Alessandro Lomi and Eric R. Larsen, eds., *Dynamics of organizational societies.* (Cambridge, MA: AAAI/MIT Press, 2001), 63-92; Kathleen Carley and Ju-Sun Lee, "Dynamic Organizations: Organizational Adaptation in a Changing Environment", *Advances in Strategic Management: A Research Annual*, Vol. 15 (1998), 269-297.

8. Lichtenstein *et al.*, "Complexity Leadership Theory: An Interactive Perspective on Leading in Complex Adaptive Systems", 4.

9. Uhl-Bien, Marion and McKelvey, "Complexity Leadership Theory: Shifting Leadership from Industrial Age to the Knowledge Era", 299.

10. Schneider and Somers, "Organizations as Complex Adaptive Systems: Implications of Complexity Theory for Leadership Research", 358.

11. Uhl-Bien, Marion and McKelvey, "Complexity Leadership Theory: Shifting Leadership from Industrial Age to the Knowledge Era", 299.; Lichtenstein, *et al.*, "Complexity Leadership Theory: An Interactive Perspective on Leading in Complex Adaptive Systems", 3.

12. Isa Engleberg, "Working in Groups: Communication Principles and Strategies", My Communication Kit Series (New York, NY: Allyn & Bacon, 2006), 126-129.

13. John Levine and Dick Moreland, "Small groups", in Daniel T. Gilbert, Susan T. Fiske and Gardner Lindzey, eds., *The Handbook of Social Psychology* (New York, NY: McGraw-Hill,

1998), 415-469; Brad Pinter, Tim Wiklschut, Chester Insko, Jeffrey Kirchner, Matthew Montoya and Scott Wolf, "Reduction of Interindividual-Intergroup Discontinuity: The Role of Leader Accountability and Proneness to Guilt", *Journal of Personality and Social Psychology*, Vol. 93, No. 2 (2007), 250-265.

14. Engelberg, "Working in Groups: Communication Principles and Strategies", 126-129.

15. Hilary Bradbury and Benyamin Lichtenstein, "Relationality in Organizational Research: Exploring the Space Between", *Organization Science*, Vol. 11 (2000), 551-564.; Seiler and Pfister, "Why did I do this? Understanding Leadership Behavior Based on the Dynamic Five-Factor Model of Leadership", 42; Lichtenstein *et al.*, "Complexity Leadership Theory: An Interactive Perspective on Leading in Complex Adaptive Systems", 4.

16. Uhl-Bien, Marion and McKelvey, "Complexity Leadership Theory: Shifting Leadership from Industrial Age to the Knowledge Era", 299.

17. Jürgen Bolten, "Interkulturelle Personalentwicklungsmaßnahmen: Training, Coaching und Mediation" [Intercutural personnel development treatments: Training, coaching and mediation] in Günter K. Stahl, Wolfgang Mayrhofer and Torsten M. Kühlmann, eds., *Internationales Personalmanagement* (Munich, Germany: Hampp, 2005), 307-324.; Christopher Earley and Soon Ang, *Cultural intelligence: An analysis of individual interactions across cultures* (Palo Alto, CA: Stanford University Press, 2003).

CHAPTER 7

NEW SECURITY ECONOMICS: A CHALLENGE FOR FUTURE LEADERS[1]

*Dr. Mie Augier & Dr. Robert M. McNab**

INTRODUCTION

There are close links between economics, economies, and security that are often overlooked. Recent events, however, provide good illustrations of these links and food for thought. The security implications of the financial crisis, and possible future crises, pose challenges for current and future generations of leaders. But despite the fact that the financial crisis has resulted in significant cuts to defense expenditures in several NATO countries (and warnings from outgoing US secretary of defense, Robert Gates, of the resulting possible "irrelevance" of NATO), a discussion of the interrelations between economics and security and its implications for strategy, curiously, is absent.

These events illustrate the need for a discussion on the nature of strategy in a post-Cold War environment, including an examination of how shifting economic balances influence matters of national and international security. Given the interdependencies between economics and security, examining emerging threats to economic security and the possible impact on national security is also a necessity. For current and future leaders to make swift and effective strategic decisions, awareness of these (and other) issues will be essential.

Therefore, the purpose of this chapter is to explicate some key issues that are important to future leaders in defense and security regarding the nature of strategy and the security implications of the changing economic balances. Emphasizing the organizational nature of strategy, this chapter explores some of the strategic implications of the financial crisis. Additionally, this chapter takes a few initial steps towards providing a framework for leaders to think about the new security economics and their role in security competition.

Much of the intellectual lacuna and missing dialogue between the fields, lack of communication across journals, professional associations, and academic

---

* The views expressed in this chapter are those of the authors and do not necessarily reflect the official policy of the United States Navy or the Department of Defense.

departments for example, has arisen because of some key misunderstandings about strategy and the unfortunate centrifugal forces that often exist within social science disciplines. Often times, social scientists see little outside of their own discipline when trying to find explanations for phenomena. In the wake of the financial crisis, for example, many economists could have taken this opportunity to revise their economic models but were unwilling to do so.[2] In addition, they are often unwilling to admit just how fundamental the changes in economic gravity are and how they will be in the near future (i.e., declining empires do not want to admit that they are declining – that has been known since the time of the Vikings!). This, in turn, essentially blindfolds current and future leaders to the possible strategic implications of changing economic balances.

To take off the blindfold, refocus the discussion and enable leaders to learn from current and future challenges, we suggest outlining a framework for thinking about strategy and the nexus of economic and security issues. While we call it "New Security Economics" (NSE), it is important to emphasize that NSE is a multi-disciplinary approach to complex strategic problems. Senior leaders face much more complex security issues than any one discipline can offer since real world problems rarely (if ever) fit one single discipline. The "Arab Spring,"[3] for example, resulted from shifts in issues such as information technology, economic decline, and cultural dynamics; yet, the security implications of this event are not well understood and are likely to unfold over the coming years. NSE is an emerging framework that seeks to understand strategic challenges and events through a combination of economics, strategic, psychological, cultural, and political lines of inquiry.

For leaders to have a better understanding of the future challenges, they must begin with a better understanding of the nature of the strategic situation and strategies. But all too often, one hears discussion about an international security strategy based on either flawed assumptions about a country's economy (e.g., refusing to see which countries really are in decline); its culture (do they really want democracy and what are their essential values?), or about the nature of strategy and strategies, where "strategy" appears to be merely a list of goals. This method is fundamentally the wrong way to conceptualize, or not conceptualize, really, the strategic challenges facing future leaders and their possible strategic processes. On a conceptual level, it does not capture the essence of strategic thinking and what strategy is. On a practical level, unrealistic assumptions will almost never lead to the intended results. Thus, if leaders base their strategies on fundamentally flawed understandings of what strategy is and what the economic underpinnings influencing strategies are, the policies for dealing with the competition, and so on, also become very suspect. In the context of modern warfare, such misunderstandings can be (very) damaging and dangerous for the long-term survival of current military balances.

In the following, we endeavour to (1) provide some clarification on the nature and the process of strategy in the current and future security environments, emphasizing the organizational nature of strategy, (2) explicate some of the current strategic issues that are economic in nature surrounding the implications of the financial crisis, and (3) argue that there is a need for a long-term perspective in strategy around the NSE. These three aims/focuses are interrelated and have implications for how to conduct strategy-based assessments in the future.

The next section will introduce the concept and discuss the central issues of strategy using some existing definitions of the organizational nature of strategy. We then explore the impact of the global financial crisis on national and international security in the third section. The fourth section presents an initial framework for NSE and the concluding section offers suggestions for leaders and for future research.

HOW (NOT) TO THINK ABOUT STRATEGY

> *Strategy without tactics is the slowest route to victory. Tactics without strategy is the noise before defeat.*

Sun Tzu[4]

Understanding the nature of strategy is one of the central elements of leadership; this challenge will only increase for future leaders, as the strategic competition will continue to be more and more complex and ambiguous. An interesting paradox is that while the concept and practice of strategy and strategic thinking are essential for leaders of nations and military organizations, there are many factors in those environments that work against strategic thinking and against developing pro-active strategies; these leaders and organizations may possibly even confuse strategy and strategic thinking with tactics.

The lack of good practice in the area furthers the problem. Thinking strategically is difficult and the literature on strategy is substandard; additionally, people are unwilling to admit strategic mistakes, which in turn prohibits them from learning. Failures to learn, to anticipate, and to adapt are commonplace.[5] Thus, lack of experience and literature constitute a poor basis for learning strategy and for leaders to understand the key strategic issues.

Chapter 7

To add further complexity, there are many definitions of strategy (e.g., in business, in the military, in leadership and in other contexts), different understandings of strategy which illustrate how historical and cultural context also influences words, and at times strategy is confused with tactics, as Sun Tzu and others warned against. Consider for instance some of the definitions of strategy among military organizations. NATO, for example, defines strategy as: "That component of national or multinational strategy presenting the manner in which military power should be developed and applied to achieve national objectives or those of a group of nations".[6] The US Joint Chiefs of Staff, on the other hand, define strategy as: "A prudent idea or set of ideas for employing the instruments of national power in a synchronized and integrated fashion to achieve theater, national, and/or multinational objectives."[7]

Perhaps the most important shortcoming in many traditional definitions is that there is too much emphasis on strategy as goals. This approach neglects the importance of the process of strategy, not to mention, it makes it impossible to understand the barriers that exist to strategy-making if one simply focuses on the desirable goals (that may be unachievable and/or unrealistic). If leaders are focused on desirable goals instead of realistic strategies, the resulting decision-making process is unlikely to be effective. Simply put, "desirable goals", when pursued with no regard for the reality, are likely to produce quite undesired outcomes.

Attempts to foster "institution building" or to "prevent falling regimes," for example, may appeal to senior leaders unwilling to address a failing course of action. Much like an individual unable to separate himself/herself from sunk costs, senior leaders may define strategy in terms of desired outcomes and then ask for courses of action to achieve these unrealistic outcomes. By focusing on what is desired, senior leaders may ignore significant evidence, which suggests that such outcomes are poorly understood and require of effort. Even though governments have spent billions of dollars over previous decades to reduce corruption in developing and transitional countries, the relative position of many countries has remained reasonably static. It is therefore somewhat fanciful to suggest that we can "build institutions" or "prevent state failure" when we do not well understand the processes of how institutions come into being or how states fail. It also seems somewhat arrogant to assume that we know the cultural and human values of the nations whose institutions we try to "build." Those values are shaped through centuries and do not change overnight just because policies may.

A further complication is the ambiguity of words. The concept of strategy has multiple interpretations and meanings; it can refer to issues such as "(how) should we respond to unrest in neighboring countries," "how do nations behave," "who are our allies," "what determines success or failure in the international strategic competition?" Some may think that a "strategy" means a policy to defend Europe (if we can afford it?), or for Europe to defend interests abroad – in which case a strategy may seem to mean a "policy" to adhere to certain guidelines, which our actions will follow. However, since strategy is a complex process involving numerous players, multiple (often conflicting) and ambiguous goals, uncertainty and unpredictability, a more forward looking, dynamic and realistic conception of strategy might seem more appropriate than "if-then" thinking. Before clarifying what some of these conceptual elements are, we can summarize some of the shortcomings in the existing conceptions of strategy around language, substance, context/culture, and implementation.

Leaders need to be aware of these issues in order to develop better alternatives. First, there is the problem of language. Many discussions of strategy do not distinguish between levels of strategy or the focus of strategy, making the term "strategy" both too broad and too inclusive. Second, there are problems of substance. The tendency exists to talk about strategy as a list of "good things" or goals one would like to achieve. Such a definition neglects the fact that strategy is a process; it also ignores the fact that it is a process we can shape. Strategy should be a pro-active tool. Third, problems of context and culture exist. The ambiguity surrounding the concept of strategy itself across different cultures and contexts adds to the confusion. The Russian definition of strategy, for example, differs from the Chinese definition. To what extent then do these differences in definitions reflect their style of strategic thinking, and implementation of strategy in the countries militaries? Finally, there are problems of implementation. Discussions of strategy often assume the automatic implementation of strategy or at least fail to consider the many (often organizational) existing barriers to strategy. Those barriers exist on our side, as well as on our opponents'. Understanding the nature of strategy and the importance of strategy requires future leaders to examine these problems and issues. A good definition is also important to getting the strategy right further in the process of implementation, and for understanding the strategic situation in which one exists.

THE DYNAMIC, ORGANIZATIONAL AND
LONG-TERM NATURE OF STRATEGY

Strategy is all about taking advantage of asymmetries in a situation.

Andrew Marshall[8]

Chapter 7

Strategy is the great work of the organization. In situations of life or death, it is the Tao of survival or extinction. Its study cannot be neglected.

Sun Tzu[9]

Andrew Marshall, the director of the Pentagon's Office of Net Assessment for more than three decades, has suggested a conception of strategy that does not conflate with policy and that emphasizes its essential dynamic nature, as being about "identifying or seeing or even creating asymmetric advantages in the strategic competition, that can be used or exploited to help achieve one's long-term objective, facing opponents that are trying to achieve theirs".[10] A well-known business strategist, Alfred Chandler, also noted the long-term nature of strategy: "Strategy is the determination of the basic long-term goals of an enterprise, and the adaptation of courses of action and the allocation of resources necessary for carrying out these goals."[11] In what follows, we will adopt the spirit of this dynamic and evolutionary concept of strategy, and elaborate on some of the elements for thinking about strategic competition in this way.

The Organizational Nature of Strategy. Instead of building strategy on unrealistic assumptions about our allies, our opponents, or ourselves, we need to build on a realistic conception of the actors, organizations and humans constituting the competition. This involves trying to genuinely understand how other nations' cultures, histories and practices influence their decision-making. In economics, behavioural and evolutionary organization scholars have taken steps towards a more empirically realistic foundation for understanding behaviour.[12]

An important premise in these approaches is that one needs to understand both the limitations to human rationality and computational capability, and the ways in which organizational (and other social) structures influence and constrain decision-making. When looking at the emerging economic (or military) powers and understanding their future paths, for example, one needs to also recognize their domestic behavioural, cultural, organizational and institutional constraints (such as corruption or a lack of social safety nets) and how that may influence behaviours. Thus, we cannot use simplified models of behaviours to understand other nations and non-state actors (in fact, the models that we have rarely even apply to ourselves/western behaviours).

Assuming full rationality, for instance, can have unfortunate consequences. Nations, like organizations, are systems of decision-makers, rules, and hierarchies. Bounded rationalities and limited information constrain them, and rules and norms guide (or blind) them. Frequently, they have conflicting and possibly ambiguous goals. Scholars familiar with behavioural organization theory will recognize this as some of the central issues in the works of Simon, March and Cyert. Thus, as US strategist Andrew Marshall argued, nations should adopt an organizational behavioural perspective when thinking about strategic competition (at the time of his writing, that was primarily concerning the Soviet Union). According to Marshall, "the hope is to replace the current rational process model with something better, something that reflects more accurately the context and the constraints within which Soviet military posture incrementally evolves, as the result of a sequence of decisions over many years."[13] Additionally, when viewing opponents through the organizational lens, we must be careful to understand them through their own perspective and not be biased by our own assumptions and experiences.

To identify and create (strategic) asymmetries, we must accept that nations have their own distinct cultures, competencies, capabilities, and organizations. We also must consider a nations' possible strengths and weaknesses (such as geographic position), and have the ability to develop strategic organizational advantages. By understanding and influencing asymmetries, not only can we better understand the nature of the competition, but we may also be able to influence it. It may be useful here to borrow a term from business strategy and talk about "strategic capabilities." In the field of business strategy, capabilities refer to the particular (non-immutable) capacity that an organization has to shape, reshape, configure, and reconfigure its assets and its resources in order to respond to changing technologies and markets. An organization's strategic capabilities, therefore, relate to its ability to adapt; organizations adapt in order to generate and to exploit internal and external specific competencies, and to address the firm's changing environment. In terms of security, we can integrate some of the discussions above and suggest an understanding of strategic capabilities as *the ability for players to identify, generate and exploit specific competencies and capabilities (including geographic positions), to adapt, anticipate and shape the changing environment in ways favourable to their own future existence and growth.*

Acknowledging the changing dynamics of the strategic competition. The last few decades have brought change to the world in many ways; two of the most obvious are a) a change of superpowers, and b) a change from bi-polar competition to multi-polar competition. The first point may be a bit controversial if one looks only at military power, but when we adopt a more comprehensive view of national power, including the economic competition between the United States and China, it is not clear that the US will remain the dominant power even in the not too distant future, numerous predictions and estimates point to this. Declining empires, of course, have a difficult time admitting or seeing that they are in decline. Cognitive and psychological biases, and perhaps, especially the tendency to overestimate successes (rather than failures) in evaluating future outcomes can become barriers for the United States to adopt a more realistic picture of the current and future trends and powers.[14]

Current and future leaders need to be aware that organizational and institutional reform is difficult in the absence of a crisis. US Secretary of Defense (SecDef) Robert Gates recently noted that NATO has not adopted or adjusted well to the changes in the security environment in the last decades. Other critics have been more direct, suggesting that NATO is an organization in search of a mission. This relates to the point above about organizations, or the organizational barriers to strategy. Psychologists have argued since at least Kurt Lewin that people (and organizations) resist change; this implies that there are problems persuading people to accept and work towards organizational changes in institutional structures that might be desirable, even necessary, for strategy. A leader wanting to implement a strategy he/she has adopted faces implementation problems from those institutions that may not agree with the overall strategy, or simply do not desire change. A first step towards overcoming such barriers to organizational and strategic adaptation to the changes in competition is to understand them and to answer the following questions: *"Why is it that organizations have a tendency to resist change? What drives organizational behaviour? What is the relationship between the structure of the organization and the individuals, and between the resistance to change at the individual and organizational level? To what extent is the inability to change a strategic disadvantage for us and a strategic capability for our opponents?"*

The economic foundations for strategy and the strategic implications of the changing economies. We argue that not only are organizations reluctant to embrace change, but so are economies. As strategy and economics are inexorably intertwined, it is difficult to change strategy without considering the economic ramifications. Likewise, if economic power is shifting, strategy must also evolve, otherwise a nation may no longer be able to generate the resources required to implement the strategy.

Future leaders, particularly those of the US and other Western militaries, need to be better educated on the links between economics and security, and on how to prepare for possibilities of "economic warfare." An emerging economic power may free ride on the projection of US power to amass sufficient assets to monopolize key resources. For example, the presence of the US Navy provides security to all vessels in an area (seemingly) without cost, allowing states to enjoy the benefits of US defense expenditures without commiserate expenditure. An emerging economy can then use resources that would otherwise be required for defense for economic investment and for loans and grants to other countries. Soon, the emerging economy can have a significant presence in a geographical area without having deployed military forces. One only needs to examine the surge of Chinese investment into Latin American and Africa, for example, to understand that the next battlefront may not be waged by weapons, but through economic means.

The US federal government, at the time of writing, is headed towards the distinct possibility of defaulting on its debt; Greek and Portuguese sovereign bonds are rated as junk, and Chinese subnational governments are continuing to disclose hidden debts in the billions of dollars. Such economic turmoil was unforeseen by the majority of strategists ten years ago and suggests that future economic events are equally unlikely to be well known today. The question of whether the US dollar will remain the international reserve currency has been discussed repeatedly over the last decade but there is yet to emerge a serious competitor. The Euro is in obvious trouble; the decision-making processes of China are too opaque for the Yuan to take centre stage (at least for now), and so the US dollar continues. Yet, it is inevitable that another currency will replace the US dollar at some point in time, and there may be significant changes in the powers of the international financial institutions ahead. What are the implications for the United States if such a shift occurs in the next decade? Such a shift would likely dramatically impact the allies of the United States who are dependent upon the ability of the United States to project power globally. Therefore, it is important for current and future leaders to explore this and other challenges, even if the prospect of such a challenge coming true is highly undesirable.

NSE offers a framework for thinking about the strategic competition and strategy as proactive and as a long-term perspective. Strategy is neither policy nor tactics. As one strategist noted, "strategy [...] focuses on longer-term goals and reflects a cast of mind that focuses on shaping the future rather than reacting to it."[15] This is important when we consider the long-term implications of the global financial crisis; economists and political leaders often focus on short-term fixes (political leaders per definition have short-term horizons due to election cycles). Future leaders need to develop a longer-term horizon and awareness.

Chapter 7

THE IMPACT OF THE GLOBAL FINANCIAL CRISIS ON SECURITY: THE BUDGET CONSTRAINT AS A BARRIER TO STRATEGY

While the financial crisis and its ongoing effects may continue to place fiscal pressure on the US government to reduce expenditures and raise revenues, the impact of the crisis on the world's most vulnerable populations should not be overlooked. Almost 40 percent of developing countries, for example, are highly exposed to the effects of the crisis.[16.] This suggests that the financial crisis, even over the medium term, may constrain the ability of the developed nations to act while simultaneously increasing the likelihood of conflict in the world's poorest countries. One challenge for leaders is how to effectively manage the forthcoming reduction in defense resources while retaining capabilities to mitigate the influence of the financial crisis.

This section discusses the impact of the global financial crisis on the national security of the United States and its allies. If the global crisis has adversely affected the ability of the United States and its allies to project power globally in the medium-term, then this suggests a rebalancing of the global order and a significant challenge for military leadership. On the other hand, if the global crisis is a short-run issue, then the challenges of the present are likely to be the challenges of the near and, potentially, medium-term.

This section is structured as follows. We first examine the impact of the global economic crisis on the economic power of the United States and its allies. We then ask the question of what states are likely to gain in the medium-term from the crisis and whether the balance of power is significantly altered. We discuss leadership lessons from the crisis, and finally, we examine methods of attempting to improve strategy and planning.

Economic Power and the Financial Crisis. The national security of a state depends on a combination of hard and soft power.[17] The crisis has affected the ability of states to raise revenues while increasing demands for social protection expenditures. Bailouts of the financial sector have further exacerbated operating deficits in many of the Organization for Economic Cooperation and Development (OECD) member countries. While the economic power of many OECD states has diminished, other states have increased their prominence during the crisis and are unlikely to return to their former positions in the global economy. China, for example, through a combination of prudent fiscal management and an abundance of capital reserves, managed to mitigate its exposure to the financial crisis. There is now serious discussion of whether the Chinese model of economic development is more appropriate than "Western" approaches.

For the United States, the financial crisis created demands for assistance to the financial sector, the auto industry, state and local governments, and a host of other claimants. Net federal government saving, which is equal to federal revenues minus expenditures, fell from $40.5 billion in 2000 to -$245.2 billion in 2007 and continued to decline to $1,333.5 billion in 2010.[18] The significant increase in the operating deficit can be attributed to four factors: 1) the 2001 and 2003 tax cuts, 2) the wars in Iraq and Afghanistan, 3) an expansion of the public health insurance program (Medicare), and 4) the impact of the financial crisis. While a temporary decrease in net federal government saving would be warranted during a recession, especially one of such significance as the financial crisis, the size of the deficit coupled with existing levels of debt pose a significant challenge to the ability of the United States to project power in the medium-term.

The decrease in net government saving, due to the recession and the resultant bailouts and stimulus packages, negatively impacted US government debt. At the end of 2007, federal government debt equaled approximately 40 percent of Gross Domestic Product (GDP). By the end of 2011, gross federal debt will rise to approximately 70 percent of GDP, significantly above the post-Second World War average of 37 percent.[19] The opportunity cost of this debt is apparent when one considers that the interest expense on federal debt outstanding in 2010 (per US treasury) was $413,954,825,362.17.

While Social Security accounts for approximately 50 percent of the gross debt, we disagree with the argument that these debts are intergovernmental in nature and thus have no direct effect on credit markets. Gross debt held by the government represents a future obligation that must be serviced by current and future taxes; if these taxes are insufficient, then the service costs must either come from reductions in current expenditures, increases in current taxes, or increased issuance of debt. The rapid increase in the debt, the persistence of large operating deficits, and the lingering impact of the financial crisis may result in increased interest costs to the US federal government. Furthermore, given the current anti-tax climate in the US Congress, it seems likely that the interest costs of the debt will place significant pressure on discretionary expenditures, of which defence is the largest component.[20]

The financial crisis not only affected the finances of the US federal government, but also that of several OECD member states. While Greece and Italy are well known for having persistent debt-to-GDP ratios at or in excess of 100 percent, public debt has increased dramatically since 2000 in the United Kingdom, France, and others. The public debt of the United Kingdom has risen from approximately 42 percent of GDP in 2000 to approximately 86 percent of GDP in 2010. France's public debt has risen from approximately 47 percent of GDP in 2000 to 67.4 percent of GDP in 2010 (according to OECD's own documents). Other members of the OECD, notably Australia, Germany, and New Zealand, have weathered the crisis without a substantial increase in their public debt.

Yet, it is likely that the financial crisis is not over and that the ramifications are likely to continue to plague the global economic system for the foreseeable future. Sovereign default by an OECD member is likely to occur in the short-term. Yields on Greek public debt at the time of writing, for example, exceed 16 percent; this is unsustainable given the perilous nature of Greek public finances and the imbalances in the Greek economy. Contagion remains a real possibility; that is, a default by Greece, for example, could trigger defaults in Italy, Portugal, and Spain. In the best-case scenario, if Greece manages to avoid default through the provision of substantial financial assistance by the European Union (EU), then the growth prospects for Greece remain grim for the medium-term. It doesn't however seem to be a likely outcome and more plausible, the Greek crisis will likely impose significant costs on EU member states.[21]

While the financial crisis has battered the finances of the United States, Britain, and other countries in the OECD, it has also created conditions for significant shifts in economic power among developing countries. China, for example, is thought (by the World Development Indicators from the World Bank) to have weathered the financial crisis, sustaining enviable rates of economic growth. GDP growth in 2008 and 2009 was 9.6 and 9.1 percent, respectively. Yet, this ignores the relaxation of subnational borrowing constraints that funded infrastructure projects and moderated the impact of the financial crisis. Burgeoning subnational level debt threaten China's economic growth prospects. It also ignores the fact that Chinese power may be better captured not using GNP (i.e., our way of doing things) but by their own, (i.e., the so-called Comprehensive National Power); another example of the need to understand the cultural and historical aspects of nations.

Local government debt in China rose by 70 percent to approximately 7.38 trillion Yuan in 2009, increasing to approximately 10.7 trillion by the end of 2010.[22] There is increasing concern that the rapid proliferation of loans to local governments in China may constrain the ability of the public sector as a whole to respond to a double-dip recession in the OECD or an exogenous supply shock. In the best-case scenario, China's national government will face significant pressure to manage subnational debts and to address imbalances created by the 2008-2009 stimulus program.[23] In a worst-case scenario, defaults by local governments will lead to an internal Chinese financial crisis, further exacerbating social tensions.

Compounding issues for China is the persistence of corruption at all levels of government. China, for example, is ranked 78th in the world according to the Transparency International's Corruption Perceptions Index. Unlike OECD countries, there is not a clear picture of Chinese public finances, let alone an accurate measurement of defense expenditures. The lack of transparency and accountability suggests that investment inefficiency in China may be less than in other nations at similar stages of development. China's real Incremental Capital Output Ratio (ICOR), a measure of investment efficiency, was 5.1 for 1979-2000. For 1987-1997, the ICORs of Taiwan, Singapore, and Hong Kong were (on the scale of their investment efficiency) 3, 4 and 6 respectively.[24] This suggests that China is less efficient than Taiwan and Singapore and that China requires more capital to achieve comparable levels of economic growth. A significant subnational financial crisis in China would possibly constrain inflows of capital and thus retard Chinese economic growth.

What conclusions can we draw from the above discussion? First, the financial crisis highlighted the increasing interdependence of the global economy and the fragility of the global economic system. In the past, before currency integration in the EU, the Greek crisis would have resulted in the devaluation of the Greek currency and relatively small impacts on institutional investors. Today, a fiscal and financial crisis in a relatively small economy (2010 GDP = $329.92 billion, less than the US state of Massachusetts (2010 GDP = $340 billion), can threaten the stability of the banking systems of much larger economies. Globalization has lowered the cost of goods and services and financial capital but has also increased the breadth and depth of economic and financial crises.

Second, we can only expect these crises to continue in the medium-term until governments have sufficient incentive to regulate the financial industry and to impose significant losses on private investors. The financial system created incentives for firms to take on excessive risk, knowing full well that the likelihood of punishment (closure) was low, relative to the likelihood of reward (investment gain or bailout). This type of behaviour seems likely to continue until sufficient regulation occurs or the size of the bailouts grows so large that firms thought too large to fail, must do just that.

Third, the resources available for defense among OECD member states will become more constrained over the next decade and potentially beyond. In fact, one need only to think for a moment about the longer term implications of the relative defense spending over the last, say, 15 years, to get a picture of where things are going (see Table 1).

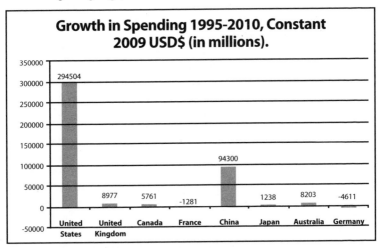

Table 1 – Data accessed from SIPRI Database

Fourth, among developing countries, defense expenditures are likely to increase on average, driven, in part, by the stated intent of China to modernize its armed forces and the response of its neighbours to this action. With fewer stable alliances (that we know of) among those nations, coalitions and conflicts may result from these changes. And perhaps not too far in the future, a situation will emerge with an attack on a US ally and no money to defend it.

We thus return to our initial thesis: the financial crisis is likely to inhibit defense resources among OECD members in the medium term. The challenge to senior leaders in this environment is to seek out efficiency and effectiveness improvements while maintaining desired capabilities. Obviously, with the discussed reductions in defense expenditures, even maintaining desired capabilities is unlikely for some countries. In the next section, we discuss the concept of NSE and how it can assist leaders in making decisions in a resource constrained, uncertain environment.

Attempts to Cope With the Evolving Economic and Security Environment. With the end of the Cold War, defence planners lost the ability to focus their efforts on the singular, conventional, and well-understood threat embodied by the Soviet Union. The emerging multi-polar security environment brought dramatic shifts in the roles of and missions of the US (and other) armed forces, often in response to previous unknown (or unplanned for) events. These shifts undermined traditional planning models, and provided an opportunity for reform towards a planning system focused on tradeoffs among competing alternatives in terms of desired outcomes rather than budgetary resources or systems.

The increasing spectrum of adversaries and environments overwhelmed the single-threat based planning system, leading to an increasingly vivid disconnect between defence plans, desired capabilities, and resource constraints. This gap, as evidenced by the inability of the existing force structure to adhere to the two major theatre war-planning scenario, created an opportunity for defence planners to revisit the central questions of SecDef McNamara's budget process reforms of the 1960s. First, what are the desired outcomes of the defence budget process? Second, what systems increase the likelihood of achieving these desired outcomes? Inter-service competition and the lack of central coordination in the US Department of Defense budget process subsumed these questions. From this perspective, defense planning on a capabilities basis is appealing, as it would entail a shift in perspective from a single (or dual) threat environment to one of multiple scenarios based upon a spectrum of threats.

Proponents of a Capabilities-Based Planning (CBP) argue that the emerging security environments require flexible and adaptive planning, one where systems of vision and direction were born joint at the start for the strategic planning process, and were useful across a continuum of threats. In this vein, proponents envision capabilities-planning as a return to the central role of the SecDef in the planning process, with planning and resourcing power shifting from the services to the Secretary. If successful, proponents argue, capabilities-planning would result in a more nimble, efficient, and effective force structure able to counter a myriad of existing and emerging security challenges.

The proponent's argument that capabilities-planning supplants threat-based planning is, in our opinion, specious. While CBP is a movement away from single-threat based planning, CBP also requires the identification of threats (or challenges) for the generation of scenarios (potential futures) about said threats. From this perspective, CBP should enable (force) planners to develop a range of threats, permutations to these threats, and to identify systems that are sufficiently flexible to span across multiple threats. This approach, if implemented, would represent a marked departure from the single-capability systems that dominated US defence procurement in the last two decades (the F-22).[25] Defence policy-makers and planners would thus be expressing an explicit preference for systems that may be potentially less capable in a single threat environment (air superiority), but able to perform multi-role missions (air superiority, ground attack, surveillance).

Yet, if this is what CBP should ideally achieve, there remains the question of what does CBP actually entail? While there exists a multitude of definitions for CBP, these definitions are general in nature. And implicit in these arguments is the idea of attempting to mitigate future risk through an analytical approach to determining potential operating environments and what potential capabilities produce the "best" outcome by reducing uncertainty in outcomes.

Yet, the literature on how to implement CBP is, in our opinion, woefully inadequate. Much of the literature that discusses CBP does so in an institutional vacuum. How does CBP integrate, for example, into the existing budget framework is a difficult question and one that produces a unique answer dependent upon the institutional conditions in each country. What documents provide the national planning objectives, which guide the development of planning scenarios? Furthermore, who should (and how) inventory the capabilities of existing systems and estimate the capabilities of proposed systems? From where will the resources come to support what will undoubtedly be an intensified analytical effort? These questions are not trivial.

MOVING TOWARDS A FRAMEWORK FOR NEW SECURITY ECONOMICS

NSE is a framework to assist decision-makers with the evolution of the strategic and the economic environment, both locally and globally. It builds on a realistic, dynamic and long-term approach to strategy and leaders' strategic decision-making (as outlined above). As noted previously, the ability of a nation to project hard power is dependent on its ability to raise revenue, which, in turn, is dependent upon a nations' economic output and that of its trading partners. A nation's "soft power" is also a function of its attractiveness in terms of values, policies, institutions, and culture. If a nation cannot observe shifts in its ability to influence events, then the resulting strategy will not produce the intended results. In this section, we develop the concept of NSE and apply it to leadership challenges in the 21st century.

We argue that security and economics are inexorably intertwined, yet have been divorced artificially in strategy discussions. CBP in the United States, for example, avoids the question of an interaction between security and economics entirely to focus on desired capabilities across multiple scenarios. A hypothetical scenario, for example, might describe a Chinese attack on Taiwan to justify the procurement and operation of air superiority, air refueling, and command and control capabilities. Various permutations on the scenario might envision different types of attack (amphibious, air beachhead, indirect fire only), but the basic thrust of the scenario demands a kinetic response.

Economic Interdependencies. While at first glance such a hypothetical scenario might be judged of some non-zero probability, an NSE approach would move the planning process before capabilities determination and ask crucial questions such as: "What does China Want?" and "What are the economic interdependencies between the potential parties to a conflict?" By focusing on the relationship between security and economics, we argue that NSE shifts the discussion to a realistic assessment of the incentives to engage in (or prevent) conflict.

As of May 2011, the number of Taiwanese investment projects in Mainland China (according to the Ministry of Commerce, PRC) reached 84,158 with a total use of $53.01 billion Taiwanese capital. Taiwan was the 2nd highest non-financial foreign direct investor in 2009, only behind Hong Kong. Taiwanese exports to China grew 37.1 percent in 2010 to $114.78 billion or 41.8 percent of total exports. Taiwan is also an important export market for China.

Conflicts and wars are much more than economic incentives, but a conflict would likely seriously disrupt trade between the countries and also lead to capital flight. Furthermore, a conflict between China and Taiwan would likely disrupt exports to the United States and would potentially threaten US Foreign Direct Investment into China. The United States, faced with an impending crisis between the two countries, could instead employ non-kinetic instruments to illustrate the significant costs to parties to the conflict. Given the significant holdings of US Treasuries by the Chinese, the United States could threaten a selective default, though such a radical action could have unforeseen consequences for US interest rates.

But nations do not act solely based on economic self-interest. Issues of history and national pride, and wish to "restore wholeness" may influence things in other directions. In addition, there are ways to take over Taiwan "gently." For example, China may use its significant capital reserves to buy and then restrict access to rare earth elements used in the production of high technology goods. It could then employ this monopoly to induce changes in Taiwanese investment policy (or political policy). A realistic exploration of strategy would thus explore non-security approaches to forestall such an outcome. It might also be useful to do more research into the psycho-biographical profiles of foreign leaders to understand how those personalities may influence the decision-making of nations.

Chapter 7

Political Interdependencies. The security of a nation depends in part on its ability to project (or foster the illusion of projection) hard and soft power in service of its national goals and objectives. An NSE approach would not only inquire about the strategic goals of a country, it would also consider the possible goals and behaviours of other parties to the conflict; kind of similar, economists may note, to a game theoretic approach where there is an interdependency of the agents at play; but unlike game theory, our players in the world are not rational, nor are the outcomes of their interactions known in advance.

Dynamics. The last part of the NSE framework is the idea of understanding economic, political, and security environment dynamics and knowing that such dynamics are inherently unpredictable and filled with uncertainty and ambiguity. As the economies of the world have grown more independent, there have been benefits and costs. Conflict is also less likely for countries with high degrees of integration in the global economy. Yet, as noted previously, globalization has lowered the price of capital but also increased the transmission of capital.

What then can leaders do in the face of an interdependent, dynamic system? Is strategic planning useless? While one is likely to not end up with neat answers (as one might using unrealistic models), we believe that a strategic framework that takes into account the relations between economies, societies and security, can assist decision makers grappling with complex, unwieldy problems that appear to defy analysis. Recognizing that a framework around new security economics is in its infancy, we have suggested some points for leaders to pay attention to.

CONCLUSION

The purpose of this chapter has been to discuss the following interrelated themes: (1) to outline some key challenges for future leaders in defence and security and to help provide a richer discussion of national security issues; (2) to encourage future leaders to think harder about the nature of strategy and the process of strategy in a multi-polar world, (3) to discuss some of the key challenges relating to the topics of economics and security, and (4) to offer a tentative outline for a framework of NSE that can be useful for leaders to think strategically about the military and economic competition now and in the future. In the process, we have suggested a different conception of strategy than that normally used by defence and we have outlined some essential security implications for the change in economic balances.

Despite the development of important insights by some contributors, it is unfortunately still the case that many misunderstandings and misconceptions exist about strategy. For instance, one often hears discussions about strategy and strategies, where strategy seems to be just a list of goals and/or about how we react to certain events or issues. This is fundamentally a wrong way of conceptualizing the strategy process and fails to capture the essence of strategy as a dynamic process and the possibilities for strategy to help shape existing competition. This has implications beyond just "getting the concepts right," for if we base our strategies on a fundamentally flawed understanding of what strategy is, our comprehension of the current and future security environment, our policies for dealing with the competition, and so on, become very suspect. In the context of modern security competition, such strategic misunderstandings can be very damaging. Instead leaders must focus on developing a richer understanding of strategy, its links to economies, and the possibilities for shaping the future security environment in order to be intellectually prepared for developing strategies in the future. Considering some implications of the global financial crisis and the importance of strategy, a framework based on new security economics might be a useful way for leaders to understand new and emerging threats. Key points in this framework include:

- Seeing the behaviour of nations and other international actors as systems of organizations, limited in their rationality and bound by institutional, cultural and organizational constraints will enable a more realistic understanding of the strategic competition and what strategies may be possible.

- Strategy as a long-term, descriptive and non-policy-prescriptive exercise – enabling a genuine understanding of the situation, not just a list of goals for a desirable one.

- Organizational barriers to strategy (and why organizations may resist change, and how that influences our security organizations' inability to adapt to the changes in the security environment).

- Realizing possible security implications of the global financial crisis and the changes in the economic powers in general (including economic warfare; changing leadership of international financial institutions, etc).

- Understanding not just economic or other quantifiable aspects of international situations; but also how human, cultural and psychological issues interact and influence national and international decision-making.

Chapter 7

ENDNOTES

1. Acknowledgement: We are grateful to Kathleen Bailey, Jeffrey Stouffer, Julie Bélanger, and Jerry Guo for help and comments on this chapter.

2. There are, however, important exceptions. For instance, the economists around the initiative "Institute in New Economic Thinking" are doing important work trying to learn the lessons for economics and economists from the crisis.

3. The Arab Spring refers to the recent wave demonstrations and revolutionary unrest that began in the Arab world in the spring of 2011.

4. Sun Tzu, *The Art of War* (Oxford University Press, 1963).

5. Eliot Cohen and John Gooch, *Military Misfortunes: The Anatomy of Failure in Warfare* (New York, NY: Free Press, 1990).

6. North Atlantic Treaty Organization, see <http://www.nato.int/cps/en/natolive/topics_56626.htm>.

7. Joint Chiefs of Staff (JSC) dictionary.

8. Andrew Marshall, personal conversation.

9. Sun Tzu, *The Art of War* (Oxford University Press, 1963).

10. Andrew W. Marshall, "Strategy as a Profession for Future Generations", in Andrew W. Marshall, James J. Martin and Henry S. Rowen, eds., *On Not Confusing Ourselves: Essays on National Security Strategy in Honor of Albert and Roberta Wohlstetter* (Boulder, CO: Westview Press, 1991).

11. Alfred Chandler, *Strategy and Structure* (Cambridge: MIT Press, 1962).

12. See Herbert A. Simon, "A Behavioral Model of Rational Choice", *Quarterly Journal of Economics*, Vol. 69, No. 1 (1955), 99-118; Herbert A. Simon, "Rational Choice and the Structure of the Environment", *Psychological Review*, Vol. 63 (1956), 129-138; Herbert A. Simon, *Administrative Behavior* (New York, NY: Free Press, 1947); James G. March and H. Simon, *Organizations* (New York, NY: Wiley, 1958); and, Richard M. Cyert and James G. March, *The Behavioral Theory of the Firm* (Englewood Cliffs, NJ: Prentice Hall, 1963).

13. Andrew W. Marshall, "Improving Intelligence Estimates thought the Study of Organizational Behavior", RAND paper for the Board of Trustees (15 March 1968). James March also noted the complications of using rational models in a complex and uncertain world: "As complexity is increased and temporal and spatial perspectives are extended, returns (both of alternatives that are adopted and of those that are rejected) are likely to be misestimated by huge amounts. This means that those alternatives that are adopted are likely to have been overestimates by huge amounts. There are many instances in which the use of a technology of rationality in a relatively complex situation has been described as leading to extraordinary, even catastrophic, failures. These include the extensive efforts of the Soviet Union to manage an economy through planning and rational analysis …. The attempts of various American firms to use learning curves as a basis for investments, pricing and output strategies ….; the attempt by the American political and military establishment to use rational analysis to develop strategies for war in Vietnam …; the attempt by Long-Term Capital Management to use rational theories to make money in the options market … and the wave of corporate merges in the United States from 1998 to 2001." (James G. March, "Rationality, Foolishness, and Adaptive Intelligence", *Strategic Management Journal*, Vol. 27 (2006), 207).

14. Dan Lovallo and Daniel Kahneman, "Delusions of Success: How Optimism Undermines Executives Decisions", *Harvard Business Review*, Vol. 81 (2003), 56-63.

15. Andrew Marshall, (1991), 303.

16. Louise Cord, Marijn Verhoeven, Camilla Blomquist and Bobn Rijker, *The Global Economic Crisis: Assessing Vulnerability with a poverty leans* (Washington DC: World Bank, 2009).

17. Joseph S. Nye Jr., "The Decline of America's soft power," *Foreign Affairs*, (May-June 2004).

18. Federal Reserve Bank of St. Louis: Net Federal Government Saving, (May, 2011).

19. Congressional Budget Office Long-Term Budget Outlook, (June, 2011).

20. At the subnational level, the finances of states and local governments have faltered due to falling employment, incomes, and housing prices. California, for example, has endured repeated multi-billion dollar operating deficits leading to reductions in public services and employment. Localities have reduced basic public protection services, to include fire and police departments. Similar fiscal pressures shut down the state government in Wisconsin during July 2011, as the state legislature and the governor were unable to agree on how to close the operating deficit. While the federal government provided "stimulus" funding to states and localities in 2009 and 2010 to offset declines in state and local revenues, this funding only partially offset recession-induced shortfalls in revenues. The state and local sectors are expected to remain a substantial drag on the US economy through 2012.

21. Of the 310.84 billion Euro estimated exposure of EU members, Germany, France, and Italy have the largest exposure at 83.76, 81.73, and 42.58 billion Euros, respectively. Under the second bailout plan, the share of Greece's debt underwritten by foreign taxpayers will rise from 26% in 2011 to 64% in 2014. Given the magnitude of the fiscal imbalance in Greece and debt-to-GDP ratios approaching 150 %, we do not believe that Greece will avoid default. Taxpayers in these countries will likely face additional cuts in discretionary expenditures and increases in taxes to service the debt secured through the EU bailouts to Greece.

22. Bloomberg: "China Crackdown on Local-Government Debt May Restrain Economy." (June, 2010).

23. Adam McKissack and Jessica Y. Xu, "Chinese Macroeconomic Management Through the Crisis and Beyond", *Asia Pacific Economic Literature*, Vol. 25, No.1 (2011), 43-55.

24. Zhang Jun, "Investment, investment efficiency, and Economic Growth in China," *Journal of Asian Economics*, Vol. 14 (2003), 713-734.

25. While the F-22 is recognized as one of the most advanced air superiority fighters in service today, it has not been deployed to Iraq or Afghanistan. The capabilities of the F-22 are unidimensional, that is, focused on the defeat of other aircraft and are of little use in an environment requiring close-air support. As former Secretary of Defense Robert Gates noted in 2008: "*The reality is we are fighting two wars, in Iraq and Afghanistan, and the F-22 has not performed a single mission in either theater. So it is principally for use against a near peer in a conflict, and I think we all know who that is.*" in Robert Gates, *Secretary of Defense, Congressional Testimony (2008).*

CHAPTER 8

PERSPECTIVES ON LEADERSHIP DEVELOPMENT IN THE AUSTRALIAN DEFENCE FORCE

*Lieutenant-Colonel Jon Hawkins**

INTRODUCTION

Leadership in the Australian Defence Force (ADF) is commonly defined as the process of influencing others to gain their willing consent in the ethical pursuit of missions.[1] In contemporary ADF and business frameworks, there is a high reliance on leadership to create value opportunities; indeed, the Australian Graduate School of Management uses six domains of leadership to assist in defining and developing management techniques.[2] The domains are relational, personal, ethical, supportive, contextual, and inspirational. These business leadership domains can be melded with the development aspects of leadership in the ADF.[3]

To examine leadership development a number of recent ADF leadership scenarios, which include operational, training and administrative events, will be reviewed against the six leadership domains. The primary method to illustrate how leaders are developed, however, is through operations. Without argument, job rotation, mentoring, formal leadership education, additional responsibility and career progression all contribute to leadership development and are highlighted in ADF leadership doctrine.[4] Operational and realistic training environments continue to represent the most confronting situations for junior leaders and provide development opportunities beyond that experienced in other surroundings. Each of the accounts described below will endeavour to illustrate that ADF leadership development is facilitated from a variety of sources. The narratives selected represent real-world events from the past 12 years: they draw on overseas deployments and domestic activities, and demonstrate that leadership development occurs in a range of environments and at various rank levels. However, the most acute leadership development appears, as mentioned above, to occur on operations, as demonstrated in the first domain of relational leadership. This type of leadership is defined as creating ties between leaders and subordinates that feel honest, accessible and human.[5]

---

* The views expressed in this chapter are those of the author and do not necessarily reflect the official policy of the Australian Defence Force.

Chapter 8

DOMAIN ONE – RELATIONAL LEADERSHIP

This category of leadership is often between two people or a small group of individuals. To illustrate the development of relational leadership, the East Timor crisis of 1999 will be used as the backdrop. Several small teams of Australian soldiers were embedded within East Timorese FALINTIL elements. These teams were deployed to provide liaison between General Peter Cosgrove's headquarters and FALINTIL's leadership. One example that highlighted the relational influence qualities of the Australian soldier occurred when the FALINTIL leadership learned of an incident in Dili and, as a consequence, was quite infuriated with the International Force East Timor (INTERFET). The decision was made to march into Dili, bearing weapons. This action however would have been contrary to the existing agreement of the cantonments and, without doubt, would have further aggravated the Dili situation.

An ADF Warrant Officer with one of the small teams was able to use the rapport he had built with the FALINTIL leadership and draw on his negotiation skills to defuse the situation. The potential for a major incident was high. Indeed, the FALINTIL elements in the cantonment threatened the Australians. However, through the repeated use of honesty, logical argument, persuasion and appealing to the senior FALINTIL leaders to look to the long term and trust the Australians, the Warrant Officer kept the FALINTIL in their cantonment.

The Warrant Officer was assisted by several more junior soldiers, who provided him with communications support to General Cosgrove's headquarters. The soldiers' ability to work through this extremely stressful situation was a testament to the value of the training they received at Army training schools in Australia and the near real-life annual exercises that had also been conducted in Australia. Relational leadership is often complemented by other leadership traits, as they reinforce the bonds formed between individuals.

DOMAIN TWO – PERSONAL LEADERSHIP

The second account also draws on an operational theatre to introduce an activity that demonstrates the use of the second leadership domain, personal leadership. This type of leadership is defined as those individual attributes, such as personality, actions, expertise and credibility that contribute to how a person projects himself/herself.[6]

High levels of personal leadership can influence others and serve as a catalyst for behavioural change.[7] This influence may be observed in many different facets, but one of the aspects that ADF personnel typically demonstrate is behavioural integrity. In essence, sailors, soldiers and airmen and airwomen exhibit congruence between their spoken values and their actions. That is, ADF personnel "walk the talk." Leaders who act according to their words develop trust and credibility, which builds subordinate/peer commitment.[8]

During a 2002 deployment to Afghanistan, many of the small teams of Australian special forces soldiers allocated to Regional Command East demonstrated personal leadership through behavioural integrity. This allowed them to influence very senior Afghan commanders to adhere to the coalition commander's campaign plan.

Teams of soldiers were allocated to Northern Alliance commanders for liaison with coalition forces. The time available for the soldiers to build trust with the Afghan commanders was limited; however, through repeated acts of selflessness and maintaining an awareness of Australian Army values, the soldiers were able to influence the Afghan commanders. The small teams positively identified, beyond any doubt, Al-Qaeda elements prior to engaging them; they paid villagers for items at the local rate so as not to adversely affect the local economy; they embraced the local customs; they respected livestock; and they also afforded Al-Qaeda women and children safe passage through combat engagements.

The small teams of Australian soldiers exhibited character traits that Afghan commanders, although not necessarily agreeing with, could recognize as Australian cultural norms. By reinforcing their values through their actions, the soldiers built trust and credibility. Indeed, their leadership, through behavioural integrity, assisted coalition commanders to achieve their intent by leveraging the Afghan Northern Alliance's capability but within the norms of Australian values.

DOMAIN THREE – ETHICAL LEADERSHIP

The third domain examines ethical leadership, which is defined as balancing competing interests and encouraging personal responsibility for advancing the greater good.[9] In particular, it focuses on the use of leadership for promoting acceptable societal values and acknowledging the group and placing individual self-interest as secondary.

In 2005, the actions of Australian and Canadian special forces soldiers demonstrated that the ADF and the CF have some of the finest, morally courageous troops in the world. Their actions in dealing with local Afghans, whether they were supporters of the central government or Taliban sympathisers, were even handed and very professional.

On one particular morning during the autumn of 2005, an Australian and Canadian special forces element, having identified a senior Taliban commander's house, was commencing an operation to apprehend the individual. An Australian patrol was inserted the evening prior to provide overwatch and cover the advance of the combined Australian and Canadian main body the following morning. During the insertion of the main body, one of the snipers in the Australian patrol engaged a Taliban spotter as he was threatening the advancing Australian and Canadian troops. Later that morning, a patrol went to clear the area where the spotter had been observed and discovered to their surprise that he was still alive. They administered first aid and an aeromedical evacuation helicopter was requested. The Taliban member was evacuated to a coalition hospital, subsequently recovered and returned to his village a month later.

The aspect of this incident that resonates is that the actions of the Australian and Canadian soldiers that morning saved the life of an adversary and allowed the Taliban to witness the philanthropic virtues of Coalition soldiers. It is possible to imagine the message that this incident left with the Taliban spotter and his fellow insurgents – "the Australians and Canadians will treat you fairly." This may go some way towards allowing Taliban members to believe that Western influences in Afghanistan are not always harmful.

DOMAIN FOUR – SUPPORTIVE LEADERSHIP

The next domain also draws on an operational deployment and introduces supportive leadership. This is defined as creating a sense of security, acceptance and confidence through providing resources, training and encouragement.[10]

Australian and Canadian troops attached to Afghan National Army units were often principally involved in teaching and training Afghan soldiers. This is known as mentoring and was provided by Australians in Tarin Kowt and by Canadians in Kandahar. At both these locations, Afghan soldiers were provided with enhanced military skills through embedded training teams; command and control systems; equipment such as vehicles, field packs and weapons; and constant encouragement and reinforcement. This mentoring also allowed for cross-cultural tolerance and curtailed ethnocentrism. The activities achieved under the mentoring programs provide the essential foundation for the Afghan National Army to eventually conduct independent operations and serve to instill a feeling of acceptance and confidence in the Kandaks (Afghan infantry battalions).

This supportive leadership is shaped by the soldiers conducting the training, and the notion of Afghan recognition through working with experienced Australian and Canadian troops. The training teams comprising Australian and Canadian soldiers provide one of the best examples of supportive leadership available.

DOMAIN FIVE – CONTEXTUAL LEADERSHIP

Domain five draws on the Sydney and Vancouver Olympic Games, providing a perspective on domestic security as the backdrop to examine contextual leadership. This leadership is defined as building group identity and creating community, which helps to bring clarity and coherence to complex tasks.[11]

During the build-up to the 2000 Sydney Olympics, particularly in 1998 to early 2000, many ADF personnel were involved in the security for the venues and coordinating the competing agendas of the various stakeholders involved. Similarly, the build up to the 2010 Vancouver Winter Games mirrored the Sydney experiences for the CF. Not least in this undertaking was the requirement to meld private commercial interests with the requirements of the Police Jurisdictions, the Governments, the Olympic Committee, and finally, the often underestimated external interests of foreign governments. The ADF and CF personnel involved were often junior officers and senior NCOs, drawn from areas such as clearance divers, sniffer dog handlers, aviation and special forces planners, all of whom had to create a grouping or community with the various domestic and international stakeholders. This sense of coherence, despite the complexity of the interrelationships, was not easily achieved, but it did provide an understanding that the Australian and Canadian governments were capable of assuring security at their respective Games.

In the early exchanges, such as desktop exercises and the preliminary counter-terrorist exercises, these junior personnel created a cooperative spirit with stakeholders including government agencies and departments. The group identity produced demonstrated the high expectations and professionalism of the ADF and CF personnel.

Additionally, as the Olympics approached, more complex activities were conducted that required increased interaction with the Sydney and Vancouver communities. These activities required consultative meetings to discuss noise abatement measures for military helicopters and watercraft. Again, these junior personnel were the face of the ADF, the CF, the Australian and Canadian governments and, very often, the security reputation of the respective Games. Through rapport building, developing a community or group identity with domestic and international stakeholders, the ADF and CF personnel involved in the introductory Games security activities were able to provide coherence to a complex system of interdependent relationships.

DOMAIN SIX – INSPIRATIONAL LEADERSHIP

The final domain will examine inspirational leadership. This type of leadership is defined as producing high expectations, raising enthusiasm, optimism and confidence.[12] Additionally, this style of leadership often requires an individual to possess all the leadership traits already mentioned. In this account, operational scenarios are used as the mechanism to demonstrate inspirational leadership.

There are many examples of inspirational leaders in the ADF, especially at the executive level. Nevertheless, an aspect that is often ignored, is the ability of junior sailors, soldiers and airmen/women to influence their peers and superiors. Reviewing the recent Victoria Cross recipients' actions provides many opportunities to be inspired by the ADF's junior ranks. The optimism, confidence and enthusiasm that the two soldiers exhibited, during what must have been seminal moments in their lives,[13] is a credit to the individuals themselves but also to the training and education provided by the ADF training institutions. Both soldiers displayed remarkable levels of inspirational leadership, by creating a feeling of optimism despite the unfavourable situations they found themselves in. Furthermore, neither of the soldiers were in a command position at the perilous moment when they provided exemplar behaviour to their peers and superiors, yet they still demonstrated the highest attributes of soldiering.

Inspirational leadership does not necessarily need to be observed from the executive level to affect or influence a situation: inspiring actions demonstrated by junior ranks can be just as beneficial in an adverse situation. This resonates both in the ADF and in business circles.

CONCLUSION

Overseas and domestic operational examples have been used to demonstrate how leadership development can occur in the ADF and CF. By using the six domains of corporate leadership: relational, personal, ethical, supportive, contextual and inspirational; and connecting them with a military event, primarily spanning operational deployments, it has been demonstrated that leadership development is accelerated during deployments and operations.

The ADF and the CF have been quite successful on recent operations and it must be acknowledged, without hesitation, that effective leadership contributed to these successes. During a speech in 2003, General Peter Cosgrove, then-Chief of the Australian Defence Force, mentioned that the starkness of being responsible for a platoon of Australian infantry in South Vietnam was very confronting at the time, but the lessons he derived from that period always remained with him.[14]

ENDNOTES

1. Australian Defence Force, *Leadership* (Executive Series, ADDP 00.6, 2007), para 1.8.

2. Australian Graduate School of Management. *Strategic Management Session 1 Notes* (Australian Graduate School of Management, 2009).

3. Australian Defence Force, *Leadership* (Executive Series, ADDP 00.6, 2007), chapter 6.

4. Ibid., para 1.8.

5. Australian Graduate School of Management. *Strategic Management Session 1 Notes* (Australian Graduate School of Management, 2009), 1.

6. Ibid., 2.

7. Australian Defence Force, *Leadership* (Executive Series, ADDP 00.6, 2007), chapter 6.

8. Ibid.

9. Australian Graduate School of Management. *Strategic Management Session 1 Notes* (Australian Graduate School of Management, 2009), 3.

10. Ibid., 4.

11. Ibid., 5.

12. Ibid., 6.

13. Defence Media Release. In describing one of the recipients, the Chief of the ADF said, "In the most dangerous and demanding of situations – when his patrol was outnumbered and his life and the lives of his mates were under extreme threat – Corporal Roberts-Smith cast aside concern for his own safety. He placed his mates' lives above his own.", retrieved on 15 July 2011 from <http://www.defence.gov.au/media/DepartmentalTpl.cfm?CurrentId=11308>; Similarly, for Cpl Mark Donaldson, the Australian Newspaper stated, "Deliberate exposure to draw enemy fire away from the wounded would have been enough for a Victoria Cross recommendation, but Trooper Donaldson then sprinted 80m over the same killing ground to save the life of a seriously wounded Afghan interpreter.", retrieved on 15 July 2011 from <http://www.theaustralian.com.au/news/nation/vc-winner-drew-fire-to-save-his-mates/story-e6frg6nf-1111118586445>.

14. General Peter Cosgrove, Chief of the Australian Defence Force, in a speech to the Disaster Conference, Brisbane Australia in 2003.

CHAPTER 9

DEVELOPING THE NEXT GENERATION INTO ADAPTIVE LEADERS THROUGH SELF-MANAGEMENT

*Lieutenant-Colonel Psalm B.C. Lew**

THE OPERATING ENVIRONMENT OF THE SINGAPORE ARMED FORCES

Since the September 11 attacks on New York, global acts of terrorism and political instability in South East Asia created a volatile security landscape. From the plans to attack the Orchard Mass Rapid Transit (MRT) Station in the heart of the city, it is clear that Singapore is not immune.[1] As the SAF transforms into a 3rd Generation fighting force,[2] it needs to raise, train and sustain units capable of conventional war-fighting but at the same time, build capacity to manage uncertainty across a full spectrum of operations to support Singapore's national interest and regional security.

Yet as the Singapore Armed Forces (SAF) engaged in a full spectrum of operations from anti-piracy missions in the Gulf of Aden to the Protection of Installations (POI) at the world's second largest oil refining centre on Singapore's Jurong Island, its leaders also began to appreciate that the inter-relationships between stakeholders is highly complex. The web of inter-related issues and stakeholders creates a great deal of ambiguity in framing the mission, the task, as well as the adversary. Together, Volatility, Uncertainty, Complexity and Ambiguity (VUCA) create an environment filled with adversities that challenge an SAF leader's capacity to be adaptive.

KEY FOCUS FOR THE SINGAPORE ARMED FORCES

Against the VUCA backdrop, Singapore's small size and population[3] and lack of natural resources, provides a *raison d'être* for its approach to defence via the implementation of National Service (NS) to meet its security requirements. When Singapore's first Minister for Defence – the late Dr. Goh Keng Swee, presented the case for NS in 1967, the SAF was given a clear

---

* The views expressed in this chapter are those of the author and do not necessarily reflect the official policy of the Singapore Armed Forces.

mandate, through NS, to become the guardian of the country's sovereignty as well as the nation building institution to engender a greater commitment to defence.[4] Over the last four decades, the practice of conscription has created the National Service (NSmen) as an "NS citizen soldier" where the SAF is a microcosm of the social trends in the larger Singaporean society.

Looking at the profile of the next generation of SAF Soldiers, it is clear that education literacy is improving tremendously. As of 2009, approximately 70.3% of the adult population had received tertiary education as opposed to 41.5% a decade earlier.[5] Even within this population, there is increasingly a perceived difference between the Generation X (Gen X) and Generation Y (Gen Y).[6] In a study within the SAF to examine the difference between both generations, it was found that Gen Y showed a strong desire for frequent performance feedback, at least monthly or at the end of each assignment, and they valued learning opportunities as much as the Gen X.[7] Both generations see work life balance as very important but Gen Ys are more tech-savvy and desire to be better connected online.[8] The concern today for a successful society, like Singapore, is that the Gen Y who grows up amidst affluence may not be tough enough to weather through a crisis or great adversity such as a terrorist attack. It would therefore seem that the need to develop Gen Y Singaporeans to possess the self-confidence to bounce back from challenging situations becomes important.

UNDERSTANDING THE NEED FOR AN ADAPTIVE LEADER

The SAF will need to continue to develop and exploit its Human Capital Development expertise especially in the behavioural, psychological and emotional competencies of its leaders as well as ensure a high level of socialization throughout the entire lifespan and metamorphosis from citizen to soldier. A preliminary study has shown that an emphasis on the SAF Leadership Competency Model (LCM) skill of Self-Management[9] lengthens leaders' perseverance to their goals when confronted with obstacles and thereby increasing their resilience in adversity. Self-Management initiatives have become increasingly important as Singapore recognizes[10] the challenge of building a resilient society, where the SAF as a nation building institution contributes to the country's future success by developing its NS Citizen Soldiers into resilient individuals who can perform in a VUCA environment.

Future SAF operating environments will demand engagements, interactions and actions that will stretch leaders cognitively. Operational commanders face challenges in making sense of situations characterized by rapid change and high levels of uncertainty, in which diverse assumptions and perspectives are held among participants acting on imperfect information. Under such conditions, situational awareness is crucial but typically difficult to attain in a timely manner, and even harder to achieve with coherency among different parts of the SAF, let alone across different organizations.[11] Future SAF leaders, especially the Gen Ys, need to spend less time worrying about their inability to establish routines or control the future, rather they should focus more on exploiting opportunities.[12]

Here, a Gen Y adaptive leader is positively balanced with the need to strive for decision superiority, without confusing it for information superiority. In short, the adaptive leader is one who is able to think and act, and spend considerable time in reflecting to learn. The need for engaging NSmen in Commitment to Defence will require SAF leaders to be adaptive in order for the SAF to be resilient. Within a VUCA operating environment, no single leader can have complete knowledge or the ability to plan and drive toward the achievement of social, political and organizational goals purely on his/her own.[13] Adaptive leaders will need to deploy adaptive thinking techniques to make sense of the SAF's jurisdiction in a complex situation and apply military expertise to manage the uncertainty while upholding SAF's professional legitimacy,[14] remaining anchored on the Core Values. They will need the necessary resilience towards uncertainty complemented by Self-Awareness and Self-Management for greater self-efficacy and effectiveness.

DEFINING THE CONCEPT OF SELF-MANAGEMENT

The SAF defines Self-Management as the ability to "control one's own emotions and impulses; remain calm and composed under stress; maintain confidence in one's abilities and adopt a positive outlook; demonstrate cognitive-behavioural flexibility in adapting to ambiguous or changing situations".[15] Self-Management lengthens an individual's persistence in persevering when confronted with obstacles, and enhances his/her resilience in the face of adversity. Hence, it is hoped that by developing Self-Management in Gen Ys, they will become Adaptive Leaders that approach difficult tasks as challenges, setting themselves challenging goals and remaining committed to them, as well as recover their sense of efficacy quickly when confronted with failure or setbacks.[16]

Confidence in the capacity to overcome adversity is vital in uncertain security environments and helps one manage his/her stress levels when confronted with difficult tasks. In contrast, leaders with low Self-Management may believe that tasks are tougher than they really are and this in turn can give rise to a sense of anxiety, stress and depression. In reviewing the SAF's definition, controlling emotion and impulses is a function of one's internal locus of

Chapter 9

control,[17] whereas adopting a positive outlook for cognitive-behavioural flexibility is a function of one's Explanation Style.[18]

Seligman's Optimism Test suggests that individuals with a high degree of Personalization believe that outcomes are related to factors internal to oneself (e.g., due to the ability to recognize change and skill), whilst an individual with low Personalization believes that outcomes are related to external forces beyond his/her control such as chance or the actions of other people.[19] For an Adaptive Leader, this is important because it determines his/her ability to recognize change.[20]

Permanence relates to whether one explains the outcomes of an event as permanent, temporary, or unlikely to recur. Pervasiveness, however, looks at whether one believes an event is specific (i.e., applicable to one specific episode) or universal (i.e., involves a person's entire behavioural repertoire). Individuals with a pessimistic explanation style characteristically attribute negative events to external ("This is due to others or circumstances"), permanent ("Things will never change") and universal ("I am stupid") causes and this puts them at risk for depression when negative events occur.

Adaptive Leaders with an optimistic explanation style would attribute negative events to internal ("This is due to my lack of skills"), temporary ("Things may be different next time"), and specific ("My skills in this aspect are not as good") causes and should recover their efficacy quickly.[21] Explanation style is an important component of the Adaptive Leader's ability to recognize change and trigger the necessary change in order to become more efficacious. Hence, it becomes critical that this is applied to help Gen Y shape their Explanation Styles so that they have Cognitive Behavioural Flexibility.

LEADERSHIP DEVELOPMENT PROCESSES TO DEVELOP SELF-MANAGEMENT

Today, one of the most efficacious methods to achieve Cognitive Behavioural Flexibility is found in Rational Emotive Behavioural Therapy (REBT).[22] Originally developed by Albert Ellis in 1955 for the treatment of Anxiety and Depression in clinical psychology, it is increasingly being used in Coaching Psychology to increase the self-efficacy and by that extension, the performance of a normal population.[23] Ellis's concept of REBT assumes that individuals possess strong tendencies to cope with adversity from birth by significantly changing their cognitive, emotional, and behavioural reaction and that some people have stronger destructive tendencies about their goals.[24] He argued that the conscious and/or implicit belief of such irrational imperatives may lead individuals to develop feelings like anxiety, depression, rage, self-pity etc., and these feelings are often accompanied by self-defeating behaviours such as procrastination, violence, and phobias.[25] Ellis (2000) states that:

> A (Adversities) may contribute heavily to C (dysfunctional emotional and behavioural Consequences): but equally important in "causing" C is B (irrational Beliefs) about A. REBT theory also hypothesizes that when therapists [or coaches] help clients to clearly see, and actively to Dispute (D) and change their dysfunctional Beliefs (B), and particularly to replace them with preferences instead of demands, they tend to wind up with E (Effective New Philosophies) that are usually accompanied by other functional E's-notably, Effective New Feelings and Effective New Behaviours.[26]

In contextualizing Self-Management for Leadership Development (LD) Processes in the SAF, the only change would be that (E) becomes Effective Goals so that it supports the preparation of (F) Follow Up Actions by SAF Leaders to guide their own growth. To draw a distinction between Ellis' original work, the SAF model of (A) Adversity, (B) Beliefs, (C) Consequences, (D) Dispute, (E) Effective goal setting and (F) Follow up actions will be termed as the Rational Emotive Behavioural Analysis (REBA) instead. With this in mind, the development of Self-Management in SAF Leaders begins with integrating REBA with the practice of Reflection and Goal Setting by SAF Leaders in their training curriculum and Individual Development Action Plans. In an Adversity, coaching with REBA would see Leaders Dispute (D) irrational and self-defeating Beliefs (B) during their Reflections and through a continuous cycle of experiential learning set (E) Effective Goals (E) and (F) Follow up on this in their Individual Development Action Plan to become increasingly self-efficacious.

The key part of REBA during Reflection is the (D) Disputation of irrational and self-defeating (B) Beliefs by correctly addressing how Permanence, Prevalence and Personalization have influenced a person's Explanation Style.[27] Reflection with REBA, thus, leads to effective Goal Setting and this is backed by strong empirical evidence[28] that goal setting has an important effect on efficacy beliefs. In the development of Self-Management, being coached with REBA allows higher levels of efficacy beliefs to complement effective goal setting. This, in turn, serves as a protective factor for emotional well-being, reducing anxiety when confronted with stressful situations and increasing the ability to adapt.[29]

In framing Goal Setting as a Leadership Development Practice, the most appropriate approach is based on Boyatzis' Intentional Change Theory.[30]

Chapter 9

Boyatzis stated that "Intentional Change is a desired change in who you are (i.e. the Real) or who you want to be (i.e. the Ideal), or both," and this is mapped as follows;

Discovery 1:	My ideal Self:	
	Who do I want to be?	
Discovery 2:	My Real Self:	
	Who am I?	
	My Strengths:	Where my Ideal and Real Self are similar.
	My Gaps:	Where my Ideal and Real Self are different.
Discovery 3:	My Learning Agenda	
	Building on my strengths whilst reducing my gaps	
Discovery 4:	New behaviour, thoughts and feelings through experimentation	
	Creating and building new pathways through practising to mastery	
Discovery 5:	Leveraging on trusting relationships to support each step in the process	

SELF-MANAGEMENT PROGRAMS FOR THE SAF

For combat adversities, the integration of Self-Management into the practice of coaching in Officer Cadet School has provided positive initial results in helping to shape the Gen Y's explanation style to develop Adaptive Leaders.[31] The integration of REBA into Reflection and Goal Setting reinforced with Self-Awareness tools in the design of all mission exercises will reinforce the development of Self-Management as an LCM skill. For example, through the introduction of ethical dilemmas, exercise planners can create mission failure adversities that will provide an opportunity to coach the leader's explanation style and hence develop their ability to bounce back from an adversity. With a greater physical and psychological impact in the training, new opportunities will be created for students to stretch them to their limits. This is extremely important as current wars[32] highlight the nature of the operating environment where even the most junior commanders need to reason through a VUCA situation to manage strategic consequences for the entire campaign.[33]

CONCLUSION

Self-Management plays a key role in human functioning and impacts other critical determinants related to one's self-concept such as goals and aspirations, outcome expectations, and perception of impediments and opportunities in the social environment.[34] Essentially, the Gen Y Adaptive Leader's ability for Self-Management influences whether he/she reasons strategically or erratically. It influences his/her courses of action, the challenges and goals he/she sets, and his/her subsequent commitment to them. Developing Self-Management skills in the Gen Y today determines how much effort future soldiers will expend in given endeavours, the outcomes they expect their efforts to produce, how long they persevere, and how much stress and depression they experience when coping with taxing environmental demands. In a VUCA environment, this will shape the SAF's future mission success.

ENDNOTES

1. Wahyudi Soeriaatmadja and Lynn Lee, "Orchard MRT station targeted by terrorists", *The Straits Times* (Singapore: Singapore Press Holdings, 19 May 2010).

2. The aspiration for the 3rd Generation SAF is to build an Armed Force that is capable of a full spectrum Operations, focused on the people and the values that make up the SAF. It would be integrated and networked across the services supported by advances in administration, planning and in the development and deployment of technology. See *C4I Asia Conference 2008 Keynote Address by Lieutenant General Desmond Kuek, Chief of Defence Force* retrieved on 20 May 2010 from the MINDEF Singapore Media Room at <http://www.mindef.gov.sg/imindef/resources/speeches/2008/18feb08_speech3.html>.

3. The total land mass of Singapore is 687 km^2 and population is approximately 4.7 million which places it as rank 191 in terms of size and 117 in terms of population, retrieved on 20 May 2011 from <https://www.cia.gov/library/publications/the-world-factbook/geos/sn.html>.

4. The late Dr. Goh Keng Swee said *"Nothing creates loyalty and national consciousness more speedily and more thoroughly than participation in defence and membership of the armed forces... the nation building aspect of defence will be more significant if its participation is spread out over all strata of society. This is possible only with some kind of national service."* See Singapore Government Press Statement Speech by the Minister of Defence, Dr. Goh Keng Swee, in moving the second reading of the National Service (Amendment) Bill in the Singapore Parliament on Monday, 13th March 1967, Document Number: PressR19670313b retrieved on 20 May 2010 from <http://www.a2o.com.sg/a2o/public/search/index.html>.

5. See *Literacy and Education, Key Annual Indicators* retrieved on 20 May 2010 from Singapore Statistics Office at <http://www.singstat.gov.sg/stats/charts/lit-edu.html>.

6. Hao Shuo, Andrew Wan and David Tang Hao, "Gen WhY – So What?", *Pointer,* Vol. 35, No. 2 (2009), 58.

7. Ibid., 64.

8. Ibid., 63.

Chapter 9

9. Psalm B. C. Lew and Cindy R. M. Tan, *Development of Self Management in Officer Cadets*, Paper presented at the 53rd International Military Testing Association Conference at Lucerne, Switzerland, 27 Sep - 01 Nov 2010.

10. See the comments made by DPM Wong Kan Seng in Alvina Soh, "Resilience building challenge for Singapore", *The Straits Times* (Singapore: Singapore Press Holdings, 11 April 2011).

11. Edward Chen, Chew Lock Pin, Foo Khee Loon, Jimmy Khoo, David Koh, Kenneth Kwok, Lee Kok Thong, Lee Shiang Long, Gerald Sim, Ravinder Singh, Tay Chee Bin and Tew See Mong, "Integrated knowledge-based command and control for the ONE SAF", *Journal of the Singapore Armed Forces*. Pointer Monograph Number 5 (February, 2008).

12. Leonard Wong, "Developing Adaptive Leaders: The Crucible Experience of Operation Iraqi Freedom", *Army War College (U.S.). Strategic Studies Institute*. (Carlisle, PA: Strategic Studies Institute, U.S. Army War College, July 2004), 11.

13. Robert Axelrod, *The Complexity of Cooperation: Agent-Based Models of Competition and Collaboration*, (Princeton, NJ: Princeton University Press, 1997).

14. Jurisdiction, Legitimacy and Expertise are commonly identified elements of the Profession. See James Burk, "Expertise, Jurisdiction and Legitimacy of the Military Profession", in Don M. Snider and Lloyd J. Matthews, *The Future of the Army Profession, Revised and Expanded, 2nd Edition* (Singapore: McGraw Hill Publishing, 2005), 48-52.

15. SAF Centre for Leadership Development. *Leadership Development Doctrine Directive 3: SAF Leadership Competency Model*. (Singapore: SAFTI Military Institute, 2004), 6.

16. Psalm B. C. Lew and Cindy R. M. Tan, *Development of Self Management in Officer Cadets*, Paper presented at the 53rd International Military Testing Association Conference at Lucerne, Switzerland, 27 Sep - 01 Nov 2010.

17. Jutta Heckhausen, Carsten Wrosch and Richard Schulz, "A Motivational Theory of Life-Span Development", *Psychological Review*, Vol. 117, No. 1 (2010), 32–60.

18. Martin E. P. Seligman, *Learned Optimism: How to change your mind and your life* (New York, NY: Knopf, 2006).

19. Patricia C. Duttweiler, "The Internal Control Index: A Newly Developed Measure of Locus of Control", *Educational and Psychological Measurement,* Vol. 44, No. 2, (Summer, 1984) 209-221.

20. Laurenz L. Meier, Norbert K. Semmer, Achim Elfering and Nicola Jacobshagen, "The Double Meaning of Control: Three-Way Interactions Between Internal Resources, Job Control and Stressors at Work", *Journal of Occupational Health Psychology,* Vol. 13, No. 3 (2008), 244-258.

21. Christopher Peterson and Martin E.Seligman, "Causal explanations as a risk factor for depression: Theory and evidence", *Psychological Review*, Vol. 9, No. 3 (1984), 347-374.

22. Martin E. P. Seligman, *Learned Optimism: How to change your mind and your* life (New York, NY: Knopf, 2006).

23. Nick Edgerton and Stephen Palmer, "SPACE: A psychological model for use within cognitive behavioural coaching, therapy and stress management", *The Coaching Psychologist*, Vol. 1, No. 2 (2005), 25-31.

24. Albert Ellis, "Rational Emotive Behaviour Therapy" in Alan E. Kazdin, ed., *Encyclopedia of Psychology, Vol. 7*, (American Psychological Association Press, 2000).

25. Ibid., 7.

26. Ibid., 8.

27. Gregory McClell Buchanan and Martin Seligman, *Explanatory Style* (Hillsdale, NJ: Erlbaum, 1995).

28. Albert Bandura and Edwin A. Locke, "Negative Self-Efficacy and Goal Effects Revisited", *Journal of Applied Psychology*, Vol. 88, No. 1 (2003), 87–99.

29. Edwin A. Locke, Elizabeth Frederick, Cynthia Lee and Philip Bobko, "Effect on Self Efficacy, Goals and Task Strategies on Task Performance", *Journal of Applied Psychology*, Vol. 69, No. 2 (1984), 241-251.

30. Richard E. Boyatzis, "Unleashing the Power of Self-Directed Learning" in Ron Sims, ed., *Changing the Way We Manage Change: The Consultants Speak.* (NY: Quorum Books, 2002).

31. Psalm B. C. Lew and Cindy R. M. Tan, *Development of Self Management in Officer Cadets*, Paper presented at the 53rd International Military Testing Association Conference at Lucerne, Switzerland, 27 Sep - 01 Nov 2010.

32. H.R. McMaster, "Preserving Soldier's Moral Character in Counter Insurgency Operations", in Don Carrick, James Connelly and Paul Robinson, eds., *Ethics Education for Irregular Warfare* (Surrey, UK: Ashgate Publishing, 2009).

33. Charles C. Krulak, "The Strategic Corporal: Leadership in the Three Block War", *Marines Magazine* (January, 2009).

34. Albert Bandura, *Self-Efficacy: The Exercise of Control* (New York, NY: Freeman, 1997).

CHAPTER 10

BECOMING AN OFFICER IN THE CANADIAN FORCES. LEADERSHIP AT THE ROYAL MILITARY COLLEGE OF CANADA, A BRIDGE BETWEEN EDUCATION AND EXPERIENCE

*Major Julie Bélanger and Dr. Daniel Lagacé-Roy**

The current CF Leadership doctrine defines effective leadership as *"Directing, motivating, and enabling others to accomplish the mission professionally and ethically, while developing or improving capabilities that contribute to mission success."*[1] As pointed out in 1970 vintage CF doctrine, leadership was described as the primary reason for the existence of officers in the CF.[2] Current CF doctrine, however, stresses that leadership does not rest solely in the domain of officers. It speaks to *distributed leadership*; a concept based on the premise that regardless of one's rank or organizational position, that they should be empowered and encouraged to exercise leadership (i.e., leadership should be shared across ranks).[3]

Andrew J. DuBrin, a leadership expert, suggested that the most effective way to foster leadership development is through education, experience and mentoring (coaching). According to him, education refers to the acquisition of knowledge without concern for its immediate application while experience allows an individual to convert knowledge into skill. DuBrin also explains that another experienced-based way to develop leadership capability is through leadership exposure delivered by a knowledgeable leader.[4]

This chapter examines one of several entry plans for the CF Officer Corps, the Regular Officer Training Plan (ROTP), through which selected individuals attend the Royal Military College of Canada (RMCC). RMCC provides the building blocks of the ROTP program to prepare Officer Cadets (OCdts) to assume their role as junior officers and future leaders in the CF.

---

* The views expressed in this chapter are those of the authors and do not necessarily reflect the official policy of the Canadian Forces or the Department of National Defence.

Chapter 10

CONTEXT

The RMCC was established by an Act of the Canadian Parliament in 1874 and the first 18 cadets commenced their program of study in 1876. Degree granting status was received from the Province of Ontario in 1959. Today, the mission of RMCC is to "produce officers with the ethical, mental, physical and linguistic capabilities required to lead with distinction in the Canadian Forces".[5] The Cadet Wing generally totals some eleven hundred OCdts spread across the four years of studies and approximately 220 Second Lieutenants are commissioned each year. This represents about 25% of the annual CF requirement for Junior Officers.

To successfully complete an undergraduate degree at the RMCC and obtain a commission, OCdts must complete a vigorous program comprised of four mandatory interlocking components (or pillars) of achievement: academic, military, athletic and language ability. All academic programs contain a compulsory number of courses (*core curriculum*), ensuring that OCdts are taught a balanced, theoretical curriculum comprised of liberal arts, science and military education.[6] Military training is designed to offer practical leadership experiences, meaning that each OCdt is required to assume different positions of increasing responsibility as they progress through their years at RMCC. Academics and military training are recognized as the most demanding. The third pillar of achievement, the Athletic Program, "is designed to provide opportunities for all OCdts to participate in physical activities and sports that are mentally demanding in order to develop their overall physical capabilities, self-confidence and leadership."[7] Lastly, Second Language (SL) training, the fourth aspect of cadet life, is designed to develop the ability to communicate in both of Canada's official languages, French and English.[8]

By providing a residential program in a military environment, RMCC attempts to socialize OCdts to the military discipline and teamwork that are required of junior leaders. Under the supervision of the Cadet Wing Staff (officers and senior non-commissioned officers), third and fourth year OCdts hold the majority of staff and command appointments and are responsible for the management and administration of many aspects of their squadron activities. In essence, leadership development goes beyond the core content of training and education as it is incorporated throughout the formal and informal elements of life at RMCC. In a holistic approach to military education, learning occurs through education, training, personal experience, observation and guidance. RMCC can be perceived as a four-year socialization process to the CF, as well as an introduction to their future responsibilities as leaders.

In recent years, a clear emphasis has been placed on the transference of values as a fundamental element of leadership development. OCdts at RMCC are exposed to various types of leadership *via* two different means of experience. The first one is presented to them when they deal with their chain of command and/or when they interact with officers that serve either as course instructors or college administrators. This encounter with "leadership" figures represents, to a certain extent, their first experience of what "leaders" are or should be. Furthermore, this first contact serves, most of the time, as the foundation for their own expression of leadership when they hold leadership positions during military activities. The First Year Orientation Period (FYOP) is a good example of a military activity in which OCdts have the opportunity to practice a leadership role. This example will be explained later in this chapter. The second opportunity for OCdts to learn more about leadership is through the presentation of theories and concepts in a classroom setting. This formal education is an important component as it is related to the acquisition of knowledge that will later serve as the background for applying leadership. The Department of Military Psychology and Leadership (MPL) at RMCC offers compulsory courses that speak directly or indirectly to the acquisition of knowledge on leadership. At this point, it would be difficult to explain the nature of these courses without briefly describing the supporting argument that led to the decision to incorporate these courses into the core curriculum of RMCC programs.

EDUCATION – UNDERSTANDING YOURSELF, THE ORGANIZATION AND ETHICAL LEADERSHIP THEORIES

The RMCC is a key leadership institution within the Canadian Forces.[9] To mark the 125th anniversary of the foundation of RMCC in 2001, Dr. John Scott Cowan, principal of RMCC at the time, wrote an article: *RMC and the Profession of Arms: Looking Ahead of Canada's Military University.* In this article, he introduced the college as a university *with a difference.*[10] For Dr. Cowan, this difference is highlighted by the fact that the college, throughout the years, became more and more attentive to changes. More importantly, this transformation is visible in the shift from courses only offered in the applied theoretical sciences such as mathematics and ballistics to the addition of courses in the liberal arts such as the study of history and ethics. To a certain extent, the necessity of these changes were called into question during the 1990s in which the CF was undeniably in a "period of darkness" following events such as the Somalia incident in 1993. The Board of Inquiry that followed pointed out in Recommendation 16.3 that RMCC, as a place of learning, is responsible in making sure that future officers of the CF receive an education that incorporates the values and principles that shape the CF culture:

Chapter 10

> [We recommend] The Chief of the Defence Staff incorporate the values, principles and processes of accountability into continuing education of officer cadets at the Royal Military College and in staff training, command and staff training, and senior command courses. In particular, such education and training should establish clearly the accountability requirements in the command process and the issuance of orders, and the importance of upper ranks setting a personal example with respect to morality and respect for the rule of law.[11]

In 1998, the Board of Governors of RMCC requested a report be written to address concerns regarding the college's *raison d'être*. The committee, chaired by General (Ret'd) Ramsey Withers, confirmed the important role played by RMCC in shaping future officers of the CF. More importantly, some recommendations of the Withers report were made to guarantee a core undergraduate curriculum with an emphasis on subjects viewed as essential for officership: leadership, ethics, psychology, Canadian history, international affairs, languages… to name few.

> Today's professional military officer must possess a body of knowledge which, taken as a whole, is unique to his or her profession. In addition to a combination of arts and sciences common to all liberal undergraduate education in Canada, there is a body of somewhat esoteric knowledge to be imparted if an officer cadet is to achieve basic level qualification for the profession of arms.[…] Last, but not least, all cadets must be involved in an intensive study of the contemporary theory and practice of leadership (including its ethical component).[12]

This core curriculum is a major feature of the Withers report along with the expansion of educational programs (Masters and PhDs), on site or by distance, to all members of the CF.

Further in his article, Dr. Cowan offered a substantial and critical reason in explaining this crucial recommendation. According to the former principal of RMCC, the changes made to the curriculum were essential for opening the college to a more *liberal arts* approach characterized by a new kind of scholastic that would ensure an adequate *formation*[13] required for future officers. Therefore, it was established that every OCdt, in conjunction with their respective program of study, would be required to pursue the same core curriculum. At convocation in May 2001, Cowan reinforced this aspect by stating:

> And yet in many respects those graduating today are a new breed of Renaissance men and women. You have learned and will learn in more

breadth about things outside your first discipline than most others in Canadian society. You will hold more varied jobs than others, and you will change jobs more often. The RMC core curriculum of liberal arts and sciences necessary for officership is predicated on the certainty that you will need to know more than others in society. Indeed, the knowledge base for the profession of arms spans most of human knowledge.[14]

With certainty, Dr. Cowan supports the contention that RMCC is the place to acquire what is needed to become a capable and knowledgeable officer in the CF. Undeniably, RMCC possesses a special "*cachet*" that encourages students to expand their skills and capabilities.

In line with the Withers report recommendations, the Military Psychology and Leadership Department (MPL) offers three courses that specifically relate to the core curriculum: *Introduction to Psychology*; *Organizational Behaviour and Leadership*, and; *Military Professionalism and Ethics*.

At first sight, *Introduction to Psychology* doesn't seem congruent with the other courses. However, when you look at the course description, it is obvious that the topics discussed are essential knowledge required of leaders concerning human behaviour.

> This course is designed to provide the student with an understanding of people as psychological beings. The essentials of the scientific method and its application to psychology will be presented. Concepts such as development, learning, memory, motivation, intelligence, stress and health, personality, and psychological disorders will be discussed.[15]

As OCdts become more familiar with the concepts and theories, they realize that a background in psychology is useful for understanding themselves and others. This knowledge therefore serves as the underpinning comprehension of how leadership is influenced by basic awareness of the makeup of human beings.

For OCdts, the study of leadership in a formal setting begins with the course on *Organizational Behaviour and Leadership*. To be specific, it is through the study of organizational systems and practices that leadership is addressed. The course description states:

> This course is designed to familiarize students with basic theories, concepts, and skills related to organizational behaviour and effective

leadership. Students will examine how individuals in organizations, groups in organizations, and organizational processes can be impacted by leaders in order to enhance organizational effectiveness.[16]

The leadership component is presented near the end of the course and addresses leadership theories along with adjacent themes such as power and influence.

The third obligatory course of the core curriculum is *Military Professionalism and Ethics*. This course is very particular to officership because its primary objective is to target the conduct of OCdts as future officers in the CF and as members of the profession of arms. As stated in the course description:

> The purpose of this course is to develop student understanding of the professional and ethical dimensions of officership. Throughout, a distinction is made between the normative ideals of behaviour prescribed by ethical and military theorists and the reality of behaviour as described and explained by cognitive, social, and other psychological factors.

More importantly, the course is designed to encourage critical thinking through the application of decision-making processes and ethical analyses. By encouraging the development of self-awareness in regards to the domain of ethical dilemmas and self-insight in dealing with ethical ambiguities, this course empowers OCdts with a valuable knowledge that would increase their chance of success when facing uncertainties.

The enterprise of offering, at the same time, courses that are compulsory in practice and developmental in nature is a tall order and presents some challenges and concerns for OCdts as well as professors. These challenges can be captured under a central theme: the acquisition of knowledge. Under this theme two major concerns are emphasized and addressed here: the first one centres on course content and the second is concerned with the method used to deliver this content. *Organizational Behaviour and Leadership* and *Military Professionalism and Ethics* will be the focus of this section. The *Introduction to Psychology* seems less problematic because it serves as a general introduction and as the foundation or prerequisite for further studies (e.g., a degree in Psychology). Some may argue that this course is not essential for all RMCC programs (e.g., Engineering). While this argument is debatable, this chapter doesn't address that particular issue. Again, some may argue that a course on *Organizational Behaviour and Leadership* falls under the same debate and might not be required of all OCdts. The difference lies in the portion dedicated to leadership. To that effect, the leadership component is – as stated earlier – the first formal introduction to leadership theories and concepts. Looking back of what the course is offering, three observations can be made. First: from a "curriculum" point of view, this course provides the adequate background in presenting how organizations are designed and function. Second: from an "educational" point of view, it is often difficult for OCdts to learn about the mechanics of civilian organizations because the linkage between the information presented (e.g., how civilian organizations work?) and their military world as an "organization" is not always obvious. As for the leadership component, it is presented in the latter part of the course and seems to serve as a tool in making the transition between civilian and military worlds. However, from a "leadership" point of view, this transition is not apparent because leadership under this approach becomes a subset of organizations instead of being its catalyst. The disadvantage of such approach is that leadership seems lost in the course content and one advantage is that OCdts, to a certain extent, are taught basic notions about leadership.

As for the course on *Military Professionalism and Ethics*, the course material has been designed with a military audience in mind. The *mélange* of topics ranging from philosophical theories to just war traditions via moral development and decision-making processes offers areas of knowledge to help OCdts formulate and probe questions on various issues. It also enables them to better articulate a sound argument to advance a hypothetical response to the various case studies debated in class. The dense readings (e.g., ethical theories such as Immanuel Kant) required for each topics could be, at times, overwhelming and OCdts have made their discontent known. However, from an "academic" point of view, criticism from students is not a solid and valid argument, especially when it is a fourth year course. While it is important to hear students' criticism or suggestions for changes in course curriculum to occur, especially when course material is concerned, the heart of the issue here is not content but the method of delivery. Let's remember that *Military Professionalism and Ethics* is a mandatory course and as such required standardization. The requirement for uniformity only serves the "instructor" that delivers the "course package". To that effect, an interesting article by Dr. David Last suggests that such "uniformity must be resisted" because the differentiation between the meaning of a university and a training school becomes indistinct.

> When a 'subject expert' prepares a 'package', which interchangeable instructors 'deliver' to students, we are treading the line between training and education. When the 'subject expert' has assembled knowledge from other sources, and cannot explain how or why something is known, then we have lost the essence of the questioning university. Pedagogy (the art of teaching) without epistemology

Chapter 10

(the philosophy of knowledge) degenerates quickly into pedantry (insistence on forms and details).[17]

This statement written in 2004 is still very much valid in 2011. It does suggest that the development of OCdts through the study of military professionalism and ethical conduct; critical knowledge and critical thinking; moral development and decision-making could be compromised by the instructor's ability to grasp and deliver the depth of the content. Nevertheless, in retrospect, the course offers a solid foundation on leadership and ethical conduct in the context of the profession of arms.

Teaching a subject such as leadership, professionalism and ethics demands a holistic approach that transcends the mere basics of teaching. When a holistic approach is used, the instructor empowers students by engaging them into discussion. In fact, the instructor *leads* the discussion and *coaches* by getting students to focus on the essence of the issue. Therefore, the instructor becomes engaged with the students in the process and his/her way of thinking is sometimes emulated (i.e. *role model*). The long-term effect of this instructor commitment to the development of OCdts is that it helps them to make the connection between theoretical knowledge and practice. The next section provides good illustrations of RMCC practical experiences of leadership.

MILITARY TRAINING

First Year Orientation Period (FYOP)

Socialization is "the process by which people learn the norms and roles that are necessary to function in a group or organization".[18] As such, socialization is designed to transform the individual from a social being into the "'desired' military person".[19] Upon arrival in Kingston, Ontario at the RMCC main campus, all OCdts complete the Initial phase of Basic Officer Training Course (I-BOTC), which lasts 5 weeks, to verify that they have the potential, motivation and ability to continue with leadership training. During this training, the recruits are taught basic military knowledge and skills common to all members of the CF and take part in a rigorous program of sports and fitness training. Upon completion of the I-BOTC, the OCdts are posted to RMCC to start their first academic year.

From then, the OCdts are assigned a squadron, and, as they start their first academic semester in their respective programs, they go through one of the first formal socialization processes at RMCC, the First Year Orientation Period. FYOP consists of five weeks of "intense training designed to familiarize the cadets with the traditions, history, rules and regulations of the College; to increase their level of physical fitness; [and] to develop the cadet's ability to work effectively within a team".[20] It culminates with the Obstacle Course and Badging Parade Ceremony, marking the first year OCdts' entry into "full-fledged" membership of their Squadron, the Wing, and the College.

According to research on newcomer socialization, individuals who are new to an organization will look to establish two types of networks, 1) formal, and 2) informal or friendship.[21] The first network is to acquire specific information about the organization culture (i.e., rules, code of conduct, etc.,) and the second allows the newcomer to get a sense and feel of being integrated into the social environment. During this early stage of socialization, the new recruit will learn important information such as norms, policies, reporting relationships, terminology, goals, history, politics, role expectations and responsibilities. Initial attitudes regarding adherence to particular organizational rules will likely take place during this period, with the enduring result being the acceptance of certain behaviours at the workgroup level. Different socialization tactics are often used to structure the first professional experiences of a new recruit and ease the socialization process.[22] More importantly, for the new OCdts attempting to define a role for themselves within the institution, FYOP serves as a collective[23] familiarization period to RMCC and an informal way to establishing a social network with peers and supervisors.

The OCdts are organized into a Cadet Wing composed of a headquarters and a number of divisions and squadrons. The squadron that a cadet belongs to represents the core affiliation that dictates who his/her immediate supervisors are, where he/she lives on campus, and who the cadet will work with during daily military squadron activities. During FYOP, the First Year cadets receive serial[24] and formal[25] socialization mainly from the Third and Fourth year cadets who assume FYOP Staff positions and senior bars under the direct supervision of commissioned officers (i.e., Squadron Commanders at the rank of Captains). These early relationships are an important part of the RMCC program as the socialization obtained through interactions with more experienced squadron members represents a primary means of maintaining organizational culture and tradition. For the new members, the most prominent and direct models of behaviours are those of their immediate workgroup, which in the RMCC context, would be found at the squadron level.

The overall objectives of FYOP, a formal and serial socialization process, are to develop cohesion and identity amongst the First Year Cadets. The FYOP After Action Survey, administered to the First Year OCdts at the end of the FYOP in 2009 and 2010, provides insights on how they perceived that experience.[26] As reported by First Year Cadets:

Overall, I feel that FYOP was a good teamwork building experience and it brought the whole flight closer together.

Although FYOP is difficult and stressful, it is a great way to make close friends, and when it is over, you feel more welcome at RMC.

Furthermore, the quantitative data collected also provides evidence that this program fosters cohesion and identity. Table 1 presents the reported means for the perception of First Year Cadets and the FYOP Staff on the cohesion scale for 2009 and 2010.[27]

Questions	Min	Max	Mean* FY Ocdts 2009	Mean* FY OCdts 2010	Min	Max	Mean* FYOP Staff 2010	Mean* FYOP Staff 2009
In my squadron we stuck together no matter what.	1	5	4.16	3.87	3	5	4.31	4.00
The people in my squadron encourage each other to work as a team.	2	5	4.36	4.16	2	5	4.28	4.07
There was a lot of togetherness among my squadron.	1	5	4.34	4.00	2	5	4.24	4.14
The people in my squadron did not get along (R).	1	5	4.06(R)	4.18(R)	1	4	4.19(R)	4.18(R)
I would describe my squadron as being one big family.	1	5	3.98	3.79	2	5	3.81	3.52
The people in my squadron cared about what happened to each other.	1	5	4.22	4.15	3	5	4.11	4.04
People in my squadron worked as a team.	1	5	4.27	4.15	3	5	4.17	4.07
Getting through FYOP would have been much more difficult without the cohesion and teamwork that we developed within my squadron.	1	5	4.57	4.38	1	5	4.06	3.73
Teamwork plays an important role at RMC.	1	5	4.78	4.76	1	5	4.28	4.23
Cumulative			**4.31**	**4.16**			**3.69**	**3.99**

*Reported on a Lickert scale from 1 – Strongly Disagree to 5 – Strongly Agree

Table 1 – Cohesion Level from FYOP Surveys 2009 and 2010

As these overall results suggest, the level of cohesion among First Year OCdts is very strong. In fact, the various activities (i.e., the busy schedule and the preparation for the obstacle course and the Badging parade) can arguably contribute to the strong level of agreement that is reported for the importance of teamwork at RMCC. In fact, these results were also replicated in a recent study and showed that First Year Cadets are displaying a stronger level of cohesion than any of the other cohorts (Second, Third and Fourth Year OCdts).[28]

Another interesting finding is that First Year Cadets identify themselves primarily as Officer Cadets as opposed to the Fourth Year Class whom strongly identify with being a Member of the CF as a designation (see Table 2). This can also suggest that the First Year OCdts perceive themselves as junior members of the CF, thus, preferring to mainly identify with their position or rank. As they progress and reach their fourth year of study, the senior OCdts are looking forward to their pending promotions and perhaps prefer to focus or better identify with the organizational identity. This provides evidence that the socialization process that takes place at RMCC gradually prepares the OCdts to fully embrace the common identity of the military culture as they are about to graduate and obtain their commission.

Question: I Identify myself primarily as ...

	First Year	**Second Year**	**Third Year**	**Fourth Year**
...a student	28.9 %	30.4 %	43.1 %	23.1 %
...an OCdt	42.2 %	30.4 %	31.4 %	27.7 %
...a CF Member	28.9 %	39.2 %	25.5 %	49.2 %

Table 2 – OCdts' Perceived Identity[29]

FYOP also provides the First Year OCdts with a very strong sense of affective commitment to RMCC and the CF. The sense of belonging to the larger "CF Family" is significantly lower for the FYOP Staff, however, the general commitment to the College and the CF seems to be fairly consistent across the different cohorts. (See Tables 3 and 4.)

Chapter 10

Questions	Min	Max	Mean* FY OCdts 2009	Mean* FY OCdts 2010	Min	Max	Mean* FYOP Staff 2009	Mean* FYOP Staff 2010
Affective Commitment								
A) I feel like "Part of the Family" at RMC.	2	5	4.33	4.16	1	5	4.11	3.85
B) I feel like "Part of the Family" in the CF.	2	5	4.05	3.74	1	5	2.96	3.02
A) RMC has a great deal of personal meaning to me.	1	5	4.25	4.18	2	5	3.91	4.04
B) The CF has a great deal of personal meaning to me.	1	5	4.07	4.15	2	5	4.09	4.13
A) I feel a strong sense of belonging to RMC.	2	5	4.32	4.14	2	5	4.00	4.00
B) I feel a strong sense of belonging to the CF.	2	5	4.04	3.95	1	5	3.83	3.72
A) I feel "emotionally attached" to RMC.	2	5	4.05	3.78	1	5	3.66	3.60
B) I feel "emotionally attached" to the CF.	1	5	3.70	3.63	2	5	3.58	3.56
As an Officer Cadet at RMC, I feel a strong connection to the CF.	2	5	4.06	3.85	1	5	2.68	2.93
General								
I am proud to be an RMC student.	1	5	4.65	4.62	1	5	4.13	4.14
I am proud to be a member of the CF.	1	5	4.62	4.59	4	5	4.52	4.64

*Reported on a Lickert scale from 1 – Strongly Disagree to 5 – Strongly Agree

Table 3 – Affective and General Commitment Reported – FYOP 2009 and 2010[30]

General	Min	Max	Mean*
I am proud to be an RMC graduate.	3	5	4.33
I am proud to be a member of the CF.	4	5	4.58

*Reported on a Lickert scale from 1 – Strongly Disagree to 5 – Strongly Agree

Table 4 – General Commitment Reported by Graduating Class of 2010[31]

Other objectives of FYOP are to instill in OCdts an appreciation for time management, proper dress and deportment, physical training, inspections and college traditions. They learn the specific demands of the college and how to respond accordingly, but more importantly, how to live and adhere to the RMCC motto: Truth, Duty, Valour. It could be argued that the CF values of Duty, Loyalty, Integrity and Courage,[32] that are at the core of the Canadian military ethos, are not the main focus of the RMCC socialization process. Indeed, the College, with its own motto, represents an organizational sub-culture of the CF. It appears, at least as face value, however, that the RMCC core values are aligned, in theory, with the values of the larger organization. The perception of OCdts as reported by First and Third Year Cadets on who follow the rules at RMCC clearly indicates that sub-culture.[33] Both groups agree that First Year OCdts are following the rules as expected, and, First Year Cadets perceived that their seniors are providing a good example. As they progress, senior OCdts expect the First Year OCdts to follow the rules but they report not following the rules themselves.

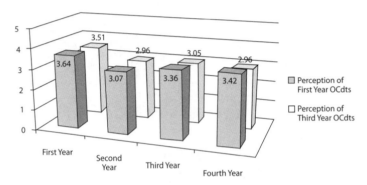

Figure 1 – Who follows the rules at RMCC?[34]

Because the goal of the RMCC is to produce officers that possess the ethical characteristics informed by the CF's ethos, it is crucial that the institution also pays close attention to the informal process of socialization that is taking place as it encourages the evaluation of values through experiences and lessons learned. Various researchers suggested that personal values develop in a social context and that certain values are essential to the value systems of good leaders (i.e., these primarily include but are not limited to honesty, integrity, concern for others, fairness, and justice).[35]

The results obtained from the FYOP After Action Surveys confirm the previous observations and provide an insight to the adherence to the CF values by the Cadets. Both groups reported a strong degree of agreement toward respect for the CF military core values. Interestingly, when exploring the alignment between the values of RMCC and the CF, senior cadets show a dichotomy between behaviours that are acceptable at RMCC and the values of the CF. The results suggest that the senior OCdts perceive a distinction between life at RMCC and their understanding of the CF reality; for them, it appears to be more acceptable to bend the rules in your squadron at RMCC than it is in the CF.

Questions	Min	Max	Mean* FY OCdts 2010	Mean* FYOP Staff 2010
A) In my squadron, it is okay to bend the rules. B) At RMC, it is okay to bend the rules. C) In the CF, it is okay to bend the rules.	1	5	1.63 1.60 1.51	2.55 2.64 1.95
Cadets in my squadron are held accountable for their actions.	1	5	4.21	3.96
Cadets in my squadron adhere strictly to regulations.	1	5	3.64	2.90
I respect the CF military value of serving country before self.	1	5	4.43	4.32
I respect the CF military value of obeying lawful authority.	1	5	4.45	4.31
I respect the CF military priorities of my mission, my troops, myself.	1	5	4.49	4.49

*Reported on a Lickert scale from 1 – Strongly Disagree to 5 – Strongly Agree

Table 5 – Values of First Year OCdts and FYOP Staff [36]

BAR POSITIONS AT RMCC – PRACTICAL LEADERSHIP EXPERIENCE AT RMCC

Previous research has reported that the College was providing a transactional model of leadership in which cadets were punished for making mistakes instead of being given the opportunity to learn from them.[37] Comments obtained from previous graduating OCdts (Class of 2007) support these findings and suggested that leadership positions were often perceived as the merely the management of information.[38]

> Most bar positions ask of us to act just as a message delivery service, and not as leader.

> There is a lack of personal and professional development as cadets' role/position within the military wing. There is always discrepancy in what is expected of us. As a senior bar, I had little responsibility or authority: pertinent information was not always provided and punishment resulted from seeking the information.

It appears that the institution made a conscious effort when putting together the RMC Transformation Project within the Cadet Wing in 2007, by empowering the OCdts in order to better develop their leadership skills through focusing on cohesion and morale, and fostering ethical behaviour in all circumstances.[39] In the last five years, graduating cadets reported that one of their most satisfying leadership experiences at RMCC was having the opportunity to serve as FYOP Staff and holding senior positions. The results from the FYOP Staff indicate that perceptions of leadership experience at RMCC are gradually changing. Their views on learning from this experience seem to contribute to their overall leadership development. FYOP Staff OCdts positively agree that this leadership role allowed them to develop leadership skills and the ability to better relate to subordinates, as suggested by the FYOP Staff Surveys in 2009 and 2010 (see Table 6). Overall, the Third Year Students that are given the opportunity to hold a FYOP Staff Position describe this as being one of the meaningful leadership experiences of their College career because it is viewed as having a direct influence on subordinates in contrast to other bar positions that are reported to require more management than leadership abilities *per se*.

Questions	Min	Max	Mean* FYOP Staff 2009	Mean* FYOP Staff 2010
Being a FYOP Staff was an important achievement for me personally.	1	5	4.29	4.00
During FYOP, rules and procedures limited discretionary behaviour of FYOP Staff.	2	5	4.29	4.15
During FYOP, mistakes from FYOP Staff were treated as learning opportunities by the COC.	1	5	2.73	2.32
As FYOP Staff, the unwritten rule was to admit mistakes, learn from them, and move on.	2	5	3.96	4.06
Personal-Professional Development: Leadership skills.	3	5	3.96	4.33
Personal-Professional Development: Ability to relate with subordinates.	3	5	4.32	4.22
Personal-Professional Development: Staff duties (military writing, staff duties, file management).	1	5	3.43	3.74
Personal-Professional Development: Training ability.	1	5	4.00	3.96

*Reported on a Lickert scale from 1 – Strongly Disagree to 5 – Strongly Agree

Table 6 – Perception of Leadership Development by FYOP Staff [40]

The organizational environment of a military academic institution is unlike any other workplace. Part of the unique environment at RMCC is the reality that the military pillar routinely cycles OCdts in and out of positions of authority within the squadron. This allows maximum exposure to a variety of roles within the Wing. A limitation of this approach, however, is reduced continuity regarding who represents a peer, a subordinate, and/or who is an authority figure throughout the academic year. This creates a certain amount of role ambiguity and increases the number of individuals who are trying to exert influence over other group members. A longitudinal study[41] described the dilemma that is created by such a subculture and it is prevalent amongst cadets because it allows them, as an example, to look after one another. In fact, their dilemma can be summarized as "What is more important: protecting my friends or enforcing college rules?". It is well known among OCdts, however, that "Truth Duty Valour" refers to knowing and understanding the rules and how to contour them in order to avoid punishment or, when in position of authority, to have to report a friend's misconduct.

Questions	Min	Max	Mean*
I would not confront a FYOP Staff for his/her wrongdoing if this FYOP Staff was a friend of mine.	1	5	2.15
I would comply with unethical assignments or rules if I were ordered to do so.	1	5	2.20
I would not report a FYOP Staff for misconduct.	1	5	2.02
I would not report a cadet under my supervision for misconduct.	1	5	2.13
It is not my duty to take action when I observe another squadron member commit unprofessional actions.	1	5	2.13

*Reported on a Lickert scale from 1 – Strongly Disagree to 5 – Strongly Agree

Table 7 – Perception of Role Ambiguity by FYOP Staff OCdt (2009)[42]

As an OCdt commented in the Annual Departure Survey of 2011 administered to the graduating class, this context can certainly prepare them for the reality of a military career and challenges their personal values.

> Recognizing that I would have to "blow the whistle" on my friends.
> I learned a considerable amount, but I didn't like it.[43]

In is important to keep in mind that OCdts are also undertaking individualized military training within their respective military occupations during the summer. Because occupational training is taking place in various CF Schools and Units across Canada, it will vary significantly in terms of content and experiences. While enhancing leadership development, this is not considered as one of the building blocks of RMCC, but rather, depends on the CF Officer Training System of each element (Navy, Army and Air). During MOC training, OCdts gain valuable exposure to the organization they belong to and their future trade. The leadership training at that level is mainly delivered by warrant officers and senior non-commissioned officers being directly involved in candidate training. This exposure has a significant effect on socialization, as experienced members of the organization try to impart their technical knowledge and experience to their future leaders.

EMPOWERING AND COACHING –
EXPOSURE TO LEADERSHIP ROLE MODELS

As RMCC provides many opportunities for senior OCdts to be appointed to staff and command positions in the Cadet Wing, it can be argued that knowledge and experience alone are not sufficient for leadership development. The practical training in leadership that occurs at RMCC is via various duties and responsibilities related to the discipline, progress and efficiency of the OCdts' squadrons. This can be an excellent environment for leadership development as it allows the OCdts to gain exposure and explore different leadership roles, some more related to management, and others more associated with the supervision of personnel. Bass suggested that power sharing is a process of involving subordinates in the planning and decision-making process.[44] As the OCdts are enabled by the RMCC Cadet Wing to exercise their abilities and share power, they need to be able to look to their Chain of Command and their staff, who should exemplify the best possible model of servant leadership.[45] Furthermore, empowerment is a central element in servant leadership and modeling is an important means for promulgating organizational values and developing leadership abilities.[46]

In a recent publication, Dr. Alan Okros suggested that the different leadership roles of supervisors need to be in alignment with the developmental stages of the subordinates in order to be effective.[47] Also, to achieve leadership effectiveness, one should consider the appropriate alignment of competencies, authority and responsibilities, and, in turn, foster personal growth and development of leadership abilities.

> Some people think some of the leadership roles here are useless but the fact is that these minor roles are good practice for some officer cadets, while the roles with more responsibilities are better suited for those persons who are farther along in their leadership development and who have demonstrated more leadership ability.[48]

Transformational leadership is often referred to as the most influential leadership approach. Bass's full range model of transformation leadership is comprised of four dimensions: Idealized influence, Inspirational motivation, Intellectual stimulation, and, Individualized consideration. The first dimension stresses the importance of being a role model; to be perceived as a good leader, ones should exemplify the organization values, cultivate trust and respect in his/her followers. The leader should also inspire others to achieve beyond their expectations by encouraging subordinates to contribute in the decision-making process and to achieve beyond their expectations. Lastly, leaders using individualized consideration offer respectful advices that tailor individual needs and aspirations.

Chapter 10

Social learning theory asserts that individual behaviours are learned by observing role models' behaviours and their consequences; suggesting that when there are positive and effective role models in the work environment, individuals will strive to emulate those models.[49] As such, OCdts are exposed to different role models, ranging from senior OCdts holding various positions (as junior cadets), to their Squadron Commanders (Captains) and senior officers holding higher positions inside and outside their respective Chain of Command. The level of influence will vary according to the proximity and the perception from the subordinates that the leader represents a good example.

Various surveys are administered at the College to allow the Chain of Command to obtain information about the OCdts' perceptions of leadership at RMCC. Interestingly, First Year Cadets perceive their FYOP Staff very favourably and look up to them as role models (see Table 8). In turn, the FYOP Staff' perceptions of the Squadron Commanders' leadership appears, in most cases, lower. Again, this might be explained not only in terms of perceived leadership effectiveness but as a consequence of power authority. The perceived authority (enforcing the rules) by the First Year Cadets is significantly higher than the perception of FYOP Staff toward their Squadron Commanders. Even if these results can emulate the fact that First Year Cadets are providing an evaluation based on first impression, it remains that the close bond and the expectations created within this follower-leader relationship is perceived as a very positive influence that fosters the inculcation of the sub-organization values. In contrast, FYOP Staff – Squadron Commanders proximity is not as prevalent.

	Min	Max	FYOP Staff by FY OCdts	SqCo by FYOP Staff
Overall Idealized Influence[50]	1	5	4.12	3.38
Overall Inspirational Motivation[51]	1	5	4.31	3.49
Overall Individual Consideration[52]	1	5	3.77	3.47
General Items related to Leadership				
I would consider my ... as my mentor (coach/teacher).	1	5	4.0	2.77
Were fair (treated cadets equitably).	1	5	3.9	3.36
Fully participated in squadron activities.	2	5	4.4	3.27
Interacted regularly with cadets.	2	5	4.2	3.48
Were considerate of others and ensured all people were treated with dignity.	1	5	3.8	3.61
Overall Leadership Behaviour Average	1	5	4.1	3.43

Table 8 – Comparative Perception of Leadership Behaviours Among Role Models[53]

The perception of the graduating class on similar leadership components, reported in Table 9, shows a mitigated level of agreement but that it has improved over the last five years.

Items	2003	2004	2005	2006	2007	2008	2009
Showed concern for cadets.	3.33	3.21	3.45	3.59	3.44	3.63	**3.75**
Encouraged cadets to express their views.	2.78	2.57	2.82	3.03	3.11	3.16	**3.38**
Were fair (treated cadets equitably).	2.85	2.80	3.06	3.29	3.14	3.24	**3.42**
Were very knowledgeable of military requirements and procedures that impact on cadets.	3.22	3.07	3.12	3.41	3.24	3.38	**3.69**
Interacted with cadets on a regular basis.	2.83	3.00	2.83	2.89	2.90	3.19	**3.43**
Fully participated in squadron activities.	3.18	3.36	3.32	3.27	2.72	3.21	**3.48**
Administered squadron effectively.	NA	3.17	3.19	3.50	3.08	3.42	**3.54**
Were effective leaders.	2.86	2.68	2.76	3.13	2.75	3.27	**3.44**
Were good role models.	2.86	2.65	2.76	3.21	2.80	3.22	**3.33**
Encouraged me to develop in all four pillars.	3.30	2.98	2.99	3.14	2.99	3.22	**3.53**
Encouraged me to challenge myself.	3.27	3.03	2.99	3.15	2.95	3.34	**3.50**
Were good role models in all four pillars.	NA	2.51	2.50	2.78	2.36	3.15	**3.30**
There was a squadron commander that I would consider my mentor.	2.53	2.39	2.30	2.89	2.69	2.82	**2.96**
Encouraged use of personal counselling services.	3.01	2.62	2.57	2.82	2.73	3.15	**3.15**
OVERALL AVERAGE	**3.00**	**2.86**	**2.90**	**3.14**	**2.92**	**3.30**	**3.46**

Table 9 – Perception of Squadron Commanders Leadership by Graduating Classes[54]

Despite the fact that junior leaders might have the theoretical knowledge on leadership principles, one practical difficulty with the aforementioned leadership approach remains that the training system is not designed to translate its principles into practice. In fact, transformational leadership is not formally included in any leadership assessments (e.g., the components are not described into concrete actions or behaviour on the training or periodical performance assessment). As the OCdts progress at RMCC, they receive biannual performance evaluations from their superior that include an assessment of their leadership abilities. Debriefs are given by their supervisors after each term with limited input from the subordinate in question. Coaching or mentoring clearly involves much more than a performance appraisal and the development of leadership abilities should not be based solely on the successful completion of a task. To maximize leadership development, coaching should offer constructive feedback on performance.[55] Beside providing a

Chapter 10

benchmark to evaluate perceptions of leadership, these surveys also offer a tool that describes some specific, certainly not exhaustive, transformational leadership behaviours applicable to the RMCC context.

The interest in learning more about mentoring and coaching was evident in 2010 when the RMCC military wing requested a formal presentation on the topic. Despite the fact that there is no longer an official mentoring program at RMCC for OCdts, the military staff was self-aware that they are (have to be) role models for OCdts. The information provided by the presentation reinforced the necessity for staff to be agile in their role as leaders and to recognize their privileged duty in developing future CF leaders.

OPPORTUNITIES FOR PERSONAL LEADERSHIP DEVELOPMENT AT RMCC AND BEYOND

Finally, DuBrin explains that leadership development also includes an individual self-development process: self-awareness and self-discipline. Through self-awareness,[56] OCdts should actively seek feedback to see how well their actions are received by others and learn from these experiences. Self-awareness, as an emotional intelligence competency, allows critical thinking about one's own management of resources, decision-making processes and the ability to lead. Leadership through self-discipline involves an individual taking an active and vigilant role in his/her own development. For DuBrin, self-discipline is the mobilizing of an individual's effort in order to remain focused on attaining a goal.[57] In this context, the personal and professional development of an OCdt should be focused on internalizing the norms and values of the CF and becoming an effective junior officer. As previously mentioned, the core curriculum is mandatory for all OCdts and is required for them to obtain their diploma from RMCC. Along with these courses, the MPL department offers electives that specifically address the subject of leadership such as *Advanced Leadership* and *Applied Military Psychology*. It is recognized that RMCC has the tools to provide the adequate education in the domain of leadership. The different "method of training" occurring at RMCC (education, experience and mentoring/coaching) provides the foundation for leadership development. In addition, RMCC offers a unique environment that allows OCdts to be placed in and experiment with a variety of leadership positions and roles under the guidance and supervision of experimented staff. Beyond the mandatory curriculum (comprised in all four Pillars of development at RMCC), it remains in the hands of the OCdts to seize the opportunities for leadership self-development and to strive for excellence.

ENDNOTES

1. National Defence, *Introduction to Leadership*, retrieved from <http://www.cda-acd.forces. gc.ca/cfli-ilfc/Introtoleadership-eng.asp>.

2. Canada. "The Professional Officer", *Leadership, Vol. 1, Art. 202*, Canadian Forces Publication: A-PD-131-002-PT-001 (July, 1973), 2-10.

3. Canada, *Leadership in the Canadian Forces: Doctrine.* (Ottawa: DND, 2005b), retrieved from <http://www.cda-acd.forces.gc.ca/cfli-ilfc/doc/dnddoc-eng.pdf>.

4. Andrew J. DuBrin, *Leadership: Research findings, practice, and skills (Sixth Edition)* (Mason, OH: South Western, 2010), 444-455.

5. National Defence, *Cadet Wing Mission*, retrieved on 15 Sept 2010 from <http://www.rmc-cmr.ca/mil/mission-eng.asp>.

6. "Core curriculum contains within it two very separate themes. The first theme is the minimum standard for mathematics and science (which is also seen as encompassing logic and information technology) which all officers need to have. The second theme is the basic requirements in the humanities, social sciences and applied social sciences which underlie the profession of arms in a Canadian context." See: Board of Governors, *Balanced Excellence: Leading Canada's Armed Forces in the New Millenium (Whithers Report).* (Kingston, ON: Royal Military College of Canada, 1998).

7. National Defence, *Athletics Department*, retrieved on June 2011 from <http://www.rmc.ca/da-ds/index-eng.asp>.

8. National Defence, *Language Training*, retrieved on June 2011 from <http://www.rmc.ca/aca/lc-cl/index-eng.asp>.

9. Ramsey Withers and John Cowan, *RMC Undergraduate Study Group, Report of the RMC Board of Governor's Study Group: review of the undergraduate program at RMC, 30 April 1998: balanced excellence: leading Canada's Armed Forces in the new millennium* (Kingston, ON: Royal Military College of Canada, 1998); Phyllis Browne, *The socialization of officer cadets at the Royal Military College of Canada: Focus groups results (CFLI TM/2006-01),* (Kingston, ON: Canadian Defence Academy – Canadian Forces Leadership Institute, 2006); the Honourable Peter MacKay, RMC Chancellor and Minister of National Defence, RMCC Convocation Address, 14 May 2008, Kingston, Ontario.

10. John Scott Cowan, "RMC and the Profession of arms: looking ahead of Canada's military university", *Canadian Military Journal,* Vol. 2, No. 3 (Autumn 2001), 5-12. Also available at <http://www.journal.dnd.ca/vo2/no3/doc/5-12-eng.pdf>.

11. Canada, Report of the Somalia Commission of Inquiry, retrieved on June 2011 from <http://www.forces.gc.ca/site/reports-rapports/som/vol0/vol0som29-eng.asp>.

12. Board of Governors, *Balanced Excellence: Leading Canada's Armed Forces in the New Millenium (Whithers Report)* (Kingston, ON: Royal Military College of Canada, 1998). Also available at <http://www.rmc.ca/bg-cg/rep-rap/withers/ap-pa-eng.asp>.

13. The term *formation* here is understood as it is defined in French language: a more holistic approach of education in which individuals are invited to embrace different fields of study in order to analyze issues from different points of view.

14. Cowan (2001), 6.

15. National Defence, *Undergraduate calendar 2011-2012. Military Psychology and Leadership course descriptions,* retrieved on May 2011 from <http://www.rmc.ca/aca/ac-pe/ug-apc/mpl-pml/course-cours-100-eng.asp#pse-psf-103>.

Chapter 10

16. Ibid., retrieved on May 2011 from <http://www.rmc.ca/aca/ac-pe/ug-apc/mpl-pml/course-cours-300-eng.asp#pse-psf-301>.

17. LCol (ret'd) David Last, "Military degrees: How high is the bar and where's the beef?", *Canadian Military Journal*, Vol. 5, No 2. (Summer 2004), 29-36. Also available at <http://www.journal.dnd.ca/vo5/no2/doc/military-militaire-eng.pdf>.

18. Gary Johns and Alan M. Saks, *Organizational behaviour: Understanding and managing life at work (6th ed.)* (Toronto, ON: Prentice Hall, 2005).

19. Phyllis Browne, *The socialization of cadets at the Royal Military College of Canada* (Kingston, ON. Canadian Forces Leadership Institute, 2005).

20. LCol Anthony J. O'Keeffe, RMCC Director of Cadet, interview posted on RMCC Club 30th September 2008. See also "Director of Cadets – Quickly Making a Mark" retrieved on July 2011 from <http://everitas.rmcclub.ca/?m=200809>.

21. Elizabeth W. Morrison, "Newcomers' relationships: The role of social network ties during socialization", *Academy of Management Journal*, Vol. 45, No. 6 (2002), 1149-1160.

22. John Van Maanen, "People processing: Strategies of organizational socialization", *Organizational Dynamics*, Vol. 7 (1978), 19-36.

23. **Collective socialization tactic** refers to: "The degree to which individuals are socialized and processed through an identical set of experiences, with relatively similar outcomes. When a group goes through a socialization program together […] individual changes in perspective are built on an understanding of the problem faced by all members of the group.", Van Maanen, 24.

24. "The **serial** socialization process, whereby experienced members grooms newcomers about to assume similar roles in the organization, is perhaps the best guarantee that an organization will not change over long periods of time.", Van Maanen, 31-32.

25. **Formal socialization tactic** is described as: "The formality of a socialization process refers to the degree to which the setting in which it takes place is segregated from the ongoing work context and to the degree to which an individual's newcomer role is emphasized and made explicit. […] In other words, formal processes work on preparing a person to occupy a particular status in the organization.", Van Maanen, 22.

26. Julie Bélanger, FYOP Questionnaires 2009 – After Action Report, (Kingston, ON: Military Psychology and Leadership Department, Royal Military College of Canada, 2009); Julie Bélanger, FYOP Questionnaires 2010 – After Action Report, (Kingston, ON: Military Psychology and Leadership Department, Royal Military College of Canada, 2010).

27. Ibid.

28. NCdt (IV) Tyson Babcock, *The Effect of Socialization on Ethics and Identity at The Royal Military College of Canada. Undergrad Thesis, Bachelor of Arts (Honours) in Psychology* (Kingston, ON: Military Psychology and Leadership Department, Royal Military College of Canada, 2010).

29. Ibid.

30. Bélanger, FYOP Questionnaires 2009; Bélanger, FYOP Questionnaires 2010.

31. Julie Bélanger, Departure Survey Results Academic Year 2009-2010 – Report, (Kingston, ON: Military Psychology and Leadership Department, Royal Military College of Canada, 2010).

32. Canada, *Duty with Honour: The Profession of Arms in Canada*, DND, 2003b.

33. NCdt (IV) Tyson Babcock, *The Effect of Socialization on Ethics and Identity at The Royal Military College of Canada. Undergrad Thesis, Bachelor of Arts (Honours) in Psychology* (Kingston, ON: Military Psychology and Leadership Department, Royal Military College of Canada, 2010).

34. Ibid.

35. Sydney Finkelstein and Donald Hambrick, *Strategic Leadership: Top Executives and Their Effects on Organizations* (St. Paul, MN: West Publishing Company, 1996); James G. Clawson, *Level Three Leadership: Getting below the Surface* (Upper Saddle River, NJ: Prentice-Hall, 1999), 46-49; James M. Kouzes and Barry Z. Posner, *Credibility: How Leaders Gain and Lose It, Why People Demand It* (San Francisco, CA: Jossey-Bass Publisher, 1993).

36. Bélanger, FYOP Questionnaires 2009; Bélanger, FYOP Questionnaires 2010.

37. Phyllis Browne, *The socialization of officer cadets at the Royal Military College of Canada: Focus groups results (CFLI TM/2006-01)* (Kingston, ON: Canadian Defence Academy – Canadian Forces Leadership Institute, 2006).

38. Julie Bélanger, Departure Survey Results Academic Year 2006-2007 – Report, (Kingston, ON: Military Psychology and Leadership Department, Royal Military College of Canada, 2007).

39. "I will lead and manage all the new changes within the Cadet Wing. I will also continue to foster a good learning framework by working closely with the Academic Wing. I will also give more freedom of action to OCdts in order to better develop their leadership skills. We will focus on leadership and military training. We will also move forward with new changes as part of RMC transformation in order to focus on cohesion and morale. We will make every effort to manage timely decisions, action and success. We will foster ethical behaviour in all circumstances." Colonel Bernard Ouellet, Director of Cadets Address, 10 September 2007, Kingston, Ontario.

40. Bélanger, FYOP Questionnaires 2009; Bélanger, FYOP Questionnaires 2010.

41. Phyllis Browne and Justin Wright, *Tradition and Changes –The Socialization of the Officer Cadet at the Royal Military College of Canada – Final Report on the Interview Protocol* (Kingston, ON: Canadian Force Leadership Institute Technical Report 2007-03, 2007).

42. Bélanger, FYOP Questionnaires 2009.

43. Julie Bélanger, Departure Survey Results Academic Year 2010-2011 – Report, (Kingston, ON: Military Psychology and Leadership Department, Royal Military College of Canada, 2011).

44. Bernard M. Bass, *Leadership and Performance Beyond Expectations* (New York, NY: Free Press, 1985).

45. Servant leaders display several attributes which include the functional attributes of trust, appreciation of others and empowerment. See Robert F. Russell, "The Role of Servant Leadership", *Leadership & Organization Development Journal*, Vol. 22, No. 2 (2001), 76-83.

46. Ibid.

47. Alan Okros, *Leadership in the Canadian Military Context; Monograph Series, Leadership* (Kingston ON: Canadian Forces Leadership Institute, Canadian Defence Academy, November 2010), 20-21.

48. Phyllis Browne and Justin Wright, *Tradition and Changes –The socialization of the Officer Cadet at the Royal Military College of Canada – Final Report on the Interview Protocol* (Kingston, ON: Canadian Force Leadership Institute Technical Report 2007-03, 2007).

Chapter 10

49. Albert Bandura, *Social Learning Theory* (New York, NY: General Learning Press, 1977); and David M. Mayer, Maribeth Kuenzi, Rebecca Greenbaum, Mary Bardes and Rommel (Bombie) Salvador, "How low does ethical leadership flow? Test of a trickle down model", *Organizational Behavior and Human Decision Processes*, Vol. 108, No. 1 (2009), 1-13.

50. The Idealize Influence dimension includes the following items: Used the language of the week, Avoided being condescending in his/her role as leader, Demonstrated enthusiasm toward tasks, Met challenges with a positive attitude, displayed good deportment in and out of uniform, Put the interests of others before his/her own, Were good role models, Were good role models for the Academic Pillar, Were good role model for the Second Language Pillar, Were good role model for the Military Pillar, Were good role model for the Athletic Pillar.

51. The Inspirational Motivation dimension includes Promoted the Importance of peer support, Maintained a positive attitude towards College/FYOP activities, Communicated enthusiastically to motivate others, Encouraged me to challenge myself, Encouraged me to challenge myself in the Academic Pillar, Encouraged me to challenge myself in the Second Language Pillar, Encouraged me to develop in the Military Pillar, Encouraged me to develop in the Athletic Pillar.

52. Individual consideration is comprised of the following items: Showed concern for cadets, Were respectful of cadets, Were available to cadets, Encouraged cadets to express their views, Provided cadets with advices as needed, took time to become acquainted with me, Acknowledge and praised my success, Recognized my strengths and weaknesses, Was aware of the personal factors that affected my performance, Knew how I was doing.

53. Bélanger, FYOP Questionnaires 2009.

54. Julie Bélanger, Departure Survey Results Academic Year 2008-2009 – Report, (Kingston, ON: Military Psychology and Leadership Department, Royal Military College of Canada, 2009).

55. DuBrin (2010), 456.

56. Andrew J. DuBrin, *Essentials of management (8e)* (Mason, OH: South Western, 2008), 158.

57. DuBrin (2010), 444-446.

CHAPTER 11

LEADERSHIP QUALITIES IN THE NEAR FUTURE FOR THE DUTCH DEFENCE ORGANIZATION

*Major Yvonne C.J. Schroeder**

INTRODUCTION

Leadership in the Dutch Defence Organization (DDO) is based on the theories of situational leadership[1] and transformational leadership.[2] These are the pillars on which the DDO leadership vision of 2007 was established. A new leadership vision looking out to the next ten to fifteen years is to be written shortly and an update will then follow for the years 2025 to 2035. This chapter looks at the latter period and presents the vision of the Royal Netherlands Army's Centre of Excellence for Leadership and Ethics on future leadership within the DDO. In short, in approximately fifteen years (2025), it is anticipated that the DDO will require leaders who are self-aware, who can provide more individually-tailored directions, who have strong communication skills for stimulating and motivating followers, and who understand and use the power of peer networks. Given societal and generation differences in Dutch society, it will likely be an even more difficult challenge to forge individually-minded followers into a team, but it will still be necessary to do so. For this, we need leaders whose leadership is genuinely relationship-oriented; in other words, leaders with not only high intelligence (IQ), but who are also emotionally intelligent.

This chapter reflects critically on the leadership literature and its current insights, and proposes a new leadership philosophy for future military leaders. Firstly, we will look at the current military situation and leadership philosophy within the DDO. Secondly, we will examine (global) developments that are starting to and will likely continue to be dominant in the future as well as the leadership qualities the DDO will need in that near future in response to these developments.

---

* The views expressed in this chapter are those of the author and do not necessarily reflect those of the Royal Netherlands Army or the Netherlands Ministry of Defence.

Chapter 11

PRESENT

Current Shifts Within the Dutch Defence Organization

Military operations are becoming increasingly complex. Peace (enforcing) operations (such as those in Bosnia, Iraq and Afghanistan) are currently the primary activity inherent in Netherlands Armed Forces missions. One consequence of the shift from war operations to peace operations, is that the features of military operations have changed.[3] Examples of peace operations features that were not as prevalent in war missions include individual accountability for decisions and actions, increased media intensity, military personnel who are responsible for a wider range of activities (both humanitarian and military), and cultural diversity among our partners (UN, NATO, etc.) that are working together.[4]

The DDO provides support for its personnel in general, and its leaders in particular, so that they can perform effectively in such complex circumstances. Leadership and its development, therefore, occupy a prominent place in the organization and the following section will look at how that currently comes about.

Leadership Within the Dutch Defence Organization

For years, situational and transformational leadership have been embraced by the DDO. Both leadership models involve task as well as relationship-based behaviour.[5] In practice, the Dutch style of leadership would appear to be amicable and social, but is in fact highly directive and sometimes overly task-based.[6] Recent years have witnessed a growing focus on the social aspects of leadership, which will be discussed in further detail in the next section. In my opinion, although the organization acknowledges the need for more relationship-based leadership, this is only put into practice by summarizing the relationship-based approach in checklists and standard procedures.[7] One example of this can be found in ethical decision-making models. It is also the case in practice that operational processes often force leaders to adhere to systems and reporting obligations, which prevents them from providing active leadership to their personnel.[8] This often means a reduced presence of leaders in the workplace. Following a number of incidents involving undesirable behaviour, the State Secretary for Defence ordered an inquiry by the Staal Commission in 2006.[9] This commission made recommendations in four areas, each of which were fully adopted. One of the recommendations concerned the issue of leadership. The aim of the program of leadership measures is to ensure that leadership is more person-oriented and that leaders are in turn supported by the organization in the performance of their difficult task. This is all set out in the *Vision on Leadership* in the Defence Organization.[10]

2007 *Vision on Leadership*

One of the measures stemming from the Staal Commission[11] is a new vision on leadership. In December 2007, the Defence-wide *Vision on Leadership* was presented to all leaders in the Defence Organization, both civilian and military.[12] This vision was developed in consultation with all elements of the organization. Specific attention is oriented on the training and supervision of leaders, at all levels, focusing particularly however, on junior leaders (personnel who are starting out on their career as a leader). Also, a centralized leadership office has been set up to coordinate the different organizational elements and, thus enhance the quality of leadership in the DDO. The new *Vision on Leadership* uses the following definition: "Leadership is the ability to purposely inspire people and guide their behaviour in order to collectively achieve the objectives set."[13] It also states that leadership within the DDO is mainly based on situational leadership and transformational leadership models.

Situational leadership is based on the principle that a leadership style can only be effective when it takes the competence and involvement of the individuals being led into account. This means that the leaders respond, on the one hand, to the various strengths and weaknesses of individual employees and, on the other, to the circumstances under which tasks and assignments have to be carried out. In other words, changing circumstances means finding a balance between task-oriented and person-oriented leadership. Leadership in this perspective is all about the right mix of leading, coaching, supporting and delegating. It is about developing, inspiring, leading from the front and spreading confidence. Leadership is more than just managing! A manager focuses on the present, strives for order, minimises risk and allows himself to be governed more by reason than by feelings.[14] A leader, on the other hand, focuses on the future, embraces change, dares to take risks and allows himself to be governed by reason as well as feelings. A manager is more a controller than an innovator. "The leader puts the ladder in the right place (selects the right objective) and the manager climbs it (ensures that the objectives are achieved)."[15]

Bernard Bass defined transformational leadership in terms of how the leader affects followers. With transformational leadership, the followers feel trust, admiration, loyalty, and respect for the leader, and they are motivated to do more than they were originally expected to do.[16] According to Bass, the leader transforms and motivates followers by (1) making them more aware of the

Chapter 11

importance of the task outcomes, (2) stimulating them to transcend their own self-interest for the sake of the organization or team, and (3) activating their higher-order needs.[17] Transformational leadership involves four dimensions: charisma, intellectual stimulation, inspirational motivation and consideration for one's employees.[18] Whereas situational leadership focuses on the qualities of the employee, transformational leadership focuses more on the leader as an individual. The tone of communication, listening skills and the ability to spread confidence are, next to the collective mission, central to transformational leadership.[19]

As stated in the definition, the *Vision of Leadership* talks about purposely inspiring others and guiding their behaviour to collectively achieve the objective. It also specifies a number of guiding core values: "honesty and clarity," "courage," "empathy and connection," "helpfulness," "inspiration" and "authenticity."[20] To substantiate these core values, it is essential that each leader demonstrates conscious action which is only possible if he/she has a high degree of self-awareness and the courage to take a critical look at himself/herself. Self-awareness requires knowledge of his/her conditioning and an understanding of where his/her thoughts and feelings come from. Self-awareness reveals an individual's core values, which are strictly personal and cannot be imposed or adopted.[21] Core values are those that belong to the very essence or core of an individual. They are not primarily behaviours, but rather abilities that one can tune into. They stem from more deeply underlying motives and have to do with who someone actually is in their very essence.[22] According to Van Gils, a vision on leadership must not, therefore, "prescribe" core values, but should above all, be an invitation to the leader to discover his/her own core values and, subsequently, the leader within himself/herself.[23] This "self-awareness" is called self-leadership.[24]

As indicated earlier, leadership has proven in practice, to be insufficient in terms of being relationship-based.[25] In training, leadership skills are learned by focusing on a specific task or mission and on the situation rather than on the leader's behaviour and the reasons for it. Unfortunately, however, the emphasis often lies on task behaviour and not on relationship behaviour. The assumption made during this learning process is that if the leader can demonstrate the appropriate leadership style (behaviour), at the right moment, he/she will provide effective leadership. In this case, good leadership is a question of demonstrating a particular form of acquired behaviour at the right moment. In this respect, too little attention is paid to the relationship between the leader and his/her personnel and the mutuality of leadership and followership.[26] In short, and for the DDO, more relationship-based leadership, and not in the form of checklists, is a must and, for that, self-leadership is essential. This will require a change of culture in the years to come.

Chapter 11

Extra Tools for Leaders: Social Aspects of Leadership and Coaching

When implementing the measures from the Staal Commission, the DDO opted for a positive approach in which the focus was on "encouraging desirable behaviour." This more positive approach makes it possible to focus on the further professionalization of leadership within the DDO, by generating support instead of resistance. The expectation was that the intrinsic motivation of leaders and followers to demonstrate desirable behaviour would increase and that undesirable behaviour could thus be mitigated or prevented. Several tools for leaders have been developed on that basis, tools which focus structural attention on the development of leadership in the Defence Organization.[27] These tools are resources that leaders can use when they take the responsibility to grow as a leader.

One such important tool concerns the promotion of a more socially-based style of leadership. This is communicated to the organization by focusing on what we have designated as the seven Social Aspects of Leadership (SAoL). These aspects are:

1. Stimulating desirable, morally responsible behaviour and identifying, discussing and correcting undesirable, morally irresponsible behaviour.

2. Creating, stimulating and reinforcing good, morally responsible mutual relations and etiquette and the early identification and correction of any problems in this respect.

3. Gaining and giving trust and finding the right balance between the position of leader and group member.

4. Demonstrating genuine concern, respect, sensitivity and understanding for the interests and needs of personnel and recognising, discussing and sensitively resolving problems, including those of a personal nature.

5. Demonstrating self-reflection and stimulating it in personnel, as well as coaching personnel in their professional and personal development.

6. Recognizing group-dynamic processes and being able to influence them effectively.

7. Creating the conditions for pleasant and secure working and living conditions for individuals as well as the group.

These SAoL correspond to the various behaviours that make up one dimension of transformational leadership, namely personal consideration. The SAoL serve as teaching objectives for basic and career training and for the specially developed SAoL training. This training was given to approximately 10,000 leaders who serve in the various elements of the Defence Organization. One of the intended effects is that the leader is (even) more capable of dealing with group-dynamic processes and that he/she is more accessible to his/her personnel, thus, providing him/her with a better idea of what is going on in the unit. During the annual performance interviews, the leader's superiors are prompted to discuss how the leader is coping with the seven SAoL.

Another important tool is peer coaching. In 2009 and 2010, training was given to a total of 350 coaches (in peer positions) to support their fellow leaders in the development of their (personal) leadership. A leader who wants to be coached can choose from a published list of coaches, either in or outside the hierarchical chain. This guarantees a sense of security that is necessary for an effective coaching program. Coaching helps in the development of self-reflection and the ability to pick up on signals from the environment. These are important aspects for leaders in the teams that they lead, of which they are also members. Few leaders, however, have signed up for a coaching program. Leaders appear to feel some ambivalence towards coaching: on the one hand they commend it as a useful tool; on the other hand, the tool is little used (by themselves) and labelled as "soft." As a result, the tool has not got off to the preferred or a very good start within the organization. Moreover, not all commanders use it to allow personnel who are performing well to develop further, but instead, as a way to evaluate personnel who are not performing so well. Consequently, coaching has taken on a somewhat negative connotation for many.

In summary, it is fair to say that the organization provides leaders with the necessary tools to enable them to be good leaders. Current policy in respect of leadership stems from experience in the organization and developments in society as a whole, a society that is well and truly on the move. The future begins today. That is why the DDO and its leadership philosophy needs to continue to evolve further in a constant learning process. The next section will examine future developments in society and their implications for the organization and its leaders.

FUTURE

Future Trends and Developments: Global, in Europe and the Netherlands

The following seven dominant trends and developments will have a huge impact in the near future on the DDO: global economic integration, conflict, governance, information, technology, population and urbanization, and resource management and climate change.[28]

Global Economic Integration, Governance and Conflict

I would like to specify the emerging economies as the first trend. In 2007, Brazil, Russia, India and China, the so-called BRIC countries, made up 30% of the global economy and 47% of world growth.[29] This growth is expected to continue in the coming years. Countries with strong economic potential (because of, for instance, raw materials, production potential or outlet markets) are gaining influence and a larger number of countries may well acquire modern weapon systems, including long-range weapons and weapons of mass destruction and mass effect. By 2025, the sum of the GDPs of the BRIC economies could equal half the equivalent of the G-6 countries (United States, Japan, Germany, United Kingdom, France, and Italy). By 2040, assuming strong and sustained growth rates, they could overtake the G-6 altogether. Globalization stimulates international governance and cooperation, thus reducing the national influence of individual states. Dynamic, innovative and strategic partnerships between governments, civil society, the private sector, and international institutions will be necessary to address the many challenges ahead. National governments are no longer the most powerful actors, nor do traditional international governing institutions hold the clout they once did. So not only states, but also individuals, groups and multinationals are playing an increasingly important role in international relations and the balance of power.[30]

The Netherlands is expected to preserve a central role in international relations. The Netherlands is a country whose current and future welfare and necessary economic growth depends on a globalizing world, which is why it is, and will remain externally oriented. Upholding the international rule of law, human rights and alleviating human suffering continue to be core values in Dutch policy. If the Netherlands wants to keep pace with other countries to be an internationally competitive high-quality knowledge-based economy, it will place heavy demands on government authorities and organizations and their leaders. The knowledge-based economy will then become a network economy. Organizational boundaries will blur and, along with technological innovation, social innovation will play a key role.[31]

Information and Technology

Innovations in technology are fundamental in our lives and will certainly be so in 2025. By then, a massive amount of digital information will be transferred around the world. As well as data transmission on a massive scale, information will also be shared faster and more easily among all strata of the population, certainly as a result of the emergence of social media. In 2025, social media and their social functions will be commonplace in the digital experience. The thought of not having socially-enhanced experiences will seem illogical. The next evolution of the web, as we know it, is most likely to be the semantic web. In a semantic web world, search engines, for example, will anticipate the best search results for us based on what they know about us (such as all our public social networking profiles). Online social media have become entwined with the physical world. As well as the physical "me," there is also a virtual "me." Consider not only a "second life" but also local online networks such as Foursquare and Yelp, combinations with augmented reality and the "Internet of Things."[32]

New technological developments in fields such as robotics, nanotechnology, miniaturization, biotechnology, space travel and developments in the information domain will present new opportunities.[33] In nanotechnology, you can think of an ant holding a micro screw, or technologies such as nanochips, nanotubes, quantum wires, quantum dots, smart dust and molecular switches. Advancing technological developments and their ever-increasing global spread can carry security risks. Information and Communication Technology (ICT) infrastructure represents a target for cyber attacks using expertise and resources that are relatively easy to obtain. Within the weapons industry, demand for unmanned weapon systems, precision weapons and non-lethal weapons will further increase, and, this has implications for those who are going to work with them.[34] According to US military expert Peter Singer at the Rhetoric Society of America Conference USA 2010: Wired for War: The Robotics Revolution and 21st Century Conflict, the ratio of soldiers to robots is growing incredible fast since the beginning of the war in Iraq.[35] Although the DDO is having to make huge cuts, no cuts will be made in 2011 in terms of this new digital information dimension (cyberspace): cyber warfare is booming. This new, non-human kind of warfare brings with it new morally ethical dilemmas, with a crucial role for military leaders.[36] We also now know that the best operators of these robots are teenagers who have spent endless hours gaming with a joystick.[37]

Population & Urbanization

While Western democracies are expected to face stagnating or shrinking population growth and aging populations in the future, it will be a different story in developing countries. The world population is growing by 2.5 people per second and is expected to increase by at least 1.2 billion, reaching a total of 8 billion people, between now and 2030. Ninety percent of that growth comes from developing countries. In EU countries, mortality rates are expected to be higher than birth rates by 2015.[38]

The population of the Netherlands is still growing and is estimated to reach 17 million around 2025. The population continues to age and the number of over-65s will increase from 2.5 million (15%) in 2009 to 4.5 million (26%) around 2040. The number of under-20s is expected to remain relatively stable, and, according to the prognosis, this group will shrink from 3.9 million in 2009 to a mere 3.7 million in 2025. According to the same prognosis, the potential workforce will shrink from 10.1 million in 2009 to 9.2 million around 2040, and then, it is then expected to increase again to about 9.4 million in 2060.[39]

In 2030, it is expected that 1.4 billion people will be 60 or older; an ageing population has all sorts of implications. First of all, the workforce will decrease, causing shortages and potential tensions in the labour market. Companies and government bodies will find it increasingly difficult to recruit and retain sufficient personnel. In addition, age-related social provisions will become increasingly expensive for the government. The Defence Organization will need to continue to present itself as an attractive employer in order to recruit and retain sufficient personnel and leadership potential. And it will need to adapt to the behaviour of these potential applicants: the so-called "Generation Z."

Generation Z, also referred to as *digital natives*,[40] was born between 1992 and 2010;[41] in a time characterized with abundant digital technology. This is in contrast to previous generations which, to a greater extent, grew up in times in which one had to actively search out and learn to use digital technologies. These older generations have been referred to as *digital immigrants*.[42] In other words, immigrants versus the natives. The digital natives were born in an era of digital technology, in a world of plenty with few limitations. They live in the belief that any setbacks will be absorbed by their parents or the government, a belief that is constantly reaffirmed. Despite the recession of recent years, the average income of young people, for example, rose by 7% between 2007 and 2009. Generation Z still has, therefore, complete confidence in the future.

It is difficult to say precisely what educational level and what disciplines of study will be required for the DDO when Generation Z starts entering the workforce in 2020. What we do know is that since the beginning of the 1990s, is that the number of students at the preparatory secondary vocational education level has fallen while the number of senior general secondary education and pre-university education students has increased. Even though there have been complaints about the decline in the level of senior general secondary education, it is still fair to say that, on average, young people are leaving school more highly qualified.

Despite the fact that it is dangerous to generalize, it is safe to say that Generation Z has grown up in a 24/7 information society. It is also often said that it is a generation characterized by a short attention span – they get bored quickly. This also means that they can find and filter information at high speed, although, sometimes this information is being processed superficially. Further, gaming is clearly very popular and television is losing ground in the popularity stakes. Besides casual gaming, the internet has an ever increasing and primary social function. National and international social networking sites like Hyves, Facebook and Twitter and applications such as WhatsApp and Ping are immensely popular. Access to the mobile internet and the use of smart phones have become basic necessities of life, like access to clean water, food and medical treatment: one cannot actually properly function without them.[43] A negative effect is that this generation is overweight and anti-social, although the latter contradicts the fact that their main occupation is to engage in social activities on the internet. This generation is, therefore, not accustomed to dealing with setbacks, while setbacks (including those in the form of traumatic events) typify the military profession. In addition, for instance, access to digital information networks are not necessarily guaranteed in a mission area. As well as physical and mental fitness, "digital fitness" may well become a new job requirement for operators of unmanned aerial vehicles (UAVs), also known as remotely piloted aircraft (RPAs), and we may select potential personnel and/or leaders who are highly skilled in operating video game controllers such as joysticks.

Over the next 20 years, most of the growth in the world population will be in urbanized environments. Urbanization is being intensified by migration from rural areas. It is expected that 60% of the world population will be living and working in urbanized areas in 2030. The number of megacities numbering more than 10 million inhabitants will increase significantly. This will go hand-in-hand with the necessary challenges in terms of infrastructure, public services, refuse disposal and crime. It will also put huge pressure on the quality of local government. Because of urbanization and the almost unlimited opportunities for travel, infectious diseases will be able to spread more rapidly and develop into pandemics, although advances in medical science and technology will allow for better prevention and control. The potentially ongoing development of the Common Foreign and Security Policy (CFSP) will mean that the EU will have a more efficient comprehensive approach to resolving security problems.[44] Urbanization can also greatly increase the impact of terrorist attacks. Military personnel have to be able to operate in densely populated areas and, at the same time, win the hearts and minds of the population. Leaders must find the right balance between the two activities and they need to have developed some sort of cultural sensitivity.

Resource Management & Climate Change

The relative and absolute scarcity of raw materials is threefold. Firstly, there is the expectation that a shortage of the basic necessities of food and water will rise. Demand is increasing because of the world's growing population. Each generation needs 50% more water and food production than the one before. At the same time, agricultural capacity is being used to produce bio-energy and other forms of "clean" energy in response to the demand for cleaner energy or less reliance on fossil fuels. Food and water will become scarce because of inadequate distribution of global food and water supplies. Secondly, fossil fuels, which are still the main sources of energy and will remain so for the foreseeable future, will become increasingly scarce. And thirdly, supplies of raw materials such as steel, aluminium, wood and chemicals will start to run out. These are needed for the production of goods and services and thus for economic development.[45] Dutch energy consumption could increase by some 50% by 2040 in the event of substantial growth in the population and the economy. Renewable energy is still far more expensive than energy from fossil fuels and thus depends on government intervention. Wind energy, biomass and solar power will meet no more than 10% of the total demand for energy.[46] Oil is still being imported in large quantities from Russia.

The disproportional distribution and scarcity of raw materials could generate security risks. States – and private companies – feel obliged to protect or secure energy resources and raw materials. The Netherlands is prepared to deploy military means for this, crossing borders if necessary. This year, 2011, vessel protection detachments (VPDs) have already been deployed.[47] All marine units are being set to work, just as on a mission, in what is for them an unfamiliar culture of merchant shipping. And here too, a young leader and his/her team are individually accountable for decisions and actions with potentially major (international) repercussions. Even countries which do not have fossil fuels or raw materials, but play a role in the distribution because of their location, are becoming strategically more important. The protection of this distribution network (for example, pipelines, ports, supply routes) and critical objects (such as power stations) will thus, also become increasingly important.

Chapter 11

Although the views on climate change differ widely, the trend that the earth is warming up is generally accepted.[48] The melting of the polar icecaps, the rise in sea levels by between 0.2 and 0.6 metres or more and climatological changes could have serious consequences. For instance, fertile agricultural areas could suffer from water shortages, conflicts could erupt at or near the poles in connection with the extraction of minerals that are now accessible, and also the use of new shipping routes and routes that are accessible year-round. A large number of countries will have to allocate financial resources to protecting themselves against the threat of rising sea levels. The global water economy is changing. This could lead to famine, disease and natural disasters such as flooding. Although there is enough water available, drinking water is scarce because of, for example, pollution, inadequate distribution facilities and the costs associated with drinking water production.[49]

Because of its position in a delta, the Netherlands is one of the countries which will be hit relatively hard by climate change. Nevertheless, the Netherlands has a huge potential capacity to adapt technologically and socially. The Netherlands can and will adapt.[50] Over the next few decades, Dutch coastal regions will have to cope with a variety of effects related to climate change. In some places, such as the North Sea, sea levels could rise by 0.5 metres. Storms will be more violent, waves will be higher, river outlets will change and acidity levels will rise in the sea. The consequences will be intensified by a growing population in coastal regions, where most of our large cities are located. River flooding will also increase, as will flooding in coastal regions as a result of rising sea levels. The risk of heat waves in the summer will increase and extremes in precipitation will be more frequent. This is the picture given in the climate scenarios produced by the Royal Netherlands Meteorological Institute.[51]

National and international security risks associated with these phenomena include interstate conflicts over raw materials. Organized crime will also see opportunities in terms of, for example, circumventing national and international environmental regulations and procedures.[52]

FUTURE LEADERSHIP IN THE DUTCH DEFENCE ORGANIZATION

Following on from this future picture of the world and the Netherlands (2025-2035), the DDO will look different from the way it looks now in terms of task and population. Operations will have become more complex, but will be of shorter duration because of limited sustainability. It is logical that the leadership will also have to be adapted to this future picture. This section will examine leadership qualities appropriate for that situation.

The Defence Task

The Netherlands will continue to be an active member of the UN and a loyal ally within NATO. Despite the far-reaching integration within Europe, each country will continue to make its own autonomous decisions and will not give up its political say on the deployment of instruments of power such as the armed forces for the foreseeable future. In its "National Security Strategy," the Dutch government states that: "National security is at stake if vital interests of the Dutch state and/or its people are threatened to such an extent that there is – potential – social dislocation." Vital interests are defined as: territorial security, economic security, ecological security, physical security and social and political stability. The coalition agreement of February 2007 sets out under column VI, that security policy will be tailored to the new global situation and will focus on peace missions, counter-terrorism, conflict prevention and reconstruction.

As well as global and national trends, military-operational developments also mean that we have to be able to operate in an increasingly complex environment in future military operations. We are conducting joint, combined and interagency operations in which we apply the effects-based approach within a networked environment. This requires adaptability, and technological and demographic developments demand high-quality, multifunctional and flexible personnel, whom we should value and protect.[53]

The Defence Population

Looking at the pace of technological developments, demographic trends and social change, we can build a picture of our future Defence population in 2025 and of the pros and cons this will present for leaders. The population will consist of different generations, a large part of which will be made up of people from Generation Z. Of course, no-one will know exactly what the world will look like in reality, but we can prepare our Defence Organization and its leaders, in part, for that future.

Generation Z will be entering the DDO from 2010 onwards. They will have grown up in a world in which networks are the norm. Everything is shared (temporarily) in digital networks. An important feature of these social networks is that they are structured organically. The number of connections you have and the amount you communicate determines whether you are in the centre of the network or more on the periphery. It also depends not on whom you are following, but on who is following you. You no longer distinguish yourself online by the number of friends you have, but by the quality of your followers. Another feature, everyone talks to everyone without prejudice. It is in this organic world that Generation Z is growing up, and it is this which largely determines their social framework.[54]

Just like most companies, the DDO is still organized hierarchically. It has a clear power structure expressed in the form of a pyramid and clear organizational charts. Unlike social networks, the DDO has a clear hierarchical chain of command and the organizational structure is clearly segmented. This means, for example, that (technical) specialists from different Services have little or no contact with each other. A social network is never surrounded by a fence with a barrier, but barracks are. A large number of young networkers will be arriving on the shop floor around 2020. These youngsters will not be accustomed to thinking in terms of hierarchical organizational structures and defined boundaries. What is more, the old work ethic – "work hard, do what the boss says, keep your mouth shut and be loyal to the company" – is unfamiliar and irrelevant. Wishes, ambitions and problems are taken straight to the highest level and that is the level from which the answers must come. Autonomy goes without saying. This generation demands a different approach, while they still have to work with the old hierarchical thinkers who will still be active. For the leaders of 2025, the challenge will be: how do I deal with this *"clash of cultures?"*[55]

The increasingly far-reaching developments in the fields of information and technology will lead to a huge information overload, in which it will become more and more difficult to distinguish between important and unimportant information and to process more information in the same space of time. In my opinion, Generation Z will rely more on information from peers, often shared though social media, than on information shared through the hierarchical chain. After all, they cannot relate to hierarchical structures. In this near future, therefore, young leaders will use their peer networks, as they too are from Generation Z, while older leaders will only be able to connect if they gain the trust of the young personnel and are themselves sufficiently flexible and curious to keep up with developments. The clash of cultures does not have to be a clash if older leaders change their methods from giving orders to providing challenges. Tasks must be specific and clear and the context in which they are performed is important.

Generation Z has had less pressure to share material possessions. Unlike previous generations, Generation Z all have their own room, a television, iPod or computer; they download their own music from their own computer onto their own iPod. They watch their own choice of TV programs. For them, "sharing" has a different meaning. In a non-digital environment, sharing means by definition that you have less yourself. But if I share a song or a game online, I am just making it available. So sharing is multiplying. If you make something available to your social network, you just gain, you never lose. Scarcity has become an unknown phenomenon. And that is the way this generation also regards their work. They assume that they will be able to get everything they want without making any sacrifices themselves. This is, after all, how they have grown up.[56] For a Defence Organization that has to operate in times of scarcity, and as a result, all resources are shared, it will be a challenge to recruit personnel who feel drawn to such a situation. In the light of all this, leaders themselves and their personnel will have to learn to deal with scarcity. Generation Z will find this stressful. Through training and education, Generation Z may or will have to learn to live without their virtual self and without their digital social contacts at any given moment of the day. Comradeship and team spirit are also unfamiliar to them. They are self-confident and willing to disclose anything on social networks such as Facebook or Hyves, but are in all likelihood, unaccustomed to relying on others completely. They will have to learn to make real friends or buddies. The advantage of the absence of a sense of comradeship is that young leaders are less likely to experience the tension between superiors and subordinates: the "mates" dilemma. It is also more likely that they will find it easier to make less popular decisions than older generations of leaders did, and they can also perform many tasks at the same time (multitasking). The only problem is that the quality of the outcome will possibly be lower. In addition, leaders can easily use social networks to exchange information quickly with their personnel. Tasks can, for example, be coordinated quickly, easily and at any given time. Members of Generation Z are also prepared to stand up for themselves and they are good at expressing themselves. From an early age, they have been at the centre of their (virtual) world and this is an advantage for a leader. The disadvantage is, however, that they are not as good at listening. Their whole manner of communicating will be more superficial, because that is what they are used to. That will make it more difficult for the leader to cope with people-oriented competencies – exactly what will be needed in 2025.

The shortage of labour has reached an all-time high. The war for talent is in full swing. There is a gap not only in terms of absolute numbers, but also in terms of ambition and interest. The employee also becomes more demanding in times of severe shortages of labour. The labour market will become a seller's market and Generation Z knows that only too well. What is more, this generation has developed the self-confidence to exploit this fully. Generation Z strives for variety, flexibility and self-development. The shortages

Chapter 11

of well-educated labour in crucial sectors such as healthcare, education and also defence will mean that politicians will have to intervene in the process of career choice. This will undoubtedly lead to a mixture of rewards and restrictions. Working for several employers is one way to guarantee variety and flexibility and continue your self-development.[57] This may have the following implications for the Defence Organization. Firstly, we need to make sure that we retain Generation Z by trying to meet their need for variety, flexibility and self-development. Leaders need to provide a wide variety of tasks. The organization's requirement for multifunctionality is a major advantage in this respect. Matters such as cost-cutting are, on the other hand, a disadvantage. It is also important that challenges follow each other in quick succession. A promotion every five years is too slow. Coaching supervision whereby personnel see their position improve in small steps is more appealing. Generation Z wants to be appreciated and wants to know what they have to do to get to the next stage. Short-term bonuses serve well as a reward.[58] The leader will also need to provide more individual-based management. For this, he/she will need to get to know each individual in his/her team and what motivates them, starting with himself/herself. It is also important to invest in network structures, just as they do, and support them in their self-development.

Another point is that this generation is also used to being constantly tested. From the beginning of primary school, pupils are constantly tested and evaluated. As a result, a reliance on external feedback has developed. In other words, they want to keep hearing how they are doing from those with ultimate responsibility. And if that feedback is not given voluntarily, they will go and get it. They want to hear, through a one-to-one discussion, what is expected of them and why, and how they are doing. Horizontal organizations with a transparent communications and reward structure are the preferred option.[59] This means that leaders need good communication skills and relationship-based leadership. The boss can no longer get away with "no news is good news," but will have to provide feedback openly, honestly and transparently on the performance of subordinates that is based on sound reasoning. For them, it is important that the leader explains "the why."

For Generation Z, hard career opportunities are secondary to "where I live." This will in many cases be the big cities, as these offer Generation Z the facilities for a balanced life. They are less inclined to relocate for a job, as you can always work wherever you happen to be and at a time of your own choosing. The division between work and private life is blurred. Contact with social networks is maintained during "work time" and work is done in the evenings. Quality of life becomes a major secondary working condition. Under that heading, work must be fun for Generation Z. Whether it is fun or not is determined by the atmosphere at work. It is no longer just about salary, status or career, but also about nice work and a pleasant atmosphere. As such, it is vitally important to invest in a positive atmosphere.[60] Leaders need to be creative with ways to improve their team and create team spirit. Generation Z must, therefore, be taught how to deal with "live" social networks. One of the ways to create team spirit is to spend a lot of time with each other. This is at odds with choosing your own working times. On the one hand, therefore, the leader will need to support flexible working times and output-based management, thus trusting one's personnel to do their work. On the other hand, leaders will want their personnel to be together in order to forge a team.

Finally, we must remember that Generation Z has grown up with the disastrous consequences for the future of non-sustainable and/or dishonest entrepreneurship. "Do good" is the requirement; "do no harm" is no longer good enough. When it comes down to making an active and positive contribution to global well-being, Defence has the lead over other organizations. Recruitment personnel and leaders can emphasise this "do good" approach and thus motivate (potential) personnel. Know why you're doing the job you're doing.

Leadership Qualities

The future trends of global economic integration, conflict and resource management, climate change, and the military developments resulting in more joint and combined collaboration with other (non-)military organizations, call for leadership with a strong cultural dimension. Knowledge of and understanding of other (organizational) cultures is important in order to be able to generate military potential. Language, emotion, thought and, for instance, attitudes to time, can differ enormously from our own culture. The following features and qualities may also, therefore, be useful for leaders working in an intercultural setting: charismatic qualities, flexibility, curiosity about or interest in the socio-economic and political life in other countries, good (non-)verbal communication skills, and the ability to cope with stress, sense of humour, ability to build and work with (multicultural) teams.[61]

The leadership skills referred to in the previous section and the characteristics and qualities listed above correspond to the characteristics of relationship-based leadership. With the implementation of all sorts of measures, we are heading in the right direction, although the manner in which this is being done (in the form of models, standard procedures and the creation of checklists) is at times debatable. In 2025, the need for more relationship-based leadership will be even greater. Being more relationship-oriented starts with understanding each other and being able to identify with others and with other (organizational) cultures. That requires not only general intelligence, but also people-oriented qualities such as emotional (and social) intelligence. Emotional intelligence (EI) concerns the way in which you deal with emotions – your own and those of other people. More specifically, Daniel Goleman,[62] the founder of the emotional intelligence theory, distinguishes four aspects: 1. Self-awareness: knowing your own emotions; 2. Self-management: regulating your own emotions; 3. Social awareness: recognising the emotions of others; 4. Relationship management: dealing with relationships.

Self-awareness is the first step towards EI.[63] Given that people without self-awareness unknowingly become trapped in dysfunctional behaviour patterns (and are also poor at judging others), this is also the first step toward effective leadership.[64] Since ancient times, "Know Yourself" has meant that you first have to get to know yourself before you can understand others. Self-awareness begins with an awakening. A leader's awareness of his/her conditioning and an understanding of where his/her thoughts and feelings come from. Turning this "self-awareness" into directing the "self" is called "self-leadership." To be able to consciously direct the behaviour of others, one must therefore start by getting to know one's own motivations. If a leader does not do so, his/her actions as a leader will be subconscious and he/she will achieve random, possibly undesired effects. Leadership development is thus, to some extent, the same as the enhancement of self-awareness[65] and, as mentioned earlier, leadership begins with self-leadership.

Subsequent steps to emotional intelligence lie within the realm of social intelligence. The third and fourth aspects of emotional intelligence are mainly social in nature and are vitally important in the conscious direction of the behaviour of others. Social awareness, empathy and the ability to handle the emotions of others make people into good leaders, and that makes them popular. The standing someone has in his environment determines success and the sense of happiness.[66]

Last, but not least, there is an important trend emerging in the professional literature that is taking a more holistic view of leadership. Specifically, researchers are now examining all angles of leadership and including in their models and studies the leader, the follower, the context, the levels, and their dynamic interaction. The outcome of these studies will also be of influence on how future leaders develop.

CONCLUSION

The trail that is being blazed towards more relationship-based leadership presents opportunities for the DDO of the future. Following the future picture of the world and the Netherlands (2025-2035), combined with the future population (Generation Z), good leaders distinguish themselves in that they not only concentrate on the rational dimensions of the organization (vision, objectives, methods, roles, job descriptions, assessment and reward systems) but are also, or more, interested in irrational variables (i.e., factors such as the underlying values of corporate cultures, power and influence patterns, group dynamics, interpersonal relationships, etc.).[67] Leaders should, therefore, aim for self-development in these dimensions, starting with self-knowledge and social awareness on the path towards emotional intelligence. Three of the most fundamental skills in emotional intelligence are active listening, receptiveness to non-verbal communication and being able to focus on a wide spectrum of emotions. Active listening is not only a question of taking in facts, but also focusing attention on the underlying meaning of what is being said. It is also important to be able to deal with the feelings of others. The skills of empathizing and understanding how others feel can be both taught and learned.

In summary, it is fair to say that the leaders of 2025 will not only need to have a healthy dose of common sense, general intelligence, knowledge and skills, they will also need to be intrinsically motivated to develop self-leadership. Leaders will also need the flexibility to deal with both the "old" and "new" generations, and the quality of emotional intelligence is essential to be able to function amidst a diversity of tasks and complex, dynamic environments.

ENDNOTES

1. Paul Hersey and Ken Blanchard, *Management of organizational behaviour, Utilizing Human Resources (2nd ed.)* (Englewood Cliffs, NJ: Prentice-Hall, 1972); Paul Hersey and Ken Blanchard, *Management of organizational behaviour, Utilizing Human Resources (4th ed.)* (Englewood Cliffs, NJ: Prentice Hall, 1982).

2. Bernard M. Bass and Bruce J. Avolio, *Improving organizational effectiveness through transformational leadership* (Thousand Oaks, CA: Sage, 1994).

3. Rudy Richardson, Desiree Veweij and Donna Winslow, "Moral fitness for Peace Operations," *Journal of Political and Military Sociology*, Vol. 32, No. 1 (2004), 99-113.

4. Ibid.

5. Paul Hersey and Ken Blanchard, *Management of organizational behaviour, Utilizing Human Resources (2nd ed.)* (Englewood Cliffs, NJ: Prentice-Hall, 1972).; Ken H. Blanchard, *Leading at a higher level* (Upper Saddle River, NJ: Prentice-Hall, 2007); Bernard M. Bass and Bruce J. Avolio, Improving organizational effectiveness through transformational leadership (Thousand Oaks, CA: Sage, 1994).

Chapter 11

6. Commissie Onderzoek Ongewenst Gedrag binnen de Krijgsmacht, *Ongewenst gedrag binnen de Krijgsmacht: rapportage over onderzoek naar vorm en incidentie van en verklarende factoren voor ongewenst gedrag binnen de Nederlandse Krijgsmacht.* (Amsterdam: COOGK, 2006).

7. Marc J. Van Gils, "Zelfleiderschap en eigenaarschap als basis voor leiderschapsontwikkeling", *Militaire Spectator*, Vol. 180, No. 2 (2011), 87-97.

8. Franz P. Van Veen, "Administratieve werkbelasting: Een verkennend en beschrijvend onderzoek", (Afdeling Gedragswetenschappen, KL, rapportnr 88-16, 1988).

9. Commissie Onderzoek Ongewenst Gedrag binnen de Krijgsmacht. *Ongewenst gedrag binnen de Krijgsmacht: rapportage over onderzoek naar vorm en incidentie van en verklarende factoren voor ongewenst gedrag binnen de Nederlandse Krijgsmacht* (Amsterdam: COOGK, 2006).

10. Ministry of Defense, *Visie Leidinggeven* (Cdr Armed (NL) Forces, Workgroup Staal, 2007).

11. As a result of misbehaviour in the Netherlands Armed Forces, such as the incident of sexual harassment on the Navy frigate Tjerk Hiddes, this committee was set up in 2006 to investigate misbehaviour in the Netherlands Armed Forces.

12. Ministry of Defense, *Visie Leidinggeven* (Cdr Armed (NL) Forces, Workgroup Staal, 2007).

13. Ibid.

14. Max Landsberg, *The tools of leadership: vision, inspiration, momentum* (London: Harper Collins, 2000).

15. Ibid.; Marcel Nieuwenhuis, *Over The Art of Management* retrieved from <http://123management.nl>.

16. Bernard M. Bass, *Leadership and performance beyond expectations* (New York: Free Press, 1985); Bernard M. Bass, *A new paradigm of leadership: An inquiry into transformational leadership.* (Washington, DC: U.S. Army Research Institute for the Behavioral and Social Sciences, 1996).

17. Gary A. Yukl, *Leadership in Organizations (6th Ed.)* (UK: Pearson Education Limited, 2005).

18. Ministry of Defense, *Visie Leidinggeven* (Cdr Armed (NL) Forces, Workgroup Staal, 2007).

19. Ibid.

20. Ibid.

21. Daniel Ofman, *Bezieling en kwaliteit in organisaties* (Utrecht/Antwerpen, The Netherlands/ Belgium: Kosmos Uitgevers, 2006).

22. Ibid.

23. Marc J. Van Gils, "Zelfleiderschap en eigenaarschap als basis voor leiderschapsontwikkeling," *Militaire Spectator*, Vol. 180, No. 2 (2011), 87-97.

24. Ibid.

25. Commissie Onderzoek Ongewenst Gedrag binnen de Krijgsmacht. *Ongewenst gedrag binnen de Krijgsmacht: rapportage over onderzoek naar vorm en incidentie van en verklarende factoren voor ongewenst gedrag binnen de Nederlandse Krijgsmacht.* (Amsterdam: COOGK, 2006).

26. Marc J. Van Gils, "Zelfleiderschap en eigenaarschap als basis voor leiderschapsontwikkeling," *Militaire Spectator*, Vol. 180, No. 2 (2011), 87-97.

27. Carel E. M. Banse, "What is in it for me?", *Carré, I,* (2009), 42-45.

28. Kyle Thompson-Westra, "Seven Revolutions: Part of the Global Strategy Institute", *Center for Strategic and International Studies* retrieved from <http://csis.org/program/seven-revolutions>.

29. See the *International Monetary Funds* website, retrieved from <http://www.imf.org>.

30. Kyle Thompson-Westra, "Seven Revolutions: Part of the Global Strategy Institute", *Center for Strategic and International Studies* retrieved from <http://csis.org/program/seven-revolutions>.

31. See the *The Social and Economic Council of the Netherlands (SER)* website retrieved from <http://www.SER.nl>.

32. Freddie Laker, "Social Media 2012-11 Trends You Should Watch" posted on 7 April 2010 on *Take Me To Your Leader* website, retrieved on 20 July 2011 from <http://takemetoyour leader.com/2010/04/07/social-media-2012-11-trends-you-should-watch/>.

33. Wim de Ridder, *De wereld breekt open: Strategisch inspelen op de nieuwe tijd* (Amsterdam: Pearson Education Benelux, 2011).

34. Ministry of Defense, *Military Strategic Vision* (Cdr Armed (NL) Forces, 2010).

35. See video uploaded on Youtube on 9 March 2010, retrieved from <http://www.youtube.com/watch?v=gUSlbcCh2EE>.

36. Peter Warren Singer, *Wired for War: The Robotics Revolution and Conflict in the 21st Century* (Penguin, 2009).

37. Interview with Joe Dyer, director of iRobot, in dutch telvisionprogram *Uitgesproken*, 22 June 2011.

38. Ministry of Defense, *Military Strategic Vision* (Cdr Armed (NL) Forces, 2010).

39. CBS, *Bevolkingsprognose 2009 – 2060.* (Den Haag, The Netherlands: Centraal Bureau voor de Statistiek, 2010).

40. Marc Prensky, "Digital natives, digital immigrants," *On the Horizon, MCB University Press,* Vol. 9, No. 5 (2001), 1- 6.

41. Jos Ahlers, "Generatie Z, de onstuitbare opkomst van een digitale generatie," *EIFFEL: Magazine X,* Vol. 3 (2010).

42. Marc Prensky, "Digital natives, digital immigrants," *On the Horizon, MCB University Press,* Vol. 9, No. 5 (2001), 1- 6.

43. Jos Ahlers, "Generatie Z, de onstuitbare opkomst van een digitale generatie," *EIFFEL: Magazine X,* Vol. 3 (2010).

44. Ministry of Defense, *Military Strategic Vision* (Cdr Armed (NL) Forces, 2010).

45. Ibid.

46. Milieu- en Natuurplanbureau, "Waarheen met Nederland? Ruimtelijk beeld trendscenario 2040," *Nova Terra,* Vol. 6 (2006), 26-29.

47. See Ministry of Defense website, retrieved from <http://www.defensie.nl>.

48. Al Gore, *An Inconvenient Truth: The Planetary Emergency Of Global Warming And What We Can Do About It.* (London: Bloomsbury Publishing PLC, 2006).

49. Ministry of Defense, *Military Strategic Vision* (Cdr Armed (NL) Forces, 2010).

Chapter 11

50. Platform Communication on Climate Change, *Het IPCC rapport en de betekenis voor Nederland* (The Netherlands :Wageningen UR, 2007).

51 Geert Lenderink, Aad Van Ulden, Bart Van den Hurk and Franziska Keller, "A study on combining global and regional climate model results for generating climate scenarios of temperature and precipitation for the Netherlands," *Clim Dyn*, Vol. 29 (2007), 157-176.

52. Ministry of Defense, *Military Strategic Vision* (Cdr Armed (NL) Forces, 2010).

53. Ibid.

54. Jos Ahlers, "Generatie Z, de onstuitbare opkomst van een digitale generatie," *EIFFEL: Magazine X*, Vol. 3 (2010).

55. Ibid.

56. Ibid.

57. Ibid.

58. Ibid.

59. Ibid.

60. Ibid.

61. Manfred Kets de Vries, *The Leadership Mystique: Leading Behavior in the Human Enterprise (2nd Edition)* (Harlow: Pearson Education Limited, 2006).

62. Daniel Goleman, Richard E. Boyatzis and Annie McKee, *Primal leadership: Realizing the Power of Emotional Intelligence* (Boston: Harvard Business School Press, 2002).

63. Daniel Goleman, *Emotional Intelligence* (New York: Bantam, 1995).

64. Manfred Kets de Vries, *The Leadership Mystique: Leading Behavior in the Human Enterprise (2nd Edition)* (Harlow: Pearson Education Limited, 2006).

65. Marc J. Van Gils, "Zelfleiderschap en eigenaarschap als basis voor leiderschapsontwikkeling," *Militaire Spectator*, Vol. 180, No. 2 (2011), 87-97.

66. Daniel Goleman, Richard E. Boyatzis and Annie McKee, *Primal leadership: Realizing the Power of Emotional Intelligence* (Boston: Harvard Business school Press, 2002).; Daniel Goleman, *Social Intelligence: the New Science of Human Relationships* (New York: Bantam, 2006).

67. Manfred Kets de Vries, *The Leadership Mystique: Leading Behavior in the Human Enterprise (2nd Edition)* (Harlow: Pearson Education Limited, 2006).

CONTRIBUTORS

Mie Augier is an associate professor at the Naval Postgraduate School (NPS). She works on research on economics and security, strategy, and net assessment. Before joining NPS, she was a research associate and post doc at Stanford University, and a senior research fellow and director of strategy research at the Advanced Research and Assessment Group in the UK Defence Academy. She has published more than fifty articles in journals and books and co-edited several special issues of journals and books. Her current research interests include: the links between economics and security; the development of an interdisciplinary framework for strategic thinking & New Security Economics (NSE); Organizational Theory and behaviour; and the strategic challenges of the rise of China.

Major **Julie Bélanger** served for 11 years in the Canadian Naval Reserve (HMCS *Montcalm*) prior to taking her commission in 2001 as a Personnel Selection Officer in the Canadian Forces. She completed a bachelor degree in Psychology (1995) and is a graduate of Laval University (Master of Arts, 1999) in Education Psychology. In 2006, she was posted to the Royal Military College of Canada (RMCC), located in Kingston, Ontario. She was assigned to the Military Psychology and Leadership Department to teach courses on several topics related to military psychology, organizational behaviour, professional ethics and leadership. As part of her duties, Major Bélanger was responsible for the coordination and management of three major ongoing surveys at RMCC (i.e., Departure Survey, Harassment and Abuse Survey and First Year Orientation Program (FYOP) Survey).

Dr. **Craig Foster** is currently a Professor in the Department of Behavioral Sciences and Leadership at the United States Air Force Academy. Dr. Foster is a graduate of Washington University in St. Louis, where he completed an undergraduate major in Psychology and a minor in German. He then completed his Master's degree and PhD in social psychology at the University of North Carolina in Chapel Hill. His Master's thesis focused on the role that perceived injustice plays in motivating individuals to seek power. Dr. Foster's doctoral dissertation examined how individuals perceive others who seek power. Dr. Foster also taught several undergraduate courses while pursuing his graduate degrees, including Introduction to Psychology, Research Methods in Psychology, and Social Psychology. He also won a university-wide award for excellence in undergraduate teaching. After completing his doctoral degree, Dr. Foster joined the Department of Behavioral Sciences and Leadership at the United States Air Force Academy (USAFA). He has taught

Contributors

several courses at the USAFA including Introduction to Behavioral Sciences, Statistical Principles in Behavioral Science, Social Psychology, Personality, Psychology in Film, Psychological Operations, Foundations of Leadership Development, and Advanced Leadership. He has served in a variety of departmental roles, typically in the areas of assessment and leadership. Dr. Foster continues to conduct research in the areas of relationships, power, and leader development. Dr. Foster has also won a department teaching award and twice been a finalist for a USAFA-wide teaching award.

Dr. **Peter Greener** is Dean of the Academic Faculty at the Command and Staff College of the New Zealand Defence Force (NZDF) and Adjunct Professor in the Faculty of Health and Environmental Sciences at Auckland University of Technology (AUT). He has a Master's degree in Public Policy from Victoria University of Wellington and a PhD in Political Studies from the University of Auckland. Peter is a Research Associate at the National Centre for Peace and Conflict Studies at the University of Otago, and a research supervisor for Massey University.

Lieutenant-Colonel **Jon Hawkins,** DSM and Bar, is a Royal Australian Infantry officer who has served in a variety of regimental and staff appointments in Army and Australian Defence Headquarters. He holds a Bachelor of Mechanical Engineering; a Master of Defence Studies; and a Master of Business Administration. He worked alongside Canadian Forces in Afghanistan and completed Staff College at the Canadian Forces College in Toronto. He is currently a staff officer in Special Operations Command.

Colonel **Bernd Horn**, OMM, MSM, CD, PhD, is an experienced infantry officer who has commanded at the unit and sub-unit level. He has filled key command appointments such as the Deputy Commander Canadian Special Operations Forces Command, Commanding Officer of the 1st Battalion, The Royal Canadian Regiment and Officer Commanding 3 Commando, the Canadian Airborne Regiment. Dr. Horn has a PhD from the Royal Military College of Canada where he is also an Adjunct Professor of History. He has authored, co-authored, edited and co-edited 32 books and over 100 chapters and articles on military history and military affairs.

Lieutenant-Colonel **Rob Hoult** is the Director of the Army Leadership Centre, with responsibility for the development of leadership across all levels of the New Zealand (NZ) Army. Over his 28 years of military service Lieutenant-Colonel Hoult has completed a wide range of appointments including senior multi-national leadership roles in peacekeeping operations in Iran, Bougainville and East Timor. He has an infantry background and has specialized in the field of leadership development, including six years of leading the NZ Army's Adventurous Training Centre, the Army's experiential leadership school. He is a graduate of the Australian Army's Command and Staff College, and holds a Master's in Defence Studies. His interests include enjoying the outdoors with his family, and competing in endurance events. He has twice represented New Zealand at the Ironman Triathlon World Championship in Hawaii. He is also an enthusiastic aerobatic pilot. In the aftermath of the 22 February 2011 Christchurch earthquake, Lieutenant-Colonel Hoult was seconded to the NZ Police, where he assisted with planning and the establishment of the headquarters responsible for earthquake specific command and control.

Nick Jans, PhD, is a Brigadier in the Army Reserve. He is a Visiting Fellow in Leadership & Military Sociology at the Centre for Defence Leadership & Ethics at the Australian Defence College, and a Visiting Fellow in the School of Business at the Australian Defence Force Academy.

Dr. **Daniel Lagacé-Roy** is an associate professor at the Royal Military College of Canada in Kingston, Ontario where he teaches – amongst other courses – Military Professionalism and Ethics, and Psychology and Philosophy of Religious Conflicts. He is also an associate researcher in Military Ethics and Leadership at the Canadian Forces Leadership Institute and an associate professor at the University of Guelph. He is also the Director of the Ethics Research Board at the Royal Military College of Canada. He previously taught Ethics at the Dufferin-Peel Catholic School Board in Mississauga, Ontario at the Université du Québec in Rimouski, Québec and at the University of Alberta in Edmonton, Alberta. He served in the Canadian Forces from 1987 to 1995 (Regular) and from 1998 to 2001 (Reserves). He published *Ethics in the Canadian Forces: Making Tough Choices* (workbook and instructor manual), the Mentoring Handbook, and articles addressing various topics such as identity development and cultural intelligence. He is presently working on a book on war, religion and violence. Dr. Lagacé-Roy received his PhD (Philosophy) from the Université de Montréal, Québec.

Lieutenant-Colonel **Psalm Lew** is currently Head School Leadership Development with the responsibility to review and develop the Leadership Curriculum in all SAF schools. An Infantry Officer by vocation, he is concurrently the Commanding Officer of a National Service Infantry Battalion in the SAF Armed Forces. His past appointments include being the Chief Researcher of the Army Museum of Singapore, a Principal Staff Officer in the 3rd Singapore Division and Training Development Officer of the Officer Cadet School. Lieutenant-Colonel Lew holds a Bachelor of Science (1st Class Honours) in Psychology from the University of Birmingham, UK and a Diploma in Learning Science from the National Institute of Education, Nanyang Technological University.

Lieutenant-Colonel **Douglas Lindsay**, PhD, US Air Force, is the Deputy Department Head and an Associate Professor for the Department of Behavioral Sciences and Leadership at the United States Air Force Academy. He is a career Behavioral Scientist and has had held positions as a test psychologist, research psychologist, occupational analyst, military assistant, inspector general, deputy squadron commander, professor, and executive officer and has recently returned from a deployment to Afghanistan where he was the Deputy Communications Director in support of Operation Enduring Freedom. He received his doctorate degree in Industrial/Organizational Psychology from The Pennsylvania State University and his research interests are in the areas of leadership, leadership development, leader-follower dynamics, and followership. He has over 50 publications and presentations on these topics and has been published in journals such as *Military Psychology, Journal of Leadership Education, International Journal of Training and Development, Human Resource Development International*, and has presented at such venues as the American Psychological Association, American Psychological Society, Society for Industrial & Organizational Psychology, International Military Testing Association, and International Leadership Association. In addition, he is the co-founder and co-editor of the *Journal of Character and Leader Integration*.

Robert M. McNab is an Associate Professor of Economics at the Naval Postgraduate School in Monterey, California. Professor McNab has published in a number of peer-reviewed journals and holds a joint appointment with the Global Public Policy Academic Group and the Defense Resources Management Institute. His research interests include the outcomes of fiscal decentralization, the reform of budgeting and tax administration systems in developing and transitional countries, and new security economics. Professor McNab received his PhD in Economics in 2001 from Georgia State University in Atlanta, Georgia and his Bachelor of Arts from California State University, Stanislaus in 1991.

Dr. **Andres Pfister** is currently working as a research assistant at the Department of Leadership and Communication Studies at the Swiss Military Academy at ETH Zurich. He received his MSc in Social and Economic Psychology and Business Economics from the University of Basel and his PhD in Social and Economic Psychology from the University of Zurich. His primary research focuses on the influence of personality and culture on leadership behaviour. At the Military Academy he teaches several leadership courses as well as presentation and discussion techniques to future professional military officers. Prior to this function, he was working as a Human Resources consultant. Dr. Pfister serves as a special officer (Militia) in the Pedagogic Psychological Service of the Swiss Armed Forces, focusing on stress and drug prevention with young recruits.

Yvonne Schroeder joined the Army in 1985 as a truck driver and later volunteered for Officer school which she finished in 1990 as a Signals officer. As a junior leader, she served as a platoon commander, company commander and Ops officer within several Signal battalions, including the 1(UN) Signals battalion in Sarajevo in 1992. Before she started the Major Career Course at the Netherlands Defence College in 2001, she functioned as DACOS G6 during the Operational Readiness Test of the 11th Air Assault Manoeuvre Brigade. In 2003, she finished Bachelor's education in Governance Management & Administration in The Hague. In 2003, she made a career switch from Signals to Psychologist and received her Master's degree in Clinical Psychology and Work Psychology in August 2007. During her study at the University of Amsterdam she wrote her thesis about Post Traumatic Stress Disorder and working conditions in three different mission areas: Bosnia, Iraq and Afghanistan. Her first function as a military psychologist was that of a team leader at the Psychological Selection Centre of the Dutch Defence Organization. Since 2010, she has worked as a researcher for the Centre of Excellence of Leadership and Ethics and as an (executive) coach. Because of her interest in both work psychology and clinical psychology, her specific areas of interest are leadership, moral professionalism, work stress, team building, coaching, resilience and adaptability, and the dynamics within Gestalt therapy, Sexology and Emotional Focused Therapy. In her spare time she can be found in the Academic Medical Centre of Amsterdam as a sexologist.

Dr. **Stefan Seiler** is the Department Head of Leadership and Communication Studies at the Swiss Military Academy at ETH Zurich. He studied at the University of Fribourg and the University of Leeds and graduated with a PhD in Educational Psychology from the University of Fribourg. Since 2010, he is a Visiting Professor at Nanyang Business School, Singapore. His research interests include leadership, intercultural leadership, leadership ethics, moral decision making, human capital management, and conflict management. Prior to his appointment at the Swiss Military Academy, he was a member of senior management in the human resource department at Credit Suisse in Zurich and in New York. His responsibilities included global restructuring and implementation projects in America and Asia. Dr. Seiler serves in the

Contributors

Army in the rank of major (militia officer) and is a member of the military science workgroup in support of the Chief Land Forces. He was previously a company and deputy battalion commander.

Major **Ardisutopo Endro Tjahjono**, PhD, finished his Bachelor's degree in Psychology at the University of Indonesia (1995) and attended a Postgraduate Program in Organizational/Industrial Psychology at the University of Melbourne, Australia (2003). He was also an associate staff of the International Conflict Resolution Centre (ICRC) of the University of Melbourne (2002). His military training includes the Indonesian Armed Force Officer's School (1991) and the Indonesian Army's Advance Officer's Course (2005). In 2007, he served as a United Nations Military Observer as part of the UN-OMIG in Georgia, and in 2010, he attended the Indonesian Army's Staff and Command School. At present, he is responsible for psychological research at the Psychological Service of the Army.

GLOSSARY

1GW	First Generation Warfare
2GW	Second Generation Warfare
3GW	Third Generation Warfare
4CMBG	4 Canadian Mechanized Brigade Group
4GW	Fourth Generation Warfare
AATC	Army Adventurous Training Center
ADF	Australian Defence Force
ALC	Army Leadership Centre
ALF	Army Leadership Framework
APS	Australian Public Service
BINTER	*Pembinaan Territorial*, or Territorial Capacity-Building
BOTC	Basic Officer Training Course
BRIC	Brazil, Russia, India, & China
C³I	Courage, Comradeship, Commitment and Integrity
CAS	Complex Adaptive Systems
CBP	Capabilities-Based Planning
CBRN	Chemical, Biological, Radiological and Nuclear
CDA	Canadian Defence Academy
CDF	Chief of the Defence Force
CDS	Chief of the Defence Staff
CF	Canadian Forces
CFSP	Common Foreign and Security Policy

Glossary

CGS	Chief of General Staff
CLIIP(X)	Courage, Loyalty, Initiative, Integrity, Pursuit of Excellence, X-factor
CO	Commanding Officer
COE	Contemporary Operating Environment
DDO	Dutch Defence Organization
EI	Emotional Intelligence
EU	European Union
FYOP	First Year Orientation Period
GDP	Gross Domestic Product
Gen X	Generation X
Gen Y	Generation Y
GPS	Global Positioning Systems
HQ	Headquarters
ICOR	Incremental Capital Output Ratio
ICT	Information and Communication Technology
IEDs	Improvised Explosive Devices
IMLA	International Military Leadership Association
INTERFET	International Force East Timor
IQ	Intellectual Quotient/Intelligence Quotient
JIIMP	Joint, Interagencey, Intergovernmental, Multinational Partners
JJSC	Joint Junior Staff Course
LCM	Leadership Competency Model
LD	Leadership Development

LPT	Leadership Project Team
MND	Minister of National Defence
MPL	Military Psychology and Leadership
MRT	Mass Rapid Transit
MSI	Military Studies Institute and Leadership
NATO	North Atlantic Treaty Organization
NCO	Non-Commissioned Officer
NGO	Non-Governmental Organization
NPS	Naval Postgraduate School
NS	National Service
NSE	New Security Economics
NSmen	National Servicemen
NZ	New Zealand
NZDF	New Zealand Defence Force
OCdts	Officer Cadets
OCS (NZ)	Officer Cadet School of New Zealand
OECD	Organization for Economic Cooperation and Development
POI	Protection of Installations
PD	Professional Development
PER	Personnel Evaluation Report
REBA	Rational Emotive Behavioural Analysis
REBT	Rational Emotive Behavioural Therapy
RMCC	Royal Military College of Canada

Glossary

RNZAF	Royal New Zealand Air Force
RNZN	Royal New Zealand Navy
ROTP	Regular Officer Training Plan
RPA	Remotely Piloted Aircraft
SAF	Singapore Armed Forces
SAoL	Social Aspects of Leadership
Sec Def	Secretary of Defense
SL	Second Language
SLG	Senior Leadership Group
TAD	The Army Depot
TNI	*Tentara Nasional Indonesia*, or the Indonesian Defence Forces
UAV	Unmanned Aerial Vehicles
US	United States
USAFA	United States Air Force Academy
VPDs	Vessel Protection Detachments
VUCA	Volatility, Uncertainty, Complexity and Abiguity
WO	Warrant Officer
WODF	Warrant Officer of the Defence Force

INDEX

Index

Index

Index

Index

Index